A TRAVELLER'S WINE GUIDE TO

Germany

A
TRAVELLER'S
WINE GUIDE
TO

Germany

Kerry Brady Stewart

Photographs by Robert Dieth

Aurum Press

The *Traveller's Wine Guides*
were conceived and produced by
Philip Clark Ltd, 53 Calton Avenue,
London SE21 7DF, UK

Designed by Keith Faulkner Publishing Ltd

Edited by Philip Clark and Tony Raven

Photographs by Robert Dieth (except
where otherwise credited)

Maps by European Map Graphics Ltd,
Andrew Green and Simon Green

Copyright © Philip Clark Ltd,
1990, 1998

First Edition published in 1990

This revised and updated edition
published in 1998 by Aurum Press Ltd,
25 Bedford Avenue, London WC1B
3AT, UK

A catalogue record for this book is
available from the British Library.

ISBN 1-85410-514-0

Printed in Singapore for Imago

ACKNOWLEDGMENTS
The author and publisher would
particularly like to thank the
German Wine Institute and the
thirteen regional wine promotion
boards for their help with the
research and planning of this book.

Special thanks to Ian Jamieson
M.W. for his recommendations on
content. Many thanks also to Garry
and Marlies Grosvenor for their
unfailing help and advice.

Kerry Stewart would also like to
thank the many hospitable vintners,
hoteliers, restaurateurs and tourist
offices, especially in the Saale-
Unstrut and Sachsen regions, for so
generously sharing their time and
supplying information. Thanks are
also due to Rainer Lingenfelder,
Helmer Pardun, Kerstin Pawis,
Charles Stewart and Carol Sullivan
for help with research trips, and
Jeffrey Butler and Andreas Koch for
technical assistance.

COVER

Main illustration: Autumn colours
on Riesling vines in the famous
vineyard of Goldtröpfchen at
Piesport on the Mosel.
(Photograph: Mick Rock/Cephas
Picture Library)

Foreground photography by Darius

Treveris wine glass courtesy of
Mosel-Saar-Ruwer Wein e.V.

Road map of Germany: 1:500,000
courtesy of Ravenstein Verlag GmbH

TITLE ILLUSTRATION
Dawn mist hangs over the Mosel
valley near Zell.
(Photograph: Nigel Blythe/Cephas
Picture Library)

Contents

Page

How to Use this Book 6

Foreword 7

Introduction 8
The Language of the Label 10
Other Products of the Grape 12
Tasting the Wine 13
Travelling in Germany 14

The Ahr 16

The Mittelrhein 20
Koblenz 22
Downstream to Königswinter 23
Koblenz to Bingen 26
Kaub to Lahnstein 29

Mosel-Saar-Ruwer 30
Koblenz to Cochem 32
Cochem to Zell 34
The Middle Mosel 36
Trier 40
The Ruwer and Saar Valleys 42

The Nahe 44
Bad Kreuznach 46
The Alsenz and Glan Valleys 47
The Middle Nahe 48
The Upper Nahe 50
The Lower Nahe 52

The Rheingau 54
The Gateway to the Rheingau 56
Wiesbaden to Kloster Eberbach 58
Eltville to Rüdesheim 60
Rüdesheim 64
Rüdesheim to Lorchhausen 66

Rheinhessen 68
Mainz 70
The Rhein Terrasse 72
Worms 74
Alzey and the Countryside 75
Bingen and its Environs 76

Page

The Pfalz 78
Bockenheim to Bad Dürkheim 80
Bad Dürkheim to Neustadt 82
Speyer 84
The Southern Wine Road 86

The Bergstrasse 90

Franken 94
Würzburg 96
The Tauber Valley 98
The *Bocksbeutel* Route 100
The Steigerwald 102
The Mainschleife 104

Württemberg 106
Stuttgart 108
East of the Neckar 110
West of the Neckar 112
The Rems Valley 114

Baden 116
Heidelberg and the Neckar Valley 118
The Kraichgau 120
Baden-Baden and Ortenau 122
Freiburg and Breisgau 124
Kaiserstuhl and Tuniberg 126
Markgräflerland 128
The Bodensee 130

Saale-Unstrut 132

Sachsen 136

Reference Section 142
Summary of Appellation of Origin 142
Summary of Quality Categories 143
Grape Varieties 144
Pronunciation Guide and Glossary 146
Further Information 148

Index 149

How to Use this Book

This book provides a concise introduction to Germany's 13 wine-growing regions and their wines. Each section begins with a brief look at the geographical, historical and cultural developments that have influenced a region's character and that of its wines.

Visits to castles, churches and museums are integral to a wine tour. These monuments are the legacy of the Church and the aristocracy, who have been leading proponents of quality wine-growing for centuries. Equally important are the market squares, tithe courts and half-timbered houses – reminders of the medieval wine-growers and merchants, titled and untitled, who are just as much a part of Germany's wine tradition.

The itineraries

The suggested itineraries are designed primarily for the motorist, but hiking or cycling paths (especially through the vineyards) and boat trips are enjoyable alternatives to driving. You can also travel by train to major wine centres, such as Koblenz, Mainz, Würzburg, Stuttgart, Freiburg and Dresden, and by coach to smaller towns. Many panoramic views are recommended, not only for the beauty of the landscape, but also to help you appreciate the unique challenge of growing grapes on such steep slopes.

Meeting growers and visiting estates

Throughout this book there are references to wine festivals, 'open house' in wine villages, shops at co-operatives and estates, open-air tasting stands and dozens of wine restaurants and pubs where you can meet growers, visit estates and sample wines *without prior appointment and without being able to speak German.*

Wherever you see the sign *Weinverkauf*, wine is for sale. If hours are not posted, it is acceptable to stop at an estate from 0800-1200 and 1400-1800 on weekdays and 0900-1200 on Saturday mornings. This fortuitous method of meeting growers can be immensely rewarding, but it requires courage on your part actually to ring the doorbell of a stranger's home. It could happen that you arrive when only the grower's elderly mother or children are at home. They are not likely to speak English, nor to understand (at first) why you are there. If this happens and you are not able to establish when the grower will be back, simply smile, say *Danke* (thank you) and try your luck at another estate.

Organizing visits in advance

If you are interested in visiting a specific estate, write for an appointment (see the sample letter on page 148) to avoid disappointment and mutual embarrassment when you suddenly appear at the door and no one can be of assistance. Bear in mind that most estates are small, family operations. There are no staff for guided tours and tastings – the family deals with these, as well as tending the vines, making and selling the wine. German growers are extremely hospitable, but they appreciate being able to plan time for your visit. Please refer to page 148 for details on catalogues and books which provide descriptions and/or addresses of wine estates which are interesting to visit. Local tourist offices can also help.

Last but not least: tell your local wine merchant that you are planning a trip to Germany's wine country. He or she may be able to give you useful tips and perhaps help arrange some appointments for you to visit wineries and estates.

THE INFORMATION PANELS
Both wine pubs and more formal restaurants are listed in the information panels. Where a fax or telephone number is listed, it is advisable to make a reservation in advance.

Most restaurants offer several reasonably priced *offene Weine* (wines by the glass). Thus, you can enjoy wine with your meal without having to purchase an entire bottle.

Classic-style or sweeter German wines usually have 8-10 per cent alcohol by volume, while drier wines have more. Although this is a relatively low amount of alcohol, the quantity of wine you consume is an important consideration if you are driving. The German laws on drinking and driving are strict and they are enforced. Therefore, many of the places recommended are hotels or have guest rooms, so that you can sample several wines during a leisurely dinner and not have to worry about driving afterwards.

The regional wine promotion boards have maps, brochures and calendars of events. The addresses are listed under each wine region.

Foreword _____

Anyone looking for delicious food and wine, stunning landscapes and a warm welcome will find German wine country truly delightful. For many, such a visit is a revelation. You might be surprised at the large number of excellent, drier-style German wines – white, rosé *and* red – that you'll encounter. And few people realize that Germany is second only to France in its number of Michelin-starred restaurants.

The river valleys that have been 'home' to Germany's vineyards for centuries offer some spectacular scenery. You can enjoy a glass of wine from the terrace of a castle overlooking a river, on the deck of a steamer gliding past vine-covered slopes, or at one of the hundreds of colourful wine festivals amidst half-timbered houses lining a market square.

Last but not least: vintners' hospitality. It's been nearly twenty years since a wine-grower's family in Kallstadt (Pfalz) made my first visit to German wine country so special. They welcomed me, a total stranger, into their home and started me on a journey that fascinates me to this day – discovering the pleasure of fine German wines in the company of those who make them. Wine and travel foster friendship. I hope this book will help make your visit a memory worth treasuring.

St Urban, the patron saint of German wine-growers for centuries. The outcome of the vintage lies in his hands from the Feast of St Urban (25 May) to the harvest in autumn.

Introduction

Germany's winelands are among the most beautiful in the world. They offer a great diversity of scenery, attractions and wines within an area roughly the size of Bordeaux. In fact, Germany's modest 105,000 hectares (260,000 acres) of vineyards account for just over one per cent of the worldwide acreage devoted to viticulture. Germany's average annual harvest of about ten million hectolitres (approximately 1.3 billion bottles of wine) is equal to only four per cent of worldwide production.

Parallel in latitude (50°N) to the Scilly Isles and Labrador, Germany's vines are much more at the mercy of nature's vagaries than are their Mediterranean counterparts. Thus, vineyards are confined primarily to forest-topped, south-facing slopes, for protection from cold winds and maximum exposure to the sun. They are nearly all situated near the river Rhine, or its tributaries, which helps temper the climate and maintain a constant temperature. The grapes ripen slowly, retaining their fruity acidity as they develop sugar.

Weather conditions, microclimates, soil types, grape varieties, selective harvesting of grapes at various degrees of ripeness and the cellar-master's style all contribute to the extraordinary range of wines produced in Germany. Some of this information will be indicated on the wine's label. These subjects are explained on the following pages and summarized in the reference section at the back of the book.

Wine publications can provide guidelines on what to expect and a knowledgeable wine merchant can offer advice, but your own tasting impressions are ultimately the most meaningful. Only you can decide if a wine's bouquet and flavour are truly appealing or remarkable. Make brief notes about the wines you sample and when and where you tasted them. It is a very special experience to sample wines where they are grown or together with the winemaker (what are his or her comments about the wine?). Wines develop and mature in the bottle. It is fascinating to taste the same wine three or five years later and to compare these notes with your original observations.

Many wine writers have criticized the German system of labelling wine as too complicated. It is true that there is often a great deal of detail, often obscured by obsolete graphics and illegible Gothic script. However, if you focus on the key elements, the labels usually provide precisely the information you need in order to decide which wine is appropriate for everyday enjoyment, to accompany a meal or to enhance a special occasion.

Of the 70,000 grape growers in Germany, two thirds sell their crop or wine in bulk to co-operative or commercial wineries which make and/or bottle and market the wine.

These wineries and the highly individualistic wine estates merit your attention and can provide you with some memorable experiences. In addition to growers' hospitality, you can enjoy a variety of wines that are seldom exported but are well worth discovering.

The Language of the Label

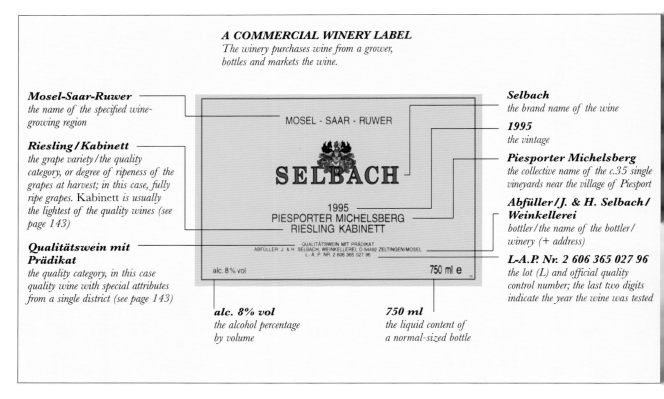

A COMMERCIAL WINERY LABEL
The winery purchases wine from a grower, bottles and markets the wine.

Mosel-Saar-Ruwer
the name of the specified wine-growing region

Riesling / Kabinett
the grape variety / the quality category, or degree of ripeness of the grapes at harvest; in this case, fully ripe grapes. Kabinett is usually the lightest of the quality wines (see page 143)

Qualitätswein mit Prädikat
the quality category, in this case quality wine with special attributes from a single district (see page 143)

Selbach
the brand name of the wine

1995
the vintage

Piesporter Michelsberg
the collective name of the c.35 single vineyards near the village of Piesport

Abfüller / J. & H. Selbach / Weinkellerei
bottler / the name of the bottler / winery (+ address)

L.-A.P. Nr. 2 606 365 027 96
the lot (L) and official quality control number; the last two digits indicate the year the wine was tested

alc. 8% vol
the alcohol percentage by volume

750 ml
the liquid content of a normal-sized bottle

The Romans used inscriptions and labels on amphorae and other vessels to identify a wine's general origin, vintage, liquid content and the name of the merchant (not producer). Modern labelling dates from the late 18th century, when wines of superior quality were bottled (albeit on a small scale) and when lithography provided a more efficient method of reproduction than woodcuts.

It was not until the 20th century, however, that bottling and labelling wines became a widespread practice. A grape variety was seldom declared and the appellation of origin often consisted only of the name of the village, without the name of a specific vineyard site.

Today, the information on the labels of German quality wines is regulated by law and must include:

region; quality category (ripeness); name and address (or ID number) of the bottler or shipper; official quality control number; liquid content and alcohol in per cent by volume. Grape variety, vintage and style are optional declarations.

Long German words, sometimes in Gothic script, can be daunting. The individual pieces of information do not always appear in the same order or in the same place on labels. Elaborate scrolls, coats of arms and pictures of the landscape or estate often obscure the label's message.

However, there is a trend among progressive producers to 'clean up' their labels, simplify the wording and print the information in more legible type. Many use established artists, and some of the resulting labels are truly collectors' items.

Wine lists

Whether you are looking at a label on a bottle or reading the names of wines on a list (such as an estate's tasting list, a price list or a restaurant's wine list) do not let the amount of detail overwhelm you. Here are the key elements to look for:

Region

German quality wine originates from one of 13 specified wine-growing regions. The more northerly regions are known for delicate, light wines with a pronounced acidity. Further south, the wines are heartier, often fuller-bodied and less acidic. The easternmost regions produce dry varietals with a rounded acidity.

Village + -er + vineyard site

If the grapes are grown in an area more narrowly defined than a region, the producer can state this on the label. The most frequently used appellation of origin is the name of a village followed by -er (ie 'from') and the name of a vineyard site.

Quality category (ripeness)

In Germany, quality categories are based on the ripeness of grapes at harvest. Ripeness is measured in terms of the amount of natural sugar that has developed in the grape.

The crop is not all harvested at one time, but rather at various stages of ripeness. This is called 'selective harvesting'. Grapes left on the vine longer (ie late-harvested) have had more time to develop natural sugar and to absorb minerals from the soil. They yield wines which are more intense in bouquet and flavour than wines made from normally ripe grapes. Overripe grapes produce extremely concentrated wines.

Grape variety

This will help you know what to expect in terms of bouquet, fullness, flavour and acidity. Most (about 80 per cent) of Germany's wines are white.

Style

Increasingly, dry and medium dry wines are identified by the words *trocken* or *halbtrocken* on the label. If neither is stated and you are not familiar with the grower's or producer's usual style of winemaking, it is best to assume the wine is medium sweet.

Producer

The producer guarantees the quality of the wine. *Abfüller* (bottler), *Erzeugerabfüllung* (producer-bottled) or *Gutsabfüllung* (estate-bottled) usually precede the producer's name.

CO-OPERATIVE WINERY LABEL
Winzer/vereinigung: Growers'/co-operative. (Growers deliver grapes to co-operative winery, which produces, bottles and markets the wine.)
Region: Saale-Unstrut
Town: Freyburg
Grape variety: Dornfelder (red)
Ripeness: Qualitätswein (QbA)
Style: not mentioned

TRADITIONAL WINE ESTATE LABEL
Guts/abfüllung: estate/bottled. (Grower produces and bottles the wine, made only from grapes grown on the estate. Equivalent to the French mis en bouteille au Château.)
Region: Pfalz
Village: Kallstadt
Vineyard site: Saumagen
Grape variety: Riesling (white)
Ripeness: Auslese (very ripe grapes selected bunch by bunch)
Style: trocken (dry)

FOR FURTHER DETAILS on region, ripeness, grape variety and style, please refer to pages 142-145.

Other Products of the Grape

1

3

5

6

2

4

7

In addition to the large and diverse selection of German wines on offer, many growers produce and/or market other products of the grape. These are often packaged in specially-sized or -shaped bottles with designer labels.

The more exclusive items, eg *Winzerbrände* (distilled spirits), are hand-crafted specialities, available in limited quantities. As such, they are not inexpensive, but they do make a lovely souvenir or gift for a gourmet friend.

Sekt or sparkling wine (**2**) is extremely popular, on its own or as an ingredient in a refreshing summer *Bowle* (punch). Those labelled *Deutscher Sekt*, *Deutscher Sekt b.A.* or *Winzersekt* are produced from wines that are 100% German in origin; for reasons of price, most of the mass-marketed brands are not, despite their very German-sounding names. German *Sekt* is usually less yeasty but fruitier in style and lower in alcohol than French sparkling wines.

Among the simpler grape- or wine-based products are *Traubensaft* (grape juice [**3**]) and for breakfast or tea,

Trauben- or *Weingelee* (**4**), jelly made from grapes or wine, respectively. *Traubenkernöl* (grape seed oil) and *Weinessig* (wine vinegar) are flavourful cooking aids. Albeit on a limited scale, the latter is also sold as a noble beverage (see panel).

The spirits that merit attention are (**5**) fruity, pungent *Trester(brand)*, the German equivalent of French Marc or Italian Grappa – a brandy distilled from grape pomace (the grape skins and pips left after the grapes are pressed); *Hefebrand* or *Weinhefe* (**6**), a rounder, softer and fuller brandy distilled from the lees, ie the yeast-rich sediment that remains after the grape juice has fermented into wine; and *Weinbrand* (**7**), the German equivalent of French Cognac, a brandy distilled from grape wine. When aged in large glass containers, the spirits are crystal clear. Oak cask-ageing yields spirits that take on a lighter or darker golden hue.

These products are sold at wine estates and speciality shops and/or grace the menus of fine restaurants that feature regional specialities.

Tasting the Wine

You will almost always have a chance to sample wine wherever it is sold, except in some self-service shops, such as supermarkets. Despite this shortcoming, the well-stocked wine departments of larger supermarkets (particularly those in the basement level of the department stores, such as Hertie or Karstadt) are interesting to visit. They are good places to buy wine, glasses and a *Korkenzieher* (corkscrew) for an impromptu picnic. Or, from the wide selection of wines available, it is easy to organize a small comparative wine tasting. You could, for example, purchase 1996 Riesling Kabinett *halbtrocken* (medium dry) wines from the Mosel-Saar-Ruwer, Rheingau and Pfalz to compare regional differences.

Wine festivals and tasting stands

At wine festivals and open-air tasting stands you select the wine(s) you wish to sample from a posted list. The wines are normally listed according to their degree of ripeness, starting with simple quality (QbA) and ending with the luscious, dessert-type wines. It is not unusual for ten to 14 wines and *Sekt* (sparkling wine) to be offered per producer.

All the different vineyard site names, degrees of ripeness, grape varieties and styles afford a wonderful opportunity to experience the diversity of German wine. Don't panic. Re-read pages 10-11 and refer to pages 142-147 to become familiar with the key terms which most often appear on labels and wine lists.

The wines are sold by the glass and by the bottle. When you order wine you will be asked to pay a *Pfand* (deposit) for glasses and/or bottles. The deposit is refunded on return. You might decide to keep the small tasting glasses, however, as an inexpensive souvenir of your visit.

Tasting at co-operatives and estates

If the tasting has not been arranged in advance, you may be asked what kind of wines you would like to taste (and handed a list from which to choose). Your host needs to know if you are interested in red (*Rotwein*), rosé (*Weissherbst*), white wine (*Weisswein*), dry (*trocken*), medium dry (*halbtrocken*) or slightly sweet (*lieblich*).

Once your preference has been determined, you will probably sit together at a table to taste and talk about the wines. Briefly note your impressions of each wine. After sampling, you can pour any wine which you do not wish to drink into the empty container on the table (are you driving?)

If you are fortunate enough to be offered a rarity (*Auslese, Beerenauslese, Eiswein* or *Trockenbeerenauslese*), the pride of every grower, it will be a small quantity and it would be a shame to pour it out. It is a common courtesy to purchase a few bottles before leaving, especially if there is no charge for the tasting. Wine glasses and accessories are often for sale as well.

The cellar-master draws a sample of new wine to check its development in cask. The cellars belong to one of Germany's internationally renowned wine estates, Maximin Grünhaus on the river Ruwer. It was once owned by the Benedictine monastery of St Maximin in Trier. The steep vineyard sites Bruderberg, Herrenberg and Abtsberg face the former monastery buildings.

Travelling in Germany

TOURIST INFORMATION

DZT – Deutsche Zentrale für Tourismus
(German National Tourist Office) Beethovenstr. 69, 60325 Frankfurt am Main.
Tel: 069/974640.
Fax: 069/751903.

DZT BRANCH OFFICES

Canada
175 Bloor Street East, North Tower, Suite 604, Toronto, Ontario M4W 3R8.
Tel: (416) 968-1570.
Fax: (416) 968-1986.

UK
Nightingale House, 65 Curzon Street, London W1Y 8NE.
Tel: 0171-495 0081.
Fax: 0171-495 6129.

USA
122 East 42nd Street, New York, NY 10168-0072.
Tel: (212) 661-7200.
Fax: (212) 661-7174.

Köln-Düsseldorfer Deutsche Rheinschiffahrt (KD)
Frankenwerft 15, 50667 Köln.
Tel: 0221/2088318.
Fax: 0221/2088345.
(KD boat excursions on the Rhine and lower Mosel; cabin cruises on the Rhine, Mosel, Saar, Main, Neckar and Elbe; details on 'The Floating Wine Seminar', a 7-day Rhine cruise with wine tastings and visits to estates.)

Deutsche Touring GmbH
Am Römerhof 17, 60486 Frankfurt am Main.
Tel: 069/790350.
Fax: 069/7903219
(Details on the Europabus.)

More than 28,000 trains travel daily throughout Germany. They are fast, reliable and comfortable.

German wine country is primarily situated in the south-west, bordered by France, Luxembourg and Switzerland. Germany's network of railways and motorways is the densest in the world, and passenger boats cruise the Rhine, Mosel, Main, Neckar, Saale, Unstrut and Elbe rivers as well as the Bodensee.

The Europabus travels famous routes, such as the *Burgenstrasse* (Castle Road) through parts of the Baden and Württemberg wine-growing regions and the *Romantische Strasse* (Romantic Road) through Franken. Last but not least, there is an impressive network of hiking trails and cycling paths in all 13 wine-growing regions. Bicycles may be hired at 150 railway stations or bicycle shops with *Fahrradverleih* (rental service).

The German Federal Railway (DB) and Köln-Düsseldorfer (KD) boat company offer many concessions. Ask about *Sparpreise* ('Saver' tickets). The KD combines boat trips with coach excursions to famous castles and other sights (*Tagestouren mit Landarrangements*).

If you are travelling on the Rhine, the lower Mosel or the Bodensee, rail and boat tickets are often interchangeable (for a supplementary fee). This is useful for round trips, as it saves time and the combination fares are more economical.

Some of the Rhine's most beautiful scenery lies between Rüdesheim and St Goarshausen. You can purchase a round-trip rail ticket in Rüdesheim: take the train to St Goarshausen (30 minutes); pay the *Übergangsgebühr* (transfer fee) at the KD landing stage in St Goarshausen; and board the boat to return to Rüdesheim (3 hours). A round trip by boat takes 5-6 hours. On your birthday (take your passport as proof) you can travel free of charge on all KD boats except the hydrofoil.

The Autobahn

Most of the itineraries suggested in the book are routed on a *Bundesstrasse* (two-lane highway, abbreviated 'B', as in B9) rather than an *Autobahn* (motorway, or 'A', as in A3). But you will probably drive on an Autobahn at some stage of your journey and it is worth pointing out that Germany's reputation for fast cars and frustrated drivers is largely justified. The practice of flashing headlights to pressure slower drivers to move to the right is illegal.

There are usually three reasons for traffic to come to a halt on the Autobahn: there has been an accident; there is a *Baustelle* (road works); or school holidays have started or ended and there is a traffic jam of monumental proportions. Thus, from mid-June to mid-September you are likely to arrive at your destination almost as quickly and with less irritation by avoiding the Autobahn.

Accommodation

Contact the organizations in the panel to the right for details on castle hotels and historic inns, as well as *Pauschal-Angebote* (package deals), ie special rates that may include gourmet meals. Guest rooms at wine-growers' estates offer an enjoyable, economical alternative. If you plan to visit a village during its wine festival, make your reservation well in advance. However, even on short notice, local tourist offices are extremely helpful in finding rooms.

The KD fleet operates from Easter to October.

HISTORIC HOTELS AND INNS
European Castle Hotels
Weinpalais,
67142 Deidesheim.
Tel: 06326/700030.
Fax: 06326/700033.

Relais & Châteaux
North America
Tel: (212) 856-0115.
Fax: (212) 856-0193.
UK
Tel: 0171-287 0987.
Fax: 0171-437 0241.

Romantik Hotels &
Restaurants International
PO Box 1144,
63786 Karlstein.

ROAD MAPS
Die General Karte by Mairs Geographischer Verlag is a good choice. Available at all Shell petrol stations and bookshops in Germany. To tour wine country you will need maps 12, 15, 16, 18, 21, 24, 36 and 37.

SPEED LIMITS
Urban areas usually 50 kph/31 mph
Normal roads 100 kph/62 mph
Motorways no legal speed limit unless indicated

DRIVING TERMINOLOGY
ADAC German auto club; for help: 01802/22 22 22
Ausfahrt exit
Autobahn-dreieck (AB-Dr.) or *-kreuz (AB-Kr.)* motorway intersection
Benzin petrol (gasoline)
Bleifrei lead-free
Panne breakdown
Polizei police; dial 110
Raststätte (R) snack shop/restaurant + WC
Selbstbedienung (SB) self-service
Tankstelle (T) petrol/gas station
Umleitung detour/diversion
Unfall accident

The Ahr

RHEIN & EIFEL

FOR FURTHER INFORMATION
Contact the regional wine
promotion board:
Touristik-Service
Ahr, Rhein, Eifel
Markt 11,
53474 Bad Neuenahr-
Ahrweiler.
Tel: 02641/97730.
Fax: 02641/977373.

*Fiery red wines with a spicy
bouquet are a speciality of the
vineyards on the Landskrone, the
flat-topped basalt cone overlooking
Heppingen and Heimersheim.*

The vineyards of Germany's 'red wine paradise' line the valley slopes of the Ahr river from near its confluence with the Rhine south of Bonn to Altenahr, only 25km (15 miles) to the west. There are magnificent views of the striking landscape from the heights of a basalt cone (Landskrone), slate cliffs and castle ruins. The main town is the elegant spa of Bad Neuenahr-Ahrweiler.

Signposts with a cluster of red grapes signal two well-marked routes through the region: for motorists, the *Rotweinstrasse* (B266 and B267); for hikers, the *Rotweinwanderweg*. Cyclists can follow the signs with the regional logo (left) along the *Ahr-Radtour*, a circular route from Remagen/Rhine through the Ahr valley and back to the Rhine. The region is popular for its natural beauty as well as for its wines. In the autumn vineyards and forests are ablaze with colour and wine festivals take place every weekend.

The Romans were probably the first to grow grapes in the Ahr valley. By the 9th century, viticulture was well established and continued to flourish throughout the Middle Ages, when the Church owned many wine estates. The period of decline caused by French invasions in the 17th and 18th centuries, secularization (1803), and a series of poor harvests, led to the formation of the first German wine-growers' co-operative, founded in Mayschoss in 1868. This helped to improve growers' income and the quality of their wines.

Today, the majority of Ahr vintners belong to one of the five co-operatives, which together produce nearly 70 per cent of the region's wine.

Red wine paradise

With 506 hectares (1250 acres), the Ahr is among the smallest and most northerly of Germany's wine regions. The vineyards are labour-intensive, planted mostly on terraced cliffs of slate, greywacke and volcanic soils. These heat-retaining soils, the tempering influence of the river and the protective Eifel mountain range create a microclimate in which even red grapes can ripen this far north.

Although introduced relatively late (1680) red vines quickly outnumbered the white and account for 80 per cent

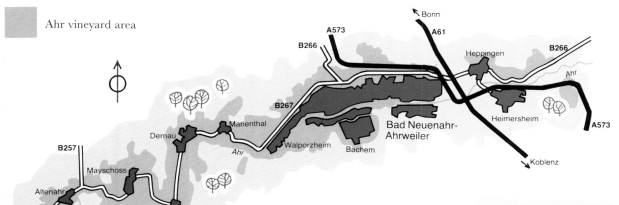

Ahr vineyard area

of production today. The entire Ahr valley produces elegant, velvety Spätburgunder, lively, fruity Portugieser and deep-coloured Dornfelder wines. Riesling and Müller-Thurgau are the main white varieties, grown primarily in Rech, Mayschoss and Altenahr.

Lower Ahr valley

The broad eastern end of the valley has orchards and fields on its lower slopes, with vineyards on the higher ground. Reorganization in the later 1960s improved working conditions and gave the vineyards a more 'groomed' look than the wild terraces of the upper valley. Loam and loess predominate, but the Burggarten vineyard below Landskrone (the flat-topped cone overlooking Heppingen and Heimersheim) also contains basalt.

Vines blossom a week earlier here, giving the grapes a longer ripening period. As a result, the red wines tend to be higher in alcohol and body than their neighbours to the west.

Near Heimersheim's market square, the late Romanesque St Mauritius Church has the oldest (13th century) stained glass windows in Germany. From the Middle Ages to the early 1800s, landlords collected *der Zehnt*, ie one tenth of the harvest, as rent from peasant growers at the 13th-century *Zehnthof* (tithe court). Don't miss the historic wine festival in mid-August.

A short drive plus a 15-minute walk (or a 45-minute walk) from the railway station in Heimersheim (on the north bank of the Ahr) will take you to the top of the Landskrone, where there is a fine view. En route you can see the thousand-year-old chapel and ruins of Burg Landskrone, built in 1205 by Philip von Schwaben as a romantic home for his bride.

REGIONAL WINE GLASSES
The *Römer* wine glass typical of the region is called a *Pokal* on the Ahr. It holds 0.2 litres of wine. For a glass of wine half that size, order a *Spezial*.

WINZERGENOSSENSCHAFTEN
(Wine-growers' Co-operatives) are located throughout the region. No appointment necessary. Mon-Fri 0800-1800, Sat 0900-1200. Some have wine pubs, too.
Bad Neuenahr
Heerstrasse 91-93.
Ahrweiler
Walporzheimerstr. 19.
Walporzheim (pub)
Walporzheimerstr. 173.
Marienthal B267 (main road).
Dernau (pub) Ahrweg 6. Also Sun.
Mayschoss (pub) Ahr-Rotweinstr. 42. Also Sun.
Altenahr (pub)
Tunnelstrasse 17.

HEIMERSHEIM
Weingut Nelles
Göppinger Str. 13.
Tel: 02641/24349.
Fax: 02641/79586.
1130-1500 Sun, 1700-2200
Tue-Sat. Guest rooms.
HEPPINGEN
Steinheuers Restaurant Zur Alten Post
Landskroner Str. 110.
Tel: 02641/7011.
Fax: 02641/7013.
1200-1400 (except Tue and
Wed), 1800-2200 (except
Tue). Closed 3 weeks
Jul/Aug. Gourmet dining,
superb wines. Also: regional
specialities at **Landgasthof
Poststuben** (same hours,
open all year). Guest rooms.
Weingut Burggarten
Landskroner Str. 61.
Wine pub from Easter to
Pentecost and Sep, Oct
from 1700 (except Mon).
BAD NEUENAHR
Weingut Lingen
Teichstr. 3. Wine pub
from 1800 (except Wed).
Weingut Sonnenberg
Heerstrasse 98. Wine pub
Oct from 1800 (except
Thu, Sun).
AHRWEILER
Prümer Hof - Ahrweinstuben
Markt 12. Hours: ask wine
promotion board. Showcase
for Ahr wines in historic
half-timbered house.
Hohenzollern
Silbergbergstr. 50. Tel: 02641/
9730. Fax: 02641/5997.
1200-1430, 1800-2130.
Outstanding view from the
restaurant terrace. Hotel.
DERNAU
Weingut Kreuzberg
Bened.-Schmittmannstr. 30.
Tel: 02643/1691. Fax:
02643/3206. Wine pub.
May-Oct (except Wed),
Sun from 1000, Sat from
1200, Mon-Fri from 1500.
Guest rooms.

Bad Neuenahr and Ahrweiler
Bad Neuenahr is an elegant spa
which is as popular with politicians
from Bonn as it is with tourists. The
heart of town is the *Jugendstil*
Kurhaus, with alkaline thermal baths,
a casino (opens daily at 1400) and
gardens (one devoted to dahlias)
along the banks of the Ahr. Nearby,
are the Willibrorduskirche (church)
dating from AD 990, and the Baroque
house where Beethoven spent his
summers from 1786 to 1792.

Ahrweiler, across the river, has
a long history. The *Römervilla*, a
magnificent Roman villa (2nd and
3rd centuries AD) unearthed in the
Silberberg vineyard testifies to the
site's warm, sunny location. Today, it is
a 'working' museum as archeologists
continue restoration (Tue-Fri 1000-
1800, Sat-Sun 1000-1700; closed mid-
Nov through March). Within the
medieval town walls and four gateways
(1248) you can see half-timbered
houses near the market square as well
as Gothic St Laurentius Church
(1269), and the Rococo town hall.

The *Weinbaulehrpfad* is a 4km (2½
mile) signposted path through the

vineyards, leading from the railway
halt 'Markt' in Ahrweiler to the
station in Walporzheim.

The soils in this area range from
slate, greywacke and quartzite (racy,
lighter wines) to heavier loam and loess
(powerful, full-bodied wines, with
milder acidity). To compare them with
wines from the entire valley, visit the
region's largest co-operative, Ahr
Winzer, in Bad Neuenahr or Dernau.

Bread and wine
In the Middle Ages, as today, few
growers had enough vineyards to make
a living from the wine alone. Many
grew grain as well, giving rise to the
establishment of community bakeries,
where growers would bring their flour
or bread dough and hire the bakery to
bake it. Bachem's 13th-century Back-
haus (bakery) is now a wine museum
(Wed 1500-1700, Sun 1000-1200).

The Frühburgunder grape is a local
speciality. These red wines have great
finesse, and are well worth sampling.

Romantic Ahr valley
From Walporzheim to Altenahr the
valley narrows, the hills are steeper
and the landscape is dominated by
terraced vineyards and rocky cliffs.

A huge greywacke-slate cliff called
Bunte Kuh (mottled cow) overlooks
Walporzheim. Drive or walk (half an
hour) to the top for the view. Try red
wines from the Kräuterberg vineyard
at the pub of the same name or from
Alte Lay and Domlay (Lay or Ley
means cliff) at Sanct Peter, the oldest
(1246) restaurant of the region.

The Staatliche Weinbaudomäne
(State Wine Domain) is the largest
estate in the region with 19 hectares
(47 acres). The estate is located in the
former Augustinian monastery of
Kloster Marienthal, founded in 1137.

The estate is sole owner of the Klostergarten (cloister garden) site. You can visit the vaulted cellars (12th-17th centuries), the remains of the monastery church and the cloister.

Dernau, Rech and Mayschoss

Half-timbered houses line Dernau's narrow alleys. The view from the Krausberg (400m/1300ft) hill on the south side of the river extends all the way to Cologne Cathedral on a clear day.

The 12th-century village of Rech straddles the Ahr and boasts the river's oldest (1759) bridge. Cliffs of weathered slate at this end of the valley yield good white and red wines.

Mayschoss lies at the foot of the ruins of the 11th-century Saffenburg fortress, the oldest on the Ahr. Walk up the hill (30 minutes) for a view of the Ahr's largest loop. There are several

The rugged cliffs of blue slate near Altenahr yield light, elegant red and white wines.

vantage points and hiking trails on the surrounding hills. The town's church contains the 17th-century black marble gravestone of Countess Katharina of Saffenburg and other art treasures.

End of the *Rotweinwanderweg*

The ancestral fortress of the Counts of Are (1100) and 18th-century Kreuzberg castle overlook the village of Altenahr. You can get a good view of the wild, romantic landscape from the ruins of Burg Are (half-hour walk or take the cable car to Ditschhardt Höhe). In town, the 12th-century church has a fine Gothic choir.

Grand Prix fans can visit the famed Nürburgring and Rennsport-Museum (historic racing cars). These are 30km (18 miles) from Altenahr via the B257.

WALPORZHEIM
Brogsitter's Restaurant
Sanct Peter (+ Vinothek)
Walporzheimer Str. 134.
Tel: 02641/97750.
Fax: 02641/977525.
Daily, 0900-2300. Gourmet restaurant, wine pub, shop.
Weingut Försterhof
Am Rotweinwanderweg 65.
1000-1800. Wine pub 1100-dusk (except Thu, Fri and from Jan through mid-Feb).
MAYSCHOSS
Hotel Lochmühle
B267, SW of Mayschoss.
Tel: 02643/8080. Fax: 02643/808445. 1200-1430, 1800-2130. Very scenic.

EXCURSIONS
About 25km (15 miles) south of the Ahr via the A61, visit Maria Laach Abbey Church (Romanesque) or from Brohl ride the 'Vulkan Express', a narrow-gauge railway.

The Mittelrhein

FOR FURTHER INFORMATION
Contact the regional wine promotion board:
Mittelrhein-Wein
Am Hafen 2,
56329 St Goar.
Tel: 06741/7712.
Fax: 06741/7723.

The Mittelrhein is the spectacular stretch of the Rhine river between Bonn and Bingen, also known as the Rhine Gorge. Here the river has carved its course through the stone hills to form a steep, narrow valley with a microclimate in which vines have thrived since Roman times.

It is a region steeped in legend (the Loreley, the Nibelungs) and has long been a source of inspiration to artists, poets and composers. The ancient castle ruins which tower over vine-covered cliffs and medieval villages are reminders of the Mittelrhein's turbulent past. Today, the robber barons are gone but many of their castles are open for visits and offer outstanding panoramic views of the Rhine valley. Visitors can sample the region's wines in the many wine pubs and garden cafés in the picturesque towns and along the tree-lined promenades.

Vineyards stretch uphill as far as the forested summits, which help to protect the vines from cold winds.

It is a real challenge to plant, care for and harvest grapes on the steeply terraced cliffs of the Mittelrhein. At 645 hectares (1594 acres) it is one of the smallest and most labour-intensive wine regions of Germany. Nearly all the work is done by hand, and winches are used to pull workers uphill on specially-designed ploughs. Not surprisingly, the number of vineyards is steadily decreasing.

Between Bingen and Koblenz, vineyards are located on both sides of the Rhine (further north they are only found on the right bank). A few vineyards are located on the south-facing slopes of the side valleys and along the Lahn river near its confluence with the Rhine at Lahnstein.

At first glance, the craggy inclines of clayish slate and greywacke seem like inhospitable sites for growing grapes (or any other crops). Yet the hills protect the vines from cold winds and they thrive on the stony, heat-retaining soils. The Rhine acts as a heat reflector during the day, while at night the mists over the water help to maintain a constant temperature. This favourable microclimate enables grapes to ripen this far north.

Mittelrhein wines are a speciality generally not available outside the region. A small amount of red wine is produced ('Dragon's Blood', see page 24) but the region is best known for steely, earthy white wines with a powerful acidity. This gives the wines a refreshing character and enables

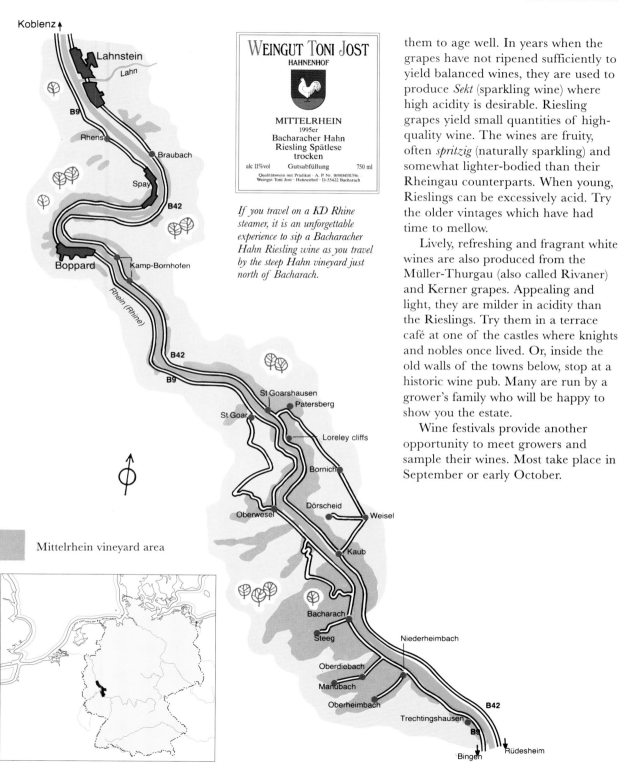

WEINGUT TONI JOST

HAHNENHOF

MITTELRHEIN
1995er
Bacharacher Hahn
Riesling Spätlese
trocken

alc 11%vol   Gutsabfüllung   750 ml

Qualitätswein mit Prädikat · A. P. Nr. 16/980403/396
Weingut Toni Jost · Hahnenhof · D-55422 Bacharach

If you travel on a KD Rhine steamer, it is an unforgettable experience to sip a Bacharacher Hahn Riesling wine as you travel by the steep Hahn vineyard just north of Bacharach.

Koblenz

Lahnstein

Lahn

B9

Rhens

Braubach

Spay

B42

Boppard

Kamp-Bornhofen

Rhein (Rhine)

B42

B9

St Goarshausen

Patersberg

St Goar

Loreley cliffs

Bornich

Dörscheid

Oberwesel

Weisel

Kaub

Bacharach

Steeg

Niederheimbach

Oberdiebach

Manubach

Oberheimbach

B42

Trechtingshausen

B9

Bingen

Rüdesheim

Mittelrhein vineyard area

them to age well. In years when the grapes have not ripened sufficiently to yield balanced wines, they are used to produce *Sekt* (sparkling wine) where high acidity is desirable. Riesling grapes yield small quantities of high-quality wine. The wines are fruity, often *spritzig* (naturally sparkling) and somewhat lighter-bodied than their Rheingau counterparts. When young, Rieslings can be excessively acid. Try the older vintages which have had time to mellow.

Lively, refreshing and fragrant white wines are also produced from the Müller-Thurgau (also called Rivaner) and Kerner grapes. Appealing and light, they are milder in acidity than the Rieslings. Try them in a terrace café at one of the castles where knights and nobles once lived. Or, inside the old walls of the towns below, stop at a historic wine pub. Many are run by a grower's family who will be happy to show you the estate.

Wine festivals provide another opportunity to meet growers and sample their wines. Most take place in September or early October.

Koblenz

KOBLENZ

Deinhard Wine Museum
shows how wine and
sparkling wine are made,
historic tools, beautiful
cellars. Visits weekdays, by
appointment only. Write to:
Deinhard AG, Export
Division, Deinhardplatz,
56068 Koblenz.
Tel: 0261/104241.
Fax: 0261/14683.

Weindorf, Rheinanlagen
Julius-Wegeler-Str. 2-4.
Eat, drink and be merry in
the midst of a reconstructed
wine-growers' village. Music
nightly. Easter-Oct, daily,
1100-2300. Nov-Easter
1100-2100 (except Mon).

Weinhaus Hubertus
Florinsmarkt. Oldest wine
tavern in Koblenz, dating
from 1689. Very cosy. From
1600 (except Tue).

Historischer Weinkeller
Mehlgasse 16. Restaurant
and wine shop in 13th-
century vaulted cellars in
old town. From 1800
(except Mon).

'THE RHINE IN FLAMES'
Spectacular fireworks
displays on the Rhine, 1st
Sat May, Linz to Bonn;
2nd Sat Aug, Braubach to
Koblenz.

EHRENBREITSTEIN FORTRESS
Excellent view from the
terrace. Ferry across from
Koblenz, then walk uphill
(1 hr) or take chairlift.
Museum shows history of
local industries and river
traffic. Mid-Mar – mid-Nov,
0900-1230 and 1300-1700.

*The Deutsches Eck (German
Corner) at the junction of the
Mosel and Rhine rivers, viewed
from Ehrenbreitstein Fortress on the
opposite bank. On the point is the
Monument to German Unity. The
Old Town is just behind the Rhine
promenade in the foreground.*

*A sparkling wine poster from the 1920s. Deinhard,
wine merchants since 1794, produce fine estate-
bottled wines as well as Sekt.*

Koblenz, situated at the confluence of
the Mosel and Rhine rivers, is the
gateway to some of Germany's most
dramatic and beautiful wine-growing
country. Founded as a Roman fort, it
prospered as the residence of the
powerful Electors of Trier (11th-19th
centuries), became the provincial
capital under Prussian rule in 1822,
and is a major administrative centre
for the wine trade.

Koblenz boasts one of the smallest
vineyards in Germany, Schnorbach-
Brückstück, located adjacent to the
charming half-timbered houses of the
Weindorf (wine village) on the
Rheinanlagen (Rhine promenade)
near Pfaffendorfer bridge. On the
other side of the bridge, walk along
the Rhine past the Schloss (Electoral
Palace), an impressive neo-Classical
structure, towards Deutsches Eck
(German Corner). Continue walking,
parallel to the Mosel, to the 14th-
century Balduin bridge and the Alte
Burg (old Electoral Castle), for a
glimpse of Koblenz's medieval past.

Downstream to Königswinter

Grapes have been grown on the steep slopes between Koblenz and Königswinter for centuries. Yet the area under cultivation is shrinking, for wine-growing here requires extraordinary dedication and hard work: about 2000 hours per hectare (about 2.5 acres). Most of the growers are 'hobby vintners' with a few rows of vines that they care for at evenings or weekends.

Grapes could not ripen in this northerly location were it not for the tempering influence of the Rhine and the soil types (slate, greywacke, volcanic stone) which quickly absorb heat in the daytime and gently release it during the night.

The wines
Located only on the right-hand side of the Rhine, for better exposure to the sun, the vineyards are planted primarily with Riesling and Müller-Thurgau grapes (white) and a small amount of Spätburgunder and Portugieser (red). Over half of the wines are dry or medium dry in style.

The Rieslings, particularly when young, are somewhat austere in character, with a pronounced, refreshing acidity. Wines from Müller-Thurgau grapes are often more elegant and lively in this region than elsewhere. The red wines are pleasantly light and fruity.

Sampling and purchasing wine
Most of the wines are available only locally. You can sample and purchase directly from a grower's wine estate or in the local wine pubs and restaurants. Even the souvenir shops sell wine. Look for signs which include words such as *Weingut*, *Weinhaus*, *Winzerhof* or *Weinkeller*. *Weinverkauf* means wine for sale.

The Schlossberg vineyard of Bad Hönningen, on the hillside below Schloss Arenfels, one of the many impressive castles along the Rhine. It is not, however, open to the public.

The villages
All the villages on this route remind us of their medieval past. Explore them on foot to discover the Romanesque and Gothic churches as well as the beautiful half-timbered houses on crooked alleyways, usually near the *Markt* or *Marktplatz* (market square). You can enjoy the local wine and scenery at cafés along the river bank. Nearly all of the tourist attractions are open from April to October, but many close during the winter.

BENDORF
Weinhaus Syré
Engersport 12. Tel: 02622/ 2581. Fax: 02622/2502. 1200-1400, 1800-2130 (except Mon, Tue).
A CURIOSITY
Visit the Garten der Schmetterlinge (Garden of Butterflies) located in the Schlosspark in Bendorf-Sayn. Apr-Nov 0900-1800.
KÖNIGSWINTER
Gasthaus Sutorius
Oelinghovener Str. 7 in the suburb Stieldorf. Tel: 02244/912240. Fax: 02244/912241. 1800-2200 Tue-Sun. Also 1200-1400 Sun. Cosy atmosphere.

LEUTESDORF
Altdeutscher Weinkeller
Hauptstrasse 18. Fri from
1700, Sat from 1500 and
Sun from 1030-2200.
BAD HÖNNINGEN
Stadtweingut
Hauptstrasse 182. Tue-Sat
1000-1230; Tue-Fri from
1630, Sat-Sun from 1600.
Closed mid-Dec – mid-Jan.
BAD BREISIG
Zum Weissen Ross
Zehnerstr. 19 (same as B9).
Daily, 1100-2400. Historic
house dating from 1628.
Weinhaus Templerhof
Koblenzer Str. 45 (B9).
Tel: 02633/9435. Fax:
02633/7394. 1200-1430
(except Wed, Thu), 1730-
2200 (except Wed). Closed 3
weeks Jan and 2 weeks Jun.
Historic house from 1657.

*The half-timbered houses on the
Burgplatz, Buttermarkt and
Marktplatz in the town of Linz
are extremely picturesque.*

Leutesdorf and Hammerstein

Vines have been cultivated for more
than 1500 years in Leutesdorf, an
important wine-growing town.
Riesling is the main variety planted
on the volcanic soils. If you are
driving on the B42 from Koblenz,
watch for the turning into the
historische Rheinstrasse (historic part of
town) along the Rhine promenade. A
2.5km (1.5 miles) *Weinlehrpfad* (marked
hiking trail through the vineyards)
starts at St Laurentius Church.

Rheinbrohl and Bad Hönningen

At Rheinbrohl, the Romans' frontier
defence line (*Limes*) reached the Rhine.
Bad Hönningen is a small health
resort, with mineral baths and thermal
pools. Its most famous vineyard,
Schlossberg, is situated on the south-
facing hillside below Schloss Arenfels,
pictured on page 23. The sandy,
loamy soil on the lower reaches of the
hill yields powerful, hearty wines.

Linz, Erpel and Unkel

These are less important towns in
terms of wine production, but they are
very picturesque and full of inviting
wine pubs and little shops.

Opposite Linz, the river Ahr flows
into the Rhine. The Ahr, one of
Germany's smaller wine-growing
regions, is known for its velvety red
wines (see pages 16 to 19).

A huge basalt cliff, the Erpeler Ley,
soars above Erpel, and the ruins of the
bridge which once spanned the Rhine
to Remagen are visible on both shores.

Unkel has manor houses dating
from the 17th and 18th centuries,
medieval half-timbered houses and a
lovely Rhine promenade. The Gothic
church is also worth seeing.

Bad Honnef and Rhöndorf

These towns lie at the foot of a range
of volcanic mountains known as the
Siebengebirge, or Seven Hills. Bad
Honnef is an elegant health resort with
lush gardens and parks and very
attractive manor houses. Konrad
Adenauer, first chancellor of the
Federal Republic of Germany, lived in
Rhöndorf. The Adenauer Memorial
established in his home is open to the
public (1000-1600, except Mon).

Dragon's Cliff and Dragon's Blood

Drachenfels (Dragon's Cliff) is the most
famous of the Seven Hills and is the
name of the steep vineyard planted
below the ruins of the 12th-century
Drachenfels fortress.

The red wine produced here is
called *Drachenblut* (Dragon's Blood),
alluding to Siegfried's battle with the
dragon that lived in a cave on this
hill (*Song of the Nibelungs*). It is a
speciality which one can enjoy in any
number of wine pubs in the popular
resort of Königswinter.

The vineyards of the kings

Königswinter takes its name from the fact that a succession of *Könige* (kings) owned vineyards (Latin *vineta*) here in the Middle Ages.

Walk along the *Hauptstrasse* (main street) of town to see a variety of architectural styles, from half-timbered houses (nos.13-15) to the Rococo-style 'Zum Rebstock' (no.100) and the 'Adler-Apotheke' (no.73) dating from 1800.

Then ascend the Drachenfels for a magnificent view of the entire Seven Hills region (you can even see Cologne Cathedral on a clear day). You can walk up via footpath, hire a horse-drawn coach, or ride Germany's oldest cogwheel train.

You can also visit the Nibelungen-Halle, a museum devoted to the dramatic legend.

Rhenish specialities

Backes-Krumbeeren are well-seasoned scalloped potatoes topped with a piece of pork and baked in the oven. *Himmel und Erde* (heaven and earth) is a mixture of mashed potatoes and chunky apple sauce topped with pan-fried slices of blood sausage. *Sauerbraten* is marinated pot roast with a sweet-and-sour raisin gravy. *Spundekäse* is whipped, spiced cheese to spread on slices of buttered bread.

The Drachenfels cliffs tower above the Rhine – the romance of the past in sharp contrast to the Rhine's commercial present.

MITTELRHEIN MOMENTE
is a series of food and wine events, often with music or entertainment, that feature the talents of the region's fine winemakers and chefs (Apr-Dec). Details from the regional wine promotion board (see page 20).

VERANSTALTUNGS-KALENDER RHEINLAND-PFALZ
is a calendar of events listing hundreds of festivals and wine and food events along the Rhine, Mosel, Nahe and Ahr rivers. Contact: Rheinland Pfalz-Information, Löhrstr. 103-105, 56068 Koblenz. Tel: 0261/915200. Fax: 0261/9152040.

Koblenz to Bingen

Magnificent Riesling vineyards soar into the misty heights at Bacharach, a delightful wine town with many reminders of its medieval past, including the ruins of the 12th-century Stahleck fortress.

Travel parallel to the Rhine along the B9 (60km/37 miles). Vineyards and castles have dominated the landscape and shaped the history of this area for centuries. Boppard, Oberwesel and Bacharach are the most important wine towns, but nearly every village has a tradition of wine-growing.

On the southern outskirts of Koblenz, the first castle comes into view – Schloss Stolzenfels, a neo-Gothic castle rebuilt in 1836 for King Friedrich Wilhelm IV of Prussia.

Rhens, known for its sparkling water as well as its wine, was politically important in the Middle Ages. The powerful Electors of the Rhineland met here to elect German emperors and in 1338 they declared they would continue to do so, with or without the Pope's approval.

The Königsstuhl (King's Throne), a tall stone structure built in 1308, stands on a hill north of Rhens. It was originally located at the site of the Electors' meeting place on the

banks of the Rhine. The town of Rhens is a good example of a 16th-century fortified city. Within the town ramparts, the half-timbered houses have intricately carved beams.

The Bopparder Hamm

From Rhens to Boppard, the Rhine makes its longest loop, known as the Bopparder Hamm. Some of the region's best vineyards are situated on these south-facing slopes. For a view of the loop and the Vierseenblick, where the Rhine looks like four large lakes, take the chairlift (daily, Apr-Oct) from Mühltal at the northern edge of Boppard (15-minute walk from town).

BOPPARD
Golfhotel Jakobsberg
12km/7.5 miles north of
Boppard (west of Spay) in
a forest high above the
Rhine. Tel: 06742/8080.
Fax: 06742/3069. Daily
1200-1400,1830-2200.
Situated in a monastery
founded in 1157.
Weinhaus Heilig Grab
Zelkesgasse 12.
Tel: 06742/2371. Fax:
06742/81220. From 1500
(except Tue), all year. Wine
pub, lovely chestnut-shaded
garden. Guest rooms.
ST GOAR
Schloss Hotel (adjacent
to castle Burg Rheinfels)
Schlossberg 47.
Tel: 06741/8020.
Fax: 06741/802802. Daily,
1200-1430, 1830-2100.
Fabulous view from terrace
and excellent wine list.
OBERWESEL
Historische
Weinwirtschaft
Liebfrauenstrasse 17.
Tel: 06744/8186. Fax:
06744/7049. From 1600
(except Tue), Mar-Dec.
500-year-old house near
Liebfrauenkirche (church).
Regional specialities. Cosy
interior. Art exhibitions.
Römerkrug Marktplatz 1.
Tel: 06744/7091. Fax:
06744/1677. 1200-1400,
1800-2130 (except Wed).
Closed Jan. Charming
house from 1458. Hotel.
Weinhaus Weiler
Marktplatz 4. Tel: 06744/
7003. Fax: 06744/7303.
1130-1330, 1800-2130
(except Thu). Closed Dec,
Jan, Feb. Historic. Hotel.
Burghotel-Restaurant
'Auf Schönburg' (castle)
Tel: 06744/93930. Fax:
06744/1613. 1200-1400,
1830-2100 (except Mon).
Closed Jan-Easter. Terrace
views. Warm atmosphere.

Boppard
Settled by the Celts, later a Roman
citadel and royal court of the Franks,
Boppard was a free imperial city in the
Middle Ages. Its historic buildings
reflect this illustrious past, and include
the remains of the 4th-century Roman
fort; twin-towered St Severus-Kirche;
Gothic Carmelite monastery church;
and medieval town houses. The Rhine
promenade is beautifully landscaped.

The valley narrows as you approach
St Goar, founded in AD 570 and
named after the patron saint of
innkeepers and potters. From Burg
Rheinfels, once the mightiest castle on
the Rhine (open daily, Apr-Oct), the
view across the river is magnificent: the
Loreley and castles Katz (cat) and
Maus (mouse).

Ruins of the 12th-century Schönburg
fortress overlook Oberwesel, the 'town
of towers'. Sixteen of the original 21
watchtowers still line the town walls.
Visible for miles, the red brick
Liebfrauenkirche (Church of Our
Lady) is one of Germany's finest High
Gothic churches. Wine-growing is
important here. Expect a mouthful of
powerful, fruity acidity in the wines.

Altar of Bacchus
Bacharach (Roman *Bacchi ara*), became
the region's most important shipping
centre for wine in the Middle Ages.
The steep Riesling vineyards of
Bacharach and Steeg (side valley)
are still among the top sites of the
Mittelrhein. Enter the village through
one of the town gates and climb the
steps to walk along the town wall,
just behind the railway line. Historic
buildings include Haus Sickingen, Alte
Post, Zollhof, Rathaus, Altes Haus and
St Peterskirche (church). Next to the
chapel ruins of the Wernerkapelle, a
gem of High Gothic architecture, take

the footpath to the ruins of Burg
Stahleck (now a youth hostel) for a
great view of the river and vineyards.

From Bacharach to Trechtingshausen, vineyards spill into the side
valleys (Diebachtal, Manubach,
Heimbachtal). If the towns are less
picturesque, the landscape is not.
Three castles, with exhibits and
period rooms, are open for visits:
Burg Sooneck, Schloss Reichenstein
and Burg Rheinstein.

Binger Loch, a very narrow, rocky
and shallow stretch of the Rhine,
and the Mäuseturm (Mice Tower)
on an island in the Rhine, signal
the approach to Bingen. There is a
Fähre (ferry) across the Rhine to
Rüdesheim. Continue on the B42:
upstream through the Rheingau or
downstream toward Koblenz.

Kaub to Lahnstein

This route runs parallel to the Rhine along the B42. It is an extension of the route through the Rheingau. It also enables you to complete a circular tour of the Mittelrhein if you followed the B9 upstream from Koblenz to Bingen. From the Bingen-Rüdesheim ferry dock, turn left and drive through the last villages of the Rheingau to Kaub.

Thirteenth-century Burg Gutenfels (now a hotel) overlooks the medieval townscape of Kaub, once the centre of the Rhenish slate quarry trade. Today, the slaty hills yield excellent Riesling wines and the vineyard area from Kaub to Dörscheid is the largest on this side of the Rhine. Walk along Metzgergasse to see the historic buildings or visit the Blücher Museum (no.6).

Burg Gutenfels overlooks the island fortress known as the Pfalz, which can be reached by boat from Kaub.

In the middle of Pfalzgrafenstein island, opposite Kaub, is a six-sided fortress shaped like a ship (tours except Mon). Known as the Pfalz, it was built as a toll station in the 14th century.

Near St Goarshausen, the Rhine narrows to about 100 metres (330ft) and the massive slate cliffs of the Loreley come into view. Justifiably renowned as one of the Rhine's most dangerous passageways, the Loreley achieved romantic fame through Heine's *Song of Loreley* (1824) about the siren on the rocky cliffs who lured sailors to their death with her singing. Equally treacherous is the reef where a river god turned 'seven virgins' into rocks because they resisted his advances. Follow the signs to the Loreley-Felsen for the view and a glass of wine from the vineyard of the same name.

Downstream to Braubach

Patches of vines cling to the slopes of Katz and Maus castles, but from here to Braubach, castles and orchards, not vineyards, dominate the landscape. Braubach has retained much of its medieval character. Visit the Marksburg fortress (12th-14th centuries) rising above the town. The only castle on the Rhine never destroyed, the buildings, interior and gardens are well worth seeing.

Lahnstein straddles the Lahn river at its junction with the Rhine. There are fine Romanesque and Gothic buildings within the town ramparts. The wild cliffs of the Ruppertsklamm are also worth a visit. The last castle on our route is the 13th-century Burg Lahneck, built to protect the nearby silver mines. The view is outstanding. There are a few vineyards along the river valley near Bad Ems (a spa resort made famous by Bismarck's 'Dispatch' which sparked off the 1870 Franco-Prussian war) and between Nassau and Obernhof.

BACHARACH
Altes Haus Oberstr. 61. Tel/Fax: 06743/1209. 1130-1600 and from 1730. Closed Wed + Nov-Easter. Historic, half-timbered house. Regional specialities.
NIEDERLAHNSTEIN
Wirtshaus an der Lahn Lahnstr. 8. Tel/Fax: 02621/7270. 1800-2200 (except Mon). Historic house, plus garden seating near the Lahn river.

'THE RHINE IN FLAMES'
Spectacular fireworks displays on the Rhine, 1st Sat Jul, Bingen; 2nd Sat Sep, Oberwesel; 3rd Sat Sep, St Goar.

SCENIC ROUTES THROUGH THE HILLS
The *Rheingoldstrasse* is an alternative route through the Hunsrück Hills, from Rhens to Niederheimbach. Best views: Königsstuhl, Jakobsberg (footpath to Vierseenblick) and Fleckertshöhe. The *Loreley-Burgenstrasse* winds through the Taunus Hills, from Kaub to the Loreley and from St Goarshausen to Kamp-Bornhofen. Best views: Kaub, Loreley, castles near Kamp-Bornhofen.

WINE HIKING TRAILS
Rhein-Wein-Wanderweg between Kaub and Kamp-Bornhofen; *Weinwanderweg* between St Goar and Trechtingshausen.

RHINE CRUISES
The KD line and smaller local companies offer many boat trips (season: from Easter or May-Oct). If time is short take an hour-long *Rundfahrt* (round trip) or travel one way by boat, return by train. Especially scenic: Bingen/Rüdesheim to St Goar (two hours).

Mosel-Saar-Ruwer

MOSEL *TREVERIS*
This is an elegant, tall-stemmed glass with a cut-glass bowl featuring a star and olive pattern (see cover). It is named after the Treveri, the Celtic tribe that once inhabited the banks of the Mosel.

The valleys of the Mosel river and its tributaries, the Saar and the Ruwer (pronounced *Roo-vair*), are the setting for some of Germany's most beautiful and romantic wine country. From Perl, at the 'three-country corner' of France, Luxembourg and Germany, the Mosel flows for 242km (145 miles) to join the Rhine at Koblenz. The Saar and the Ruwer rivers flow into the Mosel near the ancient town of Trier. Vines and forests carpet the steep slopes formed when the Mosel cut a gorge through the Hunsrück and Eifel hills. Spectacular loops mark the sites where the slate has resisted the power of the river.

The *Mosel Weinstrasse* (Mosel Wine Road) runs parallel to the river and passes through dozens of famous wine villages, such as Zell, Bernkastel and Piesport. Hikers can enjoy breathtaking panoramas from the heights of the *Moselhöhenweg* trails on both sides of the Mosel. Or you can spend a few hours savouring the landscape and its wines on a leisurely river cruise.

Viticulture has been the heart and soul of the Mosel-Saar-Ruwer for the past 2000 years. The region was settled as early as 3000 BC by a Celtic tribe, the Treveri, but their Roman conquerors were the first to cultivate vineyards systematically. During their 450 years of supremacy, the Romans developed viticulture and wine shipping into what remains the Mosel's most important industry, for the vine is still the only crop to flourish on the steep slate slopes.

Another feature of the landscape dating from Roman times is the use of single stakes to support vines. This method, still used in the steepest sites, is seldom seen outside the Mosel. Rather than stretching the vine horizontally across a wire trellis, the canes of each vine are bowed into a heart shape and tied to an individual stake. The vine benefits from improved air circulation, exposure to the sun and nutrient distribution. The growers work the rows vertically, from the bottom of the hill to the top.

The frequency of wine motifs in Roman works of art and the beautiful objects (jugs and drinking vessels), designed to enhance the pleasure of drinking wine, show that the Romans appreciated the noble beverage beyond its value as a commodity. One of the finest examples of Roman wine culture is the *Diatretglas*, a glass cup ingeniously encircled by delicate glass netting. Such art treasures and other wine-related Roman artifacts are displayed in museums throughout the region, the most notable collection being that in the Landesmuseum (state museum) in Trier.

Post-Roman era
During the turbulent reign of the Franks, the successors of the Treveri carried on the wine tradition of the Romans. From the 7th century onwards, vineyards were regularly mentioned in deeds of gift to the Church and its monasteries. At the end of the 18th century and the beginning of the 19th, when

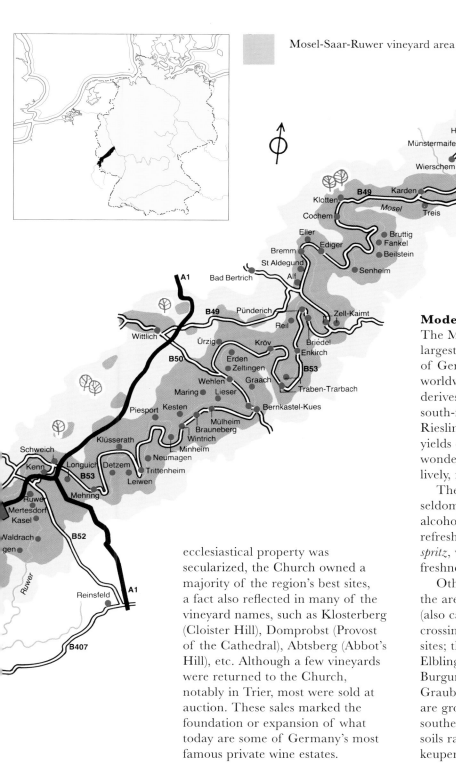

Mosel-Saar-Ruwer vineyard area

Modern times

The Mosel-Saar-Ruwer is the fourth largest (12,460 hectares/30,788 acres) of Germany's wine regions. Its worldwide reputation for fine wine derives from three elements: steep, south-facing slopes; slate soil; and the Riesling grape. This combination yields elegant, delicate wines with a wonderful fragrance balanced by a lively, fruity acidity.

They are the world's lightest wines, seldom exceeding ten per cent of alcohol by volume. Often, they have a refreshing touch of effervescence, or *spritz*, which enhances their crisp freshness and longevity.

Other grape varieties planted in the area include Müller-Thurgau (also called Rivaner); the new crossings in the alluvial soils of flatter sites; the ancient white variety Elbling; and members of the Burgundy family (Weissburgunder, Grauburgunder and Auxerrois) which are grown along the upper (ie southern) reaches of the Mosel, in soils ranging from shell-limestone to keuper and coloured sandstone.

ecclesiastical property was secularized, the Church owned a majority of the region's best sites, a fact also reflected in many of the vineyard names, such as Klosterberg (Cloister Hill), Domprobst (Provost of the Cathedral), Abtsberg (Abbot's Hill), etc. Although a few vineyards were returned to the Church, notably in Trier, most were sold at auction. These sales marked the foundation or expansion of what today are some of Germany's most famous private wine estates.

Koblenz to Cochem

Burg Eltz is a fairytale castle which has housed 30 generations of the Eltz family. There are tours daily, Easter–Oct, 0930–1700.

WINNINGEN
Gutsschänke Fährstr. 6 (near Moselstrasse). Tel: 02606/597. Fax: 02606/897. From 1700 Wed–Sat; from 1600 Sun. Closed from Xmas–Feb. Inviting, cosy indoors and lovely courtyard.

The lower Mosel
The lower Mosel extends 90km (56 miles) from Koblenz to Zell. Ancient castles and Romanesque church towers silhouette the landscape, but the vineyards are equally striking, particularly the terraced sites between Winningen and Gondorf, whose formidable slate cliffs seem to defy gravity as they sweep from the river bank to the sky. Further south, the valley widens and the contours of the hills are softer, but no less impressive.

Light, lively Riesling wines with a very pronounced acidity are the area's speciality. Especially notable are the wines of the Erzeugergemeinschaft Deutsches Eck, an association of lower Mosel and Mittelrhein producers whose high standards and strict quality controls in the vineyards and cellars have done much to enhance the area's reputation for fine Riesling wines. In the spring and autumn, growers and chefs along the *Terrassenmosel* (steep, terraced lower Mosel sites) host festive events with wine, food and music (details: Weingut Löwenstein, Bahnhofstr. 10, 56333 Winningen. Tel: 02606/1919. Fax: 02606/1909).

The Mosel Wine Road
The *Mosel Weinstrasse* has dark green signs with a stylized 'M' and grape clusters in orange. It usually corresponds to the B49 and the B53. From Koblenz to Karden, however, it runs simultaneously on both sides of the river as the B49 and the B416. Then it traverses the Mosel frequently, to include most of the important wine towns. Church spires can help you locate historic buildings and town centres, as they are not generally on the main road.

Motorists should depart from Koblenz via the suburb of Güls on the B416 to Winningen, a charming town with vine-canopied streets.

The Weinhex of Winningen
In the 17th century, the area was notorious for its witch-hunts. Imagine the surprise of the Winningen grower who finally caught the 'witch' who had been stealing wine from his best barrel, only to discover that she was his wife! Today, Weinhex (wine witch) is the collective name of the steep vineyards between Güls and Burgen.

The town of Cochem is dominated by the Reichsburg fortress. On the hills below and adjacent to the Reichsburg are the steep sites Schlossberg and Pinnerkreuzberg.

KOBERN-GONDORF
Alte Mühle
Mühlental 17 (in Kobern). Tel: 02607/6474. Fax: 02607/6848. Mon-Fri from 1700; Sat-Sun from 1200. Old mill with wine museum.
DIEBLICH
Halferschenke
Hauptstr. 63. Tel: 02607/1008. Fax: 02607/960294. 1800-2200 Tue-Sun, also 1200-1400 Sun. Closed Feb. Charming country inn with guest rooms. Known also for art exhibitions.
ALKEN
Gasthaus Burg Thurant
Moselstr. 15. Tel/Fax: 02605/3581. From 1730 (except Mon). Garden open from 1030 in summer. Closed Feb. Guest rooms.

In late August, Germany's oldest wine festival is celebrated around Winningen's Hexenbrunnen (witches' well). There is a wonderful view from the heights of the *Weinlehrpfad* (educational wine trail) that starts on Am Rosenberg at the edge of town.

Kobern-Gondorf
En route from Winningen to Kobern you will see an awesome feat of modern engineering in the bridge spanning the Mosel at Dieblich, 136 metres (446 ft) above the water. In contrast are the ruins of the 12th-century Niederburg fortress which come into view around the next bend.

Kobern's other castle, the Oberburg, is notable for its Romanesque St Matthias Chapel, reminiscent of the Holy Sepulchre in Jerusalem. Historic houses line Kobern's pretty market square, and one of Germany's oldest (1321) half-timbered houses is nearby, on Kirchstrasse 1.

Gondorf's Oberburg, formerly a moated castle, suffered a curious fate when the town fathers decided to build a road through its walls.

Excursion to Burg Thurant
Cross the Mosel at Löf and backtrack to the medieval town of Alken. Burg Thurant overlooks the town and the Burgberg vineyard. Built in 1197, the castle was besieged from 1246 to 1248 by the Archbishops of Trier and Cologne, and thereafter divided by a partition wall, with one keep for Trier and the other for Cologne. It is open daily. Wine is served in the garden.

Löf to Cochem
There are half a dozen wine villages with historic houses, churches and castle ruins between Löf and Cochem. Two sights especially recommended are Burg Eltz, in the Elzbach valley, and the Church of St Castor in Karden.

Burg Eltz is a dramatically picturesque castle. From Hatzenport, drive through the scenic Schrumpfbachtal (old mills) via Münstermaifeld (the Church of St Martin is notable) to Wierschem, where there are signs to the Burg Eltz car park. You can also drive from Moselkern or Milden to the start of marked trails through the woods to reach the castle (40 minutes).

Restored frescoes, carved tombs, a Stumm organ and Europe's only remaining terracotta altar (1420) are just a few of the treasures in the Romanesque and Gothic Church of St Castor in Karden. The church is open daily (0900-1800) and its museum from May-Oct (Sun 1000-1200 and Wed and Sat 1500-1700). The ancient town of Cochem is just past the Mosel's wide bend at Klotten.

Cochem to Zell

The ruins of Burg Metternich overlook the village of Beilstein and the Schlossberg vineyard.

RIVER BOAT EXCURSIONS ON THE MOSEL (MAY-OCT)
From Koblenz
Cochem 4½ hours.
From Cochem
Beilstein 1 hour; Zell 3 hours; Traben-Trarbach 5 hours. **From Bernkastel**
Traben-Trarbach 2 hours; Piesport 1 hour; Trittenheim 2 hours; Trier 4 hours.

ZELLER SCHWARZE KATZ
Perhaps the shape of the steep vineyards rising up behind Zell gave rise to the name 'Black Cat' ... or is the legend true?

Three wine merchants from Aachen could not decide which of 3 barrels to buy. As the grower reached to draw another sample, his black cat leaped on to the cask, arched its back and hissed. Assuming that the cat was defending the best wine, they bought that barrel and sold it as 'Black Cat' wine. For years thereafter they asked for wine from the same vineyard. Schwarze Katz is celebrated at a large annual festival in late June.

At Cochem the Mosel begins its series of scenic loops, creating a great number of south-facing slopes sheltered from the wind and ideally suited for growing grapes. The most intensively cultivated part of the Mosel-Saar-Ruwer begins here, extending nearly as far south as Trier. It is the largest unbroken stretch of Riesling vineyards in the world.

Cochem is a delightful town to explore on foot. From the 14th-century Enderttor (town gate) it is a brief walk up the Hinter Kempeln steps to the Klosterberg and former Capuchin monastery for a view of Old Town and the neighbouring heights. Descend the old monastery steps and walk along the town wall to Obergässchen, Balduinstor (town gate) and Branntweingässchen

(Brandy Alley) to see Cochem's historic houses. The Oberbachstrasse leads to the market square, with the Baroque town hall and half-timbered houses. From here it is a 15-minute walk via Herrenstrasse and Schloss-Strasse to Reichsburg Cochem (open daily, Easter-Oct 0900-1700).

For a look at the Elector of Trier's administrative buildings and Cochem's narrowest houses, follow the Herrenstrasse to Wenzelgasse. A stroll from the Burgfriedentor (town gate) along the beautiful Mosel promenade to St Martin's Church completes the circuit.

Beilstein
After you cross the Mosel at Cochem or Ernst, drive through Bruttig and Fankel to see very fine half-timbered houses with stepped gables and oriels. Beilstein is a medieval gem. Romantic alleys and stairways wind from the picturesque market square up to the castle ruins (Burg Metternich) and the former monastery church, with its Baroque furnishings and a late Gothic 'Black Madonna' of Spanish-Moorish origin. The vine-canopied terrace of Haus Lipmann's Alte Mosel Weinstuben (Marktplatz 3) is an idyllic setting for a glass of wine from Beilstein's Schlossberg vineyard site.

Ediger-Eller and Bremm
The road crosses the Mosel from Senheim to Nehren. Ediger's narrow cobbled streets are lined with half-timbered houses within remnants of the 14th-century fortifications. The church at the top of Kirchstrasse has an interesting mixture of styles. Its exterior is adorned by a Romanesque bell tower, a Gothic spire and gargoyles; inside, a Baroque high altar stands beneath an elaborate

vaulted ceiling. Also recommended is the Kreuzkapelle (chapel) overlooking town, with a unique stone relief called 'Christ in the Wine Press' (open Easter-Sept; otherwise, ask for the key from the tourist office). Signs show the way from Hochstrasse.

As the Mosel loops towards Bremm, Europe's steepest vineyard looms upon the right. The ruins of a 12th-century Augustinian convent standing in splendid isolation on the opposite shore can be seen in the photograph.

St Aldegund and Alf are pretty wine and resort towns. The side valleys offer scenic excursions to the Roman spa Bad Bertrich (late Baroque bathhouse) and to Burg Arras, a century-old fortress now housing a history museum, restaurant and guest rooms (closed Dec-Feb).

The best overall view of the Mosel loop near Zell is from the Marienburg (1129), that has served both as a monastery and as a fortress (the observation platform is open all year; restaurant, Easter to mid-Nov). This is a great setting for a glass of wine from the Marienburger vineyard or from Zell's famous site Schwarze Katz (Black Cat).

Cross the Mosel at Zell-Kaimt. From the tourist office in Zell's town hall, it is a 15-minute walk through the vineyards to Zell's landmark and last vestige of the fortifications, the Runder Turm (round tower). Historic houses are on Römerstrasse (nearest St Peter's Church) and the exterior of the late Gothic Electoral Palace is notable. Wine shops and pubs abound.

COCHEM
Hotel Alte Thorschenke
Brückenstr. 3. Tel: 02671/7059. Fax: 02671/4202. 1200-1400, 1800-2200 (except Wed in Nov, Dec). Closed Jan – mid-Mar.
EDIGER-ELLER
Hotel zum Löwen
Moselweinstr. 23 (Ediger). Tel: 02675/208. Fax: 02675/214. 1200-1400, 1800-2100 (except Tue in Nov, Dec). Closed Jan.
TRABEN-TRARBACH
Zur Goldenen Traube
Am Markt 8 (Trarbach). Tel: 06541/6011. Fax: 06541/6013. Daily, 1130-1400, 1730-2200. Guest rooms.

The Mosel loop near Bremm viewed from the Calmont vineyard, the steepest in Europe.

The Middle Mosel

Famous wine villages and vineyards, dramatic scenery and delicately fragrant wines with a taut balance of acidity and fruit are the Middle Mosel's chief attractions.

Zell to Traben-Trarbach

Briedel's vineyard Herzchen (little heart) is depicted symbolically on a sign welcoming visitors. From the B53, turn left on Hauptstrasse, then right on Zehntstrasse to see the old part of the town. The town hall (1615), Eulenturm (owls' tower) and St Martin's Church (1772) are worth seeing. Both Briedel and the next village, Pünderich (Kirchstrasse), have beautiful half-timbered houses.

Enkirch is equally charming. Turn left at Weingasse (Wine Alley), with its unusual street sign, to visit the museum and tasting room in the Rats-Weinschenke (no.20).

The 3½ km (2 mile) *Weinbaulehrpfad* through the Steffensberg vineyard north of the town affords good views and a look at some of the challenges facing Mosel growers.

The epitome of dedication: harvesting frozen grapes to make Eiswein.

The sundial (Sonnenuhr) in Wehlen's famous vineyard of the same name. It was built in 1842 by Jodocus Prüm to help growers know when it was time to stop work at lunchtime and in the evening.

Traben-Trarbach straddles the Mosel at its next loop. Watch for the turning to Trarbach, where you can see period rooms and wine-related artifacts in the Mittelmosel Museum located in the patrician's manor where Goethe stayed in 1792 (open Apr-Oct, Tue-Sun). The Grevenburg fortress ruins overlooking town are a good vantage point. You can also take in the scenery from the café inside the massive gate on the Mosel bridge.

Both parts of town have historic houses, including a number of *Jugendstil* (art nouveau) buildings, such as Hotel Bellevue on Traben's promenade. The ruins of Louis XIV's Mont Royal, once the largest fortification in Europe, are also on the Traben side. A spectacular wall of vineyards (Wolfer Goldgrube) looms up as you cross the bridge at Wolf.

Kröv to Machern

Approaching Kröv, turn right from the B53 and drive towards the spire of St Remigius Church, which is surrounded by many historic houses.

The burial chapel of the Counts of Kesselstatt on Ehrenmalstrasse is notable, as are the Echternacherhof (1764) and the half-timbered Dreigiebelhaus (1658) on the B53.

At the *Trachtentreffen* – the first weekend in July – music and dance groups in traditional costume from all over Europe make for a colourful wine festival. Kröv's famous vineyard site Nacktarsch (bare bottom) actually derives its name from the days when hedges, rather than vines, covered Kröv's high, stony cliffs.

Erden and Ürzig are famous for their steep sites Treppchen and Prälat and Würzgarten and Goldwingert, respectively. The 13th-century Cistercian monastery at Machern is worth visiting. Restored by the Schneider family of Zell-Merl, it is a setting for concerts and a remarkable museum on winemaking (tours Apr-Oct, Wed 1500, Sat-Sun 1400). There is also a shop (Schneider wines) and restaurant on the grounds. Cross the river here to reach Zeltingen.

Zeltingen to Bernkastel

Much of Germany's wine fame derives from the superb Riesling vineyards of Zeltingen, Wehlen, Graach and Bernkastel. Sonnenuhr, Himmelreich, and Doctor are but a few of the best-known sites. There is a concentration of top wine estates here, and several large estates in Trier have holdings.

For a splendid view, take the first exit at Graach, turn left at Neuer Weg and drive to Schäferei. Looking across the river, you can see Wehlen's stately manors on the shore, and on the left the large co-operative, Moselland. Its 3800 grower members collectively produce about a fifth of all Mosel-Saar-Ruwer wines. Bernkastel lies over the next hill to the left.

Bernkastel-Kues, viewed from the Doctor vineyard. The town is the setting for a large wine celebration in early September.

Bernkastel-Kues

Bernkastel is a quaint, charming town best explored on foot. Park at the river front and walk to the market square. St Michael's fountain (1606) is surrounded by half-timbered houses (16th-17th century) and the Renaissance town hall (1608). To see the legendary Doctor vineyard, walk along Hinterm Graben street near the old town gate, Graacher Tor.

Piesport's famed Goldtröpfchen site, where the Mosel is surrounded by a natural amphitheatre of Riesling vines.

Burg Landshut (castle) affords a good view. It was once a favourite summer residence of Trier's Electors and Archbishops, including Boemund II, who attributed his recovery from illness to the healing powers of the local wine, thereafter named 'Doctor'.

The Mosel Wine Museum, across the bridge in Kues, shows vintners' tools and household items and a notable collection of glasses in a building of the St Nikolaus Hospital, founded in 1458 by the theologian Nikolaus Cusanus, born here in 1401. (Cusanusstr. 2, Easter to Oct 1000-1700; 1400-1700 in winter).

Kues to Piesport

Lieser, Kesten and Minheim are on the left bank of the Mosel, with vineyards extending into the side valleys around Maring-Noviand and Osann-Monzel.

In Siebenborn (near Maring) you can visit 800-year-old cellars at

Weingut Klosterhof Siebenborn, once owned by the Himmerod monastery (daily, 1400-1800). Also see the 2nd-century Römerkelter (Roman press house) in Noviand (May-Oct, Sundays and holidays, 1400-1700).

Bernkastel to Piesport

Mülheim, Brauneberg and Wintrich are on the right bank of the Mosel, with vineyards extending into the side valleys around Veldenz and Burgen.

Mülheim is famous for 'Zeppelin' wine, Mülheimer Sonnenlay, once served on the airship Graf Zeppelin. Brauneberg's excellent sites Juffer and Juffer Sonnenuhr are on the steep slopes opposite the town. From the pretty village of Wintrich, the Mosel makes a 180° loop towards Piesport.

Piesport to Trittenheim

Turn right on Brückenstrasse and drive towards the river for a view of the vine-covered hills curving round Piesport. Its famous vineyard, Goldtröpfchen, is to the right of the village. In the old part of town across the river are the splendid Baroque interior and ceiling frescoes of St Michael's Church. The 4th-century Roman press house on the western edge of town is the largest on the Mosel.

This tombstone of a Roman wine merchant was discovered in 1874 when Constantine's 4th-century Neumagen citadel was excavated. The original is on display at the Landesmuseum in Trier.

ENKIRCH
Rats-Weinschenke
Weingasse 20. From 1800 (except Wed). Closed Nov-Mar. Tasting room of town in half-timbered house.
DREIS (SW of Wittlich)
Waldhotel Sonnora
Auf dem Eichelfeld. Tel: 06578/406. Fax: 06578/1402. 1200-1400, 1900-2100 (except Mon, Tue). Closed Jan. Gourmet restaurant with superb wines. Guest rooms.
BERNKASTEL
Doktorweinstuben
Hebegasse 5. Tel: 06531/6081. Fax: 06531/6296. 1200-1400, 1800-2200 (except Tue). Mid-Nov to mid-Mar closed. Hotel.
Ratskeller Am Markt 30. 1200-1415 and 1800-2130 (except Mon). Closed Feb.
BERNKASTEL WINE SHOPS
Moselland Co-operative
Bornwiese 6 (Kues). Mon-Fri 0900-1200, 1300-1800; Sat 0900-1230. Tours in English, Thu 1000, Easter-Oct.
Weingut J. Lauerburg Am Markt 27. Apr-Oct. Mon-Fri 1000-1700, Sat 1100-1700.
Weingut Dr Pauly-Bergweiler Gestade 15. Mon-Fri 1000-1200, 1400-1900; Sat 1500-1900. May-Oct. Guest rooms.
PIESPORT
Weinstube Moselblick
Am Berg (drive uphill through vineyards, on the road to Klausen). Tel/Fax: 06507/2267. From 1100 Sat-Sun, from 1400 Mon-Fri (except Tue), Apr-Oct. Guest rooms all year. Spectacular view.
NEUMAGEN-DHRON
Gutshotel Reichsgraf v. Kesselstatt Balduinstr. 1. Tel: 06507/2035. Fax: 06507/5644. Apr-Oct 1200-1400, 1800-2200. Nov-Mar 1800-2200. Closed Mon, and Jan – mid-Feb. Elegant country inn. Excellent food and wine.

Neumagen, said to be Germany's oldest wine village, was the site of a great Roman find: a sculpture of a wine-laden ship. Other sights include a monument to the Roman poet Ausonius, whose *Mosella* (AD 371) praised the beauty of the Mosel.

Trittenheim is in another of the Mosel's 180° loops, surrounded by its famous sites Apotheke and Altärchen. The first mention of Riesling on the Mosel is at Trittenheim, in 1562. A century earlier, the great scholar Trithemius was born here.

The Roman Wine Road
One Roman road from Trier to Mainz followed the Mosel to Leiwen and Neumagen before crossing the Hunsrück. When growers formed an association in 1986, *Römische Weinstrasse* (Roman wine road) was chosen as its name. Their logo, a

Roman transporting wine on a horse-drawn cart, appears on signposts and on the label of a medium dry Riesling wine produced in this area.

This part of the Mosel valley is rich in Roman remains. There is an important Roman villa opposite Mehring. In addition to a cellar, baths, heating system and towers, the foundations show the existence of another 18 rooms.

Leiwen's vineyard area is the Mosel's largest. The village itself is charming. Klüsserath's parish church has notable furnishings. In the former Roman village of Detzem (*ad decimum lapidem*) you can see the 10th Roman milestone on the route from Trier to Mainz or watch one of the Mosel's 14 locks in action. Longuich has fine buildings and an idyllic promenade. The ancient wine towns of Kenn and Schweich mark the end of the route.

St Klemen's Church in Trittenheim has remarkable 18th-century furnishings.

NAURATH-BÜDLICHERBRÜCK
(Dhrontal/Dhron valley; exit A1 at Mehring and/or from B325, then watch for turning to Bescheid. Or 8km/5 miles S of Trittenheim/Leiwen.)
Landhaus St Urban Tel: 06509/91400. Fax: 06509/914040. 1200-1400 (except Tue, Wed) and 1830-2200 (except Tue). Closed Jan. Gourmet restaurant with guest rooms in idyllic setting. Family's wine estate: Weingut St Urbanshof, Urbanusstr. 16, Leiwen. Mon-Fri 0800-1800.
LEIWEN
Hotel Zummethof
Panoramaweg 1 (above the vineyards of Leiwen). Tel: 06507/93550. Fax: 06507/935544. 1130-1430, 1730-2200. Closed Jan, Feb. Great view from the terrace.

Trier

St Peter's Fountain on Trier's market square dates from 1595. St Peter is the town's patron saint.

Trier is considered to be the oldest town in Germany and among the most fascinating. Its slogan 'with 2000 footsteps discover 2000 years of history' is excellent advice. Trier's wine tradition is older than its historic buildings – the Romans had planted vineyards on the slopes of the town by the middle of the first century AD, predating even its oldest (AD 100) Roman structure, the amphitheatre.

Today, as in Roman times, Trier is the region's cultural, religious, political and commercial centre. The state-owned wine domain as well as ecclesiastical, public and private wine estates carry on the legacy of the Romans and the Church.

In 16 BC Emperor Augustus founded *Augusta Treverorum* on a site which had been settled for centuries by the Celtic tribe of the Treveri. Situated at the junction of major trade routes, it quickly grew into a shipping and trading centre. The amphitheatre, Roman bridge, Barbara thermal baths and superb Roman gate, Porta Nigra, date from this early period of prosperity.

After destruction in AD 275 by Teutonic tribes, Trier was rebuilt on an even grander scale. In the late 3rd and 4th centuries, it was the imperial residence and capital of the western part of the Roman Empire, a territory extending from Britain to southern Spain. Constantine the Great built monumental public structures (imperial baths, palace with *Aula palatina*) and the first bishop's church of Germany.

Evidence of Trier's Roman wine heritage abounds. Parts of the *Horrea* (AD 330), the largest Roman warehouse north of the Alps, are Germany's oldest cellars that are still being used to store wine. (To visit, write to: Vereinigte Hospitien, Krahnenufer 19, 54290 Trier.) Highly recommended is the spectacular collection of wine-related Roman artifacts in the Landesmuseum, Ostallee 44 (Tue-Fri 0930-1700, Sat-Sun 1030-1700).

Ecclesiastical Trier

The pagan Franks conquered Trier in the 5th century. Christianity, however, eventually triumphed. Under Charlemagne, the Bishop of Trier was elevated to Archbishop, and in the 12th century, to Prince Elector. The Church restored Trier to a position of power and enriched it with splendid churches and the Electoral Palace. Viticulture flourished at the hands of the Church fathers whose far-sighted regulations governing work in the vineyards and the cellars did much to improve quality. In 1787, the last Prince Elector, Clemens Wenzeslaus,

TRIER
Palais Kesselstatt
Liebfrauenstr. 9. Tel: 0651/75101. Fax: 0651/73316. 1100-1400, 1800-2200 (except Sun, Mon). Closed Feb. Gourmet dining in a palace from 1745. Also: wine shop and light fare in **Weinstube Palais Kesselstatt**. Daily 1100-2400. Closed Feb. Rustic, cosy wine pub, with tree-shaded terrace in summer.

Zum Domstein
Hauptmarkt 5. Tel: 0651/74490. Fax: 0651/74499. 1130-2130. Cosy indoors, garden seating in summer. See the Roman artifacts on display and dine in Roman cellars Easter-Oct. Speciality: dishes prepared according to ancient Roman recipes.

Pfeffermühle Zurlaubener Ufer 76. Tel: 0651/26133. 1200-1400 (except Sun, Mon), 1830-2130 (except Sun). Gourmet dining on the river bank.

Zurlaubener Uferfest
Wine festival on the river bank of Trier's historic fishermen's quarter, July. For a fabulous view of Trier take the cable-car from Zurlauben to Weisshaus.

TRIER WINE SHOPS
Bischöfliche Weingüter Gervasiusstr./Rahnenstr. Mon-Fri 0900-1700.

Friedr-Wilhelm-Gymnasium Weberbach 75. Mon-Fri 0900-1230, 1300-1745. Also, Apr-Dec 0900-1330 Sat.

Weininformation
Konstantinplatz 11 (in the arcade opp. Basilika). Mon-Fri 1100-1300, 1330-1830. Sat 1000-1300, 1330-1600. Also, Apr-Oct 1300-1700 Sun. Wide selection of wines to sample, purchase. Information on Mosel wines.

went so far as to make the planting of Riesling mandatory throughout the Mosel valley.

Other sights

The finest examples of secular medieval architecture are on Simeonstrasse, the market square and Dietrichstrasse. The birthplace of Karl Marx, Brückenstrasse 10, has a small museum dedicated to the founder of Communism (open Apr-Oct, 1000-1800, Mon 1300-1800).

Visit or write to 'Tourist Information Trier', An der Porta Nigra, 54290 Trier (Tel: 0651/978080. Fax: 0651/44759), for excellent maps and brochures and exemplary guided walking tours, or to arrange wine tastings.

Porta Nigra, the Roman town gate. The upper storeys were once converted into a twin church.

TRIER-PFALZEL
Klosterschenke
Klosterstr. 10 (opposite bank of Mosel). Tel: 0651/6089. Fax: 0651/64313. 1200-1400, 1900-2200. Closed Jan. Lovely hotel and restaurant in 800-year-old monastery. Terrace on the river bank. Cycle path *Moselfahrradweg* starts here.

The Ruwer and Saar Valleys

MERTESDORF
Hotel Weingut Weis
Eitelsbacher Str. 4. Tel:
0651/95610. Fax: 0651/
9561150. Daily 1200-1400
and 1800-2300. Closed
Jan. Situated at the foot of
steep Ruwer vineyards.
Weingut Karlsmühle
Im Mühlengrund 1. Tel:
0651/5123. Fax: 0651/
52016. May-Oct daily,
1200-1400, 1800-2200.
Nov-Apr closed Mon. Also
closed Jan. 500-year-old mill
in park-like setting. Hotel.
SAARBURG
Burg-Restaurant
Auf dem Burgberg 1. Tel:
06581/2622. Fax: 06581/
6695. 1200-1400, 1800-
2130 (except Mon, Tue).
Closed Jan. Castle from
AD 964. Wonderful view of
Saar valley. Terrace.
AYL
Ayler Kupp Trierer Str.
49. Tel: 06581/3031. Fax:
06581/2344. 1200-1400,
1800-2200 Tue-Sat. Hotel,
wine estate daily. Closed Jan.

The Ruwer and the Saar flow into
the Mosel to the north and south of
Trier, respectively. Both valleys are an
easy drive from Trier and make for
pleasant excursions.

The finest wines of the Ruwer
and the Saar, as on the Mosel, derive
from the combination of steep, south-
facing slopes; slate soil; and the
Riesling grape. In general, the wines
are more fragrant and have a more
pronounced acidity than their softer
and fuller Mosel counterparts.

Trier and the Ruwer

Depart from Trier to the north. At
the roundabout, look for signs to the
suburb of Ruwer. After two railway
crossings, turn right to Eitelsbach, the
first important wine town on the river
Ruwer, but still officially part of Trier.

Karthäuserhofberg is the name of
the vineyard, referring to the
Carthusian monastery which owned it
in the Middle Ages. The present estate
has a most unusual label: a small
curved label affixed only to the neck of
the bottle. Mertesdorf's most famous
vineyards, Maximin Grünhaus, are
across the road from the village and
are also named after their medieval
owners, St Maximin Abbey of Trier.

Kasel and Waldrach

Several famous estates have vineyard
holdings in Kasel, testimony to the
fine reputation of its wines.

Waldrach is less well-known, but
also produces very good wine. The
Roman aqueduct that supplied Ruwer
water for Trier's baths and drinking
water started here.

Wine suburbs of Trier

To see Trier's wine suburbs, return on
the country roads through the wine
towns of Korlingen, Irsch and Olewig,

popular for its charming wine estates
and the festivals in vintners' courtyards
(*Hoffest*) in July and August. The
Weinlehrpfad from Olewig to Sickingen
Strasse, opposite the amphitheatre in
Trier, makes for an enjoyable walk.

The Saar valley

Viticulture on the Saar flourished
during Roman times, but declined
thereafter. Oak forests supplanted
vines, and tanners replaced wine-
growers. In the 19th century, when
tanning was increasingly carried out
with chemicals, many forest owners
replanted the slopes with vines. Many
vineyards are named *Kupp*, referring
to the rounded hilltops.

Depart from Trier to the south
and drive to Konz, where the Saar
flows into the Mosel. Turn left on to
the road immediately *before* the Saar
crossing. The Saar's first important
vineyards and estates are at Filzen.
The road follows the Saar's first big
loop (Hamm) and crosses the river at
Kanzem (very good, steep vineyards).

At Wiltingen, across the next bridge,
is the Scharzberg hill, whose name may
be used as a group appellation for all
Saar wines. Scharz*hof*berg is a choice
part of the hill, which is famous
because of the superb Scharzhof estate.

Ockfen and Serrig

The hills of Bockstein and Geisberg
lend their names to Ockfen's best sites.
Continuing on this side of the Saar
past Beurig, Schloss Saarfels castle at
Serrig comes into view. It is the name
of both a vineyard and an estate, as
are Schloss Saarstein and Herrenberg.
Serrig's name derives from the Latin
Serviacum, referring to the Roman
Servius, who is said to have founded
the settlement and planted the first
vines in the Herrenberg site.

Saarburg

Backtrack to the bridge at Beurig to reach Saarburg, a picturesque town of half-timbered and Baroque buildings, old gates and towers. A brook runs through the town's lanes, forming a steep waterfall that once powered the mills. You can visit the Mabilon bell foundry in Old Town, on Staden 130 (Mon-Fri 0800-1200 and 1400-1600). For a panoramic view, visit the *Burg* (fortress) overlooking the town. Also recommended are excursions to Ayl, an important wine village to the north, and Kastel-Staadt, to the south, where the *Klause* (hermitage) atop the cliffs was built as a tomb for the blind King Johann of Bohemia (1296-1346).

'Three-country corner'

Perl, gateway to the Mosel, is 30 minutes from Saarburg via the B407. The Mosel is the border between Germany and Luxembourg as it flows peacefully past vineyards, orchards, forests and wine and farm villages.

Since Roman times, Elbling has been the main grape grown on the chalky slopes. In Nennig's Roman villa, you can see the most beautiful Roman mosaic tile floors north of the Alps (Apr-Sep 0830-1200 and 1300-1800; Oct-Mar 0900-1200 and 1300-1630; closed Mon and Dec to mid-Jan). From here, you can enjoy 40km (24 miles) of idyllic landscape as the Mosel gently loops towards Trier.

Picturesque Saarburg, on the river Saar, was originally a fishing village and later a centre of tanning and weaving, as well as an important defence outpost of Trier. Colourful festivals take place in July, August and September.

FOR FURTHER INFORMATION
Contact the regional wine promotion board:
Mosel-Saar-Ruwer Wein
Gartenfeldstr. 12a,
54295 Trier.
Tel: 0651/45967 or 76621.
Fax: 0651/45443.
Their *Weinreiseführer* lists events and wine estates (in German, with pictograms).

The Nahe

The Nahe is a quiet region situated in the Hunsrück Hills between the Mosel and Rhine valleys. The part of the region of viticultural importance follows the course of the Nahe river from its confluence with the Rhine at Bingerbrück for about 60km (36 miles) south and west as far as Kirn. South of Bad Kreuznach, the largest town and an important wine-growing centre, are the dramatic porphyry cliffs of Rotenfels and Rheingrafenstein.

In this region you can follow the *Weinwanderweg Nahe* hiking trail, with its historic towns and castle ruins, or drive along the circular route of the *Nahe-Weinstrasse* (Nahe Wine Road). Simply follow the signs with a Römer wine glass bearing the letter 'N'. The unique wine festival *Rund um die Nahe-Weinstrasse* takes place in late August and early September, when 30 villages on the wine road simultaneously celebrate wine for three consecutive weekends.

LOCAL WINE GLASSES

Two wine glasses are typical of the region: the *Römer*, also called *Pokal*, and the Nahe's own *Remis'chen*, a straight-sided tumbler. Both hold 0.2 litres (c. one third of a pint).

REGIONAL SPECIALITIES ·

Füllselkartoffeln: minced liver, ground pork and cubed potatoes are spiced with marjoram and cooked together. Also used to stuff:
Spansau: roast sucking pig.
Spiessbraten: shoulder of pork sprinkled with chopped onion and spices, rolled and then roasted on a spit.
Schwenk- or Schaukel-braten: spiced steaks, usually pork, roasted by swinging (*schwenken* or *schaukeln*) the grill over a fire.

FOR FURTHER INFORMATION

Contact the regional wine promotion board:
Weinland Nahe
Dessauer Str. 6,
55545 Bad Kreuznach.
Tel: 0671/27563.
Fax: 0671/27568.

Nahewein ein Edelstein

This, the region's traditional slogan, is proudly displayed on signposts at the edge of every wine village. It means 'Nahe wine is a jewel', and refers not only to its high quality, but also to the region's mineral wealth.

The hills are full of tunnels where copper, silver and mercury were once mined. Idar-Oberstein, the centre of Germany's precious stone industry, is not far from the Nahe's westernmost vineyards.

The Romans were probably the first to cultivate grapes here, judging by the Roman wine jugs and tools found near Bad Kreuznach. Deeds of gift to the Lorsch monastery (near the Bergstrasse) contain the first written mention of wine-growing in the region (AD 766). The Church and the aristocracy expanded the vineyard area to nearly 3000 hectares (7400 acres) during the Middle Ages.

Viticulture suffered a great decline from the 16th century to the 18th, when vast tracts of land were laid waste by many wars. Recovery started slowly in the 19th century and was greatly enhanced at the turn of the century by the founding of a wine-growers' school in Bad Kreuznach and the State Wine Domain in Niederhausen, a model of quality wine production to this day.

The tasting-room of Germany

Although the Nahe is one of the smaller wine regions (4611 hectares/ 11,394 acres), it has an extraordinary range of soil types and mixtures. As a result, the Nahe has been dubbed 'the tasting-room of Germany', for its wines show a remarkable diversity.

The Nahe produces racy, piquant wines with a fine fruitiness from slate, quartzite and stony soils on steep hills. The gentle slopes and flatlands with heavier clay, loam and loess soils, often mixed with sand and gravel, produce milder, fuller and more aromatic wines. A layer of red sandstone runs sporadically through the region, adding still another dimension to the wines of some of the villages.

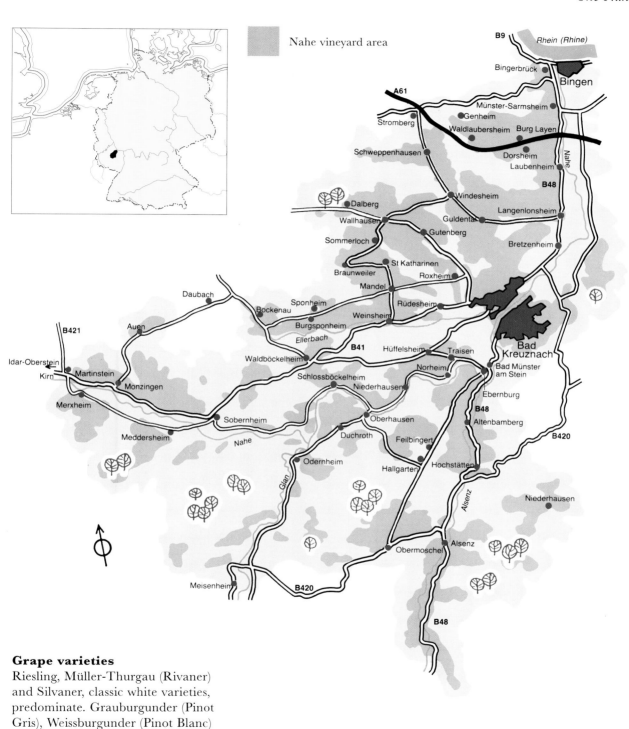

Nahe vineyard area

Grape varieties
Riesling, Müller-Thurgau (Rivaner)
and Silvaner, classic white varieties,
predominate. Grauburgunder (Pinot
Gris), Weissburgunder (Pinot Blanc)
and Kerner are also planted, as is the
red Spätburgunder (Pinot Noir).

Bad Kreuznach

Bad Kreuznach is the centre of the Nahe's 2000-year-old wine culture. Located at the junction of ancient trade routes, it has been settled since Celtic times and was part of the Roman Empire for more than 400 years.

The waters

For centuries, Bad Kreuznach has been famous for its salubrious salt-water springs and mild climate. Part of today's spa facilities date from 1743, when the first two of six graduated timber framework *Salinen* (salterns) were completed. They are still visually the most striking aspect of the spa. People sit or walk by the structures and inhale the vapours from the salt water, which evaporates as it is pumped over the framework. The springs became popular as medicinal baths in the 19th century and even more so after the turn of the century, when the presence of radon gas was believed to aid the cure of rheumatoid, circulatory and respiratory ailments.

The neo-Baroque Kurhaus (1913) served as the German Imperial headquarters during World War I. After World War II, it was the site of the first meeting (1958) between de Gaulle and Adenauer to re-establish friendship between the two nations.

The wines

Bad Kreuznach is famous equally for its wine and its waters. Nearly one fifth of the Nahe's entire vineyard area is in Bad Kreuznach and its wine suburbs.

You are more likely to become familiar with the name of a particular grower than with the nearly 40 names of the town's vineyards. A few sloping sites, however, planted mostly with Riesling grapes, are known well beyond their borders, such as Krötenpfuhl, Brückes, Narrenkappe, Kahlenberg,

Steinweg, and Rosenheck. Also try the flowery, fresh Müller-Thurgau and juicy, full-bodied Silvaner wines or one of the aromatic new crossings, such as Scheurebe or Bacchus. Wines from the Kerner grape are similar to Riesling. You will find these and Burgunder (Pinot) varieties throughout the region.

There is a fine view of Bad Kreuznach from the ruins of the 12th-century Kauzenburg fortress (now a restaurant). In the grounds of the botanical park below, there is a museum of prehistory in the Schloss (palace) and in the Römerhalle (Romans' Hall) you can see Roman artifacts and mosaics. (Both are open daily, 1000-1700.) A Roman villa has been reconstructed nearby. There is a precious gilded reliquary in the St Nikolaus Church, an early Gothic basilica, and historic half-timbered houses in the Old Town near the Eiermarkt (egg market).

Bridge houses

The Faust-Haus, next to the Wilhelms-Brücke (bridge), is today a wine pub with mementoes of the infamous magician, Dr Faust, who lived there in 1507. Cross the Nahe on the Alte Nahebrücke (bridge built in 1311) to see the unusual *Brückenhäuser* (bridge houses) built on piles in the river. In the background is the Baroque tower of St Paulus Church, where Karl Marx was married in 1843. Walk along the tree-lined Kurhausstrasse to the Kurhaus, centre of the oldest radon-salt-water spa in the world, idyllically set in the Kurpark on the banks of the Nahe river. From April to October, there is an inviting wine pub at the Elisabeth-Quelle in the park.

The 15th-century Brückenhäuser (bridge houses) on the Alte Nahebrücke. One is a wine pub.

Weinstube im Brückenhaus
Mannheimer Str. 94.
Mon, Tue, Thu 1600-2300, Fri-Sun 1200-2400.
Historisches Dr Faust Haus Magister-Faust-Gasse 47. From 1600 (except Tue), Sat-Sun also 1100-1400.
Im Gütchen Hüffelsheimer Str. 1. Tel 0671/42626. Fax: 0671/480435. Wed-Sat from 1800. Sun also 1200-1400. Regional specialities, large selection of top Nahe wines.
Oase (in Hotel Insel-Stuben) Kurhausstr. 10. Tel: 0671/ 43043. Fax: 0671/8379955. Fri-Wed 1200-1400, 1800-2200. Creative cuisine. Wine list features best Nahe estates.

The Alsenz and Glan Valleys

Vineyards are also scattered throughout the side valleys of these tributaries of the Nahe. The Alsenz flows into the Nahe where it bends west at Ebernburg. Riesling is the main grape here; further south, Silvaner predominates.

The fortress ruins of Altenbaumburg overlooking the town of Altenbamberg are worth visiting. There is also a fine panorama from the fortress ruins of Moschellandsburg, or from the Burg-Hotel near Obermoschel.

Meisenheim on the Glan has retained its medieval townscape, with historic houses on Ober- and Untergasse. The late Gothic Schlosskirche (church) has many works of art, remarkable sculpted tombs, and an organ made by the Stumm family.

Near Odernheim, at the mouth of the Glan, the monastery ruins of Kloster Disibodenberg dominate a vineyard of the same name. In the 7th century, on the site where Celts had once worshipped, the Irish monk St Disibod founded a monastery. It was greatly expanded in the Middle Ages under the Abbess St Hildegard of Bingen, the mystic famous for her music and scientific and medical writings.

Not far from the ruins is a wine and fruit estate with a shop selling cider, apples and jelly in addition to wine. Ring the old bell in the courtyard if the door is not open.

WINE AND FOLK FESTIVALS
Kreuznacher Jahrmarkt
Fri-Tue, 3rd weekend of Aug at Pfingstwiese, north edge of town. Annually, since 1361.
Nordpfälzer Herbstfest
Mid Sep in Rockenhausen, S of Bad Kreuznach via B48. Features Alsenz valley wines.
CASTLE RESTAURANTS
Altenbaumburg in the town of Altenbamberg. Mar-Dec 1200-1400, 1800-2100. Jan-Feb 1200-1400.
Burg-Hotel in the town of Obermoschel. 1100-1400, 1800-2200 (except Jan).
Ritterstube in the town of Ebernburg. 1100-1400, 1800-2100 May-Oct. Closed Mon, otherwise, and in Jan.

The Middle Nahe

The *Nahe-Weinstrasse*

The *Nahe-Weinstrasse* (Nahe Wine Road), which takes you from Bad Kreuznach to Schlossböckelheim, includes the Nahe's most dramatic scenery as well as some of its finest vineyards.

The steep sites have excellent exposure to the sun. The soils are mixtures of loam with sand, slate, loess, gravel or volcanic stone over substrata of porphyry or sandstone, rich in minerals and heat-retaining properties.

The Nahe tempers the climate and acts as a sun reflector. All in all, these are ideal growing conditions, yielding top-quality wines with a full fruitiness, spicy undertone, pronounced acidity and long-lasting flavour.

Riesling is the main grape variety. The steep Riesling vineyard Felseneck ('Cliff Corner') rises up on the right as you approach the town of Bad Münster am Stein. Wines from this site rank among the best of the region.

Bad Münster am Stein-Ebernburg

Bad Münster am Stein is also a spa and a health resort, with facilities in an 18th-century half-timbered house situated at the foot of the precipitous Rheingrafenstein. Historic buildings include the *Zehntscheuer* (1560), the barn where the tithes were stored, and the Fischerhaus (1561) on the river bank. For a fine view from the ruins of the 12th-century fortress, you should take the hand-operated ferry across the river to ascend Rheingrafenstein (half an hour's walk).

The fortress of Burg Ebernburg is perched atop another fine Riesling vineyard, Schlossberg, overlooking the village of Ebernburg. Drive or walk (half an hour) to the fortress for a good view of the rustic old town, the church with an 11th-century defence tower and the porphyry cliff of the Rotenfels, the highest rock face (180m/591ft) in mainland Europe north of the Alps.

Rotenfels cliff

The terraced vineyards nearest the river, at the foot of the Rotenfels, consistently yield the best wine. The vineyards Bastei and Rotenfels of Traisen and Dellchen and Kafels of Norheim are among the top Riesling sites.

The summit of Rotenfels is an excellent vantage point. To get there, drive from Traisen to the car park and then walk to the edge.

Norheim, mentioned in a deed of gift to Lorsch monastery in AD 766, is the oldest wine village of the Nahe.

There are many hiking trails through the forests and hills that enable you to see rare fauna and flora, such as pasque-flowers.

Porphyry cliffs make a dramatic backdrop to Bad Münster am Stein-Ebernburg.

The Rotenfels, mainland Europe's highest rock face north of the Alps.

MEDIEVAL FESTIVAL
Held on the 3rd weekend of Sep in the old town centre of Ebernburg. With costumes, jousts, a parade of knights, grilled meats, fish and local wines.

Niederhausen and Schlossböckelheim

These ancient wine towns have been synonymous with the highest quality since the Staatliche Weinbaudomäne (State Wine Domain) was established in 1902 by the King of Prussia (hence the stylized black eagle on the label). The steep hillsides were cleared and planted with Riesling vines. The site of a former copper mine (Kupfergrube) is now a famous vineyard, as are Hermannshöhle, Hermannsberg and Felsenberg.

Niederhausen's 12th-century church boasts frescoes and wall paintings with grape motifs. The *Weinwanderweg*, a 5km (3 mile) marked path through the vineyards, starts at the school on the edge of town nearest the Domäne.

Cross the Nahe on Luitpoldbrücke (bridge, 1889) to Oberhausen and Duchroth, both old wine towns with excellent vineyards.

Excursion via Feilbingert

For the best view of Niederhausen drive via Feilbingert (on the other side of the river) to the Nahe's highest hill, the Lemberg (422m/1385ft). Nearby, you can visit Schmittenstollen, a former mercury mine, or see the ruins of Burg Monfort, once the fortress of notorious robber-knights.

The Upper Nahe

The black cat of Zell/Mosel is probably the best known cat in German wine mythology. But the town of Ebernburg also has its Schwarze Katz.

In the old days, coopers who worked for a wine estate were allowed to make their own wine, for free, from the grape must left over after the first pressings. The resulting wine was, however, of lower quality.

One cooper decided to improve his situation at the expense of the estate owner. He developed the habit of tapping the kegs of the estate's better wines, and replacing the difference with his own inferior wine. The reputation of the estate's wines suffered as a result and the owner resolved to catch the thief.

He let loose a black cat in the cellars. It slept, invisible in the darkness, on the warm barrels of fermenting must. When the cooper crept in to make his customary switch, the startled cat sprang out at him from the darkness and a great commotion ensued. The cooper, caught red-handed, confessed and was locked up for a short time.

After his release he could not forego his old ways and was again caught with the help of the black cat. This time, however, he was hanged and his head placed on spikes before the estate's cellars as a warning to others. The black cat stayed on, ever-vigilant, and became a symbol of pure, unadulterated wine.

As the *Nahe-Weinstrasse* continues westwards, the valley broadens out, and the river flows at a more leisurely pace. There are vineyards on both sides of the Nahe, but they are not always visible from the road. The steep sites near Meddersheim or Merxheim, for example, are behind the villages, situated on south-facing hillsides for optimum exposure to the sun.

The Soonwald

After crossing the Nahe at its westernmost wine town, Martinstein, the route passes through rolling hills bordered by the Soonwald (Soon Forest), once the realm of the ribald bandit Schinderhannes (the Nahe's Robin Hood) and other folk heroes. The vineyards here are on steep or sloping hills, scattered amidst fields, orchards and woods. The wine villages are ancient, charming in their rustic simplicity, and most have churches worth visiting.

Bad Sobernheim

The town is a health resort known for mud bath cures (named after their proponent, Pastor Felke) with many interesting buildings, above all the St Matthias Church, with its star-vaulted choir, frescoes and Stumm organ.

South of the town, the open-air *Freilichtmuseum* shows the architecture and way of life typical of country villages centuries ago. (Open Easter-Oct, 0900-1700; restaurant 0900-2000. Both closed Mondays.)

Meddersheim to Monzingen

Meddersheim has a Renaissance town hall and a richly furnished Protestant church, as well as farmhouses and courtyards dating from the 16th and 17th centuries. En route to Merxheim you will pass the Rheingrafenberg co-operative winery (with shop), named after the town's best vineyard site.

Merxheim also has its historic houses and the Neues Schloss (18th-century palace) is the rectory of the Catholic church. At Martinstein, the route crosses the Nahe and loops east to Monzingen, with half-timbered houses said to be the prettiest of the region, particularly the Alt'sche Haus (1589) on Kirchstrasse 2.

The dark red soils (slate, stony and sandy loam over sandstone) of this part of the Nahe yield hearty, juicy wines with a fine acidity and rich bouquet.

Ellerbach valley

The route leaves the Nahe and winds through the forest past Auen and Daubach. On the way, in a cemetery, you can see the Willigis-Kapelle (chapel) built in AD 1000 and the grave of the legendary *Jäger aus der Kurpfalz* (Hunter of the Pfalz).

The Ellerbachtal (valley) is very hilly, with vineyards on steep slopes. St Laurentius Church in Bockenau, an old potters' village, is notable for its remarkable high altar. For a good view of the valley, visit the ruins of the ancestral castle of the Counts of Sponheim in Burgsponheim. The masonry of the main tower (22m/72 ft high) is exemplary for its time.

Equally impressive is the monumental Romanesque church on the hilltop of Sponheim. Next to the church, the ruins of the Benedictine monastery to which it belonged can also be visited.

The edge of the Soon Forest

The vineyards near Mandel, St Katharinen and Braunweiler, are less steep and Müller-Thurgau is the main grape. The wines have a pleasant flowery bouquet and a mild acidity. Silvaner, Riesling and Scheurebe are the other varieties planted here.

The *Nahe-Weinstrasse* continues north and east, to wine towns in the Gräfenbach and Guldenbach valleys and along the lower stretch of the Nahe river. Notable wine towns which are not directly on the *Nahe-Weinstrasse* include: Waldböckelheim (Silvaner wines are a speciality); Weinsheim and Roxheim (Riesling wines from steep sites); and Hüffelsheim and Rüdesheim (all three classic white varieties are grown).

A panorama of the vineyards near Meddersheim, from a painting dated 1875. Tractors have replaced the horse-drawn cart, but the landscape is still dominated by vineyards, orchards and meadows.

STAUDERNHEIM
(between Bad Sobernheim and Odernheim)
Bacchus Stuben
Hauptstr. 44. Tel: 06751/93230. Fax: 06751/932323. 1200-1400,1800-2200. Closed Wed and Nov-Mar. Friendly wine restaurant with guest rooms.
WALDBÖCKELHEIM
Weingut Hehner-Kiltz
Hauptstr. 4. Tel: 06758/7918. Fax: 06758/8620. 1200-1400, 1800-2200. Wine restaurant, featuring the estate's wines. Guest rooms.

The Lower Nahe

The lower Nahe includes the wine villages north and north-west of Bad Kreuznach. Vineyards are located along the valleys of three small streams, Gräfenbach, Guldenbach and Trollbach, and along the banks of the Nahe from its confluence with the Rhine at Bingerbrück.

The steeper slopes are often reserved for Riesling while Müller-Thurgau, Silvaner and newer varieties are planted on the gentler slopes and flatlands. Here, as throughout the Nahe, there are many soil types and thus there is a great diversity of wines.

Viticulture is more concentrated here than in the upper Nahe. The word *Sonne* (sun) appears frequently in vineyard names, alluding to their southern exposure.

Gräfenbach valley

Wallhausen is an old wine village at the foot of the Soon Forest. The layer of coloured sandstone below the loamy soil gives the wines a pronounced fruity bouquet and character. Felseneck and Johannisberg are good sites. Schloss Wallhausen is the home of one of the oldest wine-growing families of Germany,

descendants of the Knights of Dalberg whose vineyard holdings date from the 13th century. A *Rotweinfest* (red wine festival) takes place at the castle annually (2nd weekend May).

The Catholic church near the castle has many elaborate gravestones, and there are historic houses on the street Im Schafwinkel.

The ruins of the 13th-century Gutenburg fortress come into view on the way to the next wine village. It is the namesake of both the town and its best vineyard. You can walk up to it for a good view and to see the defence wall between the two battle-scarred towers.

Guldenbach valley

Guldental is a significant wine-growing centre, with about 500 hectares (1235 acres) of vines. Müller-Thurgau wines with a light spiciness and hearty Silvaner wines are the town's specialities. The village has an historic fountain (1584) and a 15th-century church with a Romanesque tower.

Windesheim is renowned for fine organs made by the Oberlinger family. Its church has interesting paintings on its wooden ceiling.

At Schweppenhausen, make a slight detour from the *Nahe-Weinstrasse* to visit the 12th-century fortress of Stromburg, today a hotel and gourmet restaurant. The terrace affords a good view. A famous hero of the Thirty Years' War lived here, *der deutsche Michel*, a term used today to denote a valiant person.

Trollbach valley

Returning to the wine road, drive through the 8th-century wine villages of Genheim and

From the rock sculptures in the Trollbach valley pictured here, to the precipices near Bad Münster am Stein-Ebernburg, geological formations are among the Nahe's most interesting natural attractions.

MÜNSTER-SARMSHEIM
Weingut Kruger-Rumpf
Rheinstr. 47. Tel: 06721/43859. Fax: 06721/41882. 1700-2200 (except Mon). Closed Jan. Cosy wine pub.
Hotel Trollmühle
Rheinstr. 199. Tel: 06721/44066. Fax: 06721/43719. 1130-1400, 1800-2200. Pretty surroundings.
GULDENTAL
Gasthaus Kaiserhof
Hauptstr. 2. Tel: 06707/8746. Fax: 06707/1782. 1200-1400, 1800-2200 (except Tue).

Waldlaubersheim to Burg Layen, with its picturesque castle (1200) on the hill overlooking one of the village's best sites, Schlossberg. Adjacent to Burg Layen are the steeper, stony vineyards of Dorsheim, which produce excellent Riesling wines. Goldloch and Pittermännchen are the top sites.

The bizarre reddish-brown cliff formations are named Kamel (camel), Kaffeekanne (coffee pot) and Eierfelsen (egg cliffs).

Bingerbrück to Bad Kreuznach

Stony loam over slate and quartzite yields lively, robust Riesling wines from the sloping vineyards at the mouth of the Nahe. Dautenpflänzer and Pittersberg near Münster-Sarmsheim are noteworthy vineyards.

The slopes are gentler as the wine road follows the course of the Nahe to Laubenheim and Langenlonsheim, both large wine-growing communities. Müller-Thurgau and Silvaner are the main varieties, but good Riesling is produced from Langenlonsheim's steep Rothenberg site.

The region's largest co-operative, Nahe Winzer, is located in Bretzenheim. The market square, called the *Plagge*, is the site of a wine festival and parade (2nd weekend Aug), and the Gothic cellars of the Schloss are open to all.

Bretzenheim's wide expanse of vines blends into those of Winzenheim, one of Bad Kreuznach's wine suburbs. From here it is only a few minutes' drive into the centre of town and the start of the *Nahe-Weinstrasse*.

BAD KREUZNACH
Weingalerie
Bäderkolonnade 12 (opp. Kurhaus). Shop with large selection of Nahe wines. Mon-Fri 0900-1245, 1400-1830; Sat 0900-1400.
Weingut Johanneshof
Kaiser-Wilhelm-Str. 15 (nr Kurpark). Mon-Fri 1500-1800, Sat 1000-1200. Wine shop of the Korrell family. Also: they have a wine pub, with guest rooms, at their estate in the suburb of Bosenheim: Raiffeisenstr. 4. Tel: 0671/63630. Fax: 0671/71954. Fri-Sun from 1700.

FOR CYCLING FANS
The *Radweg Nahe* is a 60km (37 mile) marked bicycle route from Bingen to Kirn.

WINE AND ART
Since 1802, the Burg Layen castle has belonged to a prestigious wine estate. In the '80s, artist Johannes Helle turned everything, from the cellars to the vineyards, into a work of art. (Tours by appointment. Contact: Armin Diel, Schlossgut Diel, 55452 Burg Layen. Tel: 06721/96950. Fax: 06721/45047.)

KULINARISCHE SOMMERNACHT
(Culinary Summer Night) Nahe wines with food prepared by top chefs. Entertainment, music, election of the Nahe wine queen. Last weekend of July. Kurpark Bad Münster.

The Rheingau

RHEINGAUER WEINBAUVERBAND

The logo of the Rheingau Wine-growers' Association.

TAG DER OFFENEN WEINKELLER
is 'open house' at wine estates throughout the region. No appointment is necessary. The cellar doors are open for you to meet growers, visit cellars and sample wines. Late Apr to early May, combined with *Schlemmerwochen* (gourmet weeks), when you can try Rheingau specialities at estates and restaurants. Also: two weekends in Sep.

RHEINGAUER WEINWOCHE
is a huge wine festival with more than 100 growers showing wines from the entire region. Nine days of food and wine, mid-Aug, in the centre of Wiesbaden.

GLORREICHE RHEINGAUER TAGE
celebrates Rheingau wine and culture with gala culinary events and an auction (at which the wines are tasted) every Nov.

FOR FURTHER INFORMATION
Contact the regional wine promotion board:
Gesellschaft für Rheingauer Weinkultur
Im Alten Rathaus Johannisberg,
65366 Geisenheim.
Tel: 06722/99540.
Fax: 06722/995440.

The Rheingau is one of the great wine-growing regions of the world. The heart of the region borders the Rhine on its east-west course from Wiesbaden to Rüdesheim, with a broad ribbon of vineyards lining the hills from the river up to the forested summit of the Taunus Hills. Monasteries, manor houses and palaces bear witness to the traditions of affluence associated with wine-growing here during the past 1200 years.

It is easy to become acquainted with the area and its wines, thanks to three well-marked routes (driving, hiking and cycling) which wind through the attractive landscape, and to nearly two dozen wine villages, most of which have open-air tasting stands. To meet growers informally, without an appointment, visit when estates 'open the cellar door'.

Viticulture in the Rheingau can be traced to Roman times, but the legacy of quality stems from the efforts of the Church and the aristocracy in the Middle Ages. From the 11th century to the 13th, peasants cleared the forested slopes of the Taunus and planted them with vines. They were rewarded with their freedom, and the Rheingau became known as the land of farmers with civil rights.

It was in the economic interests of the ecclesiastical and noble estates to strive for high quality. For several hundred years they systematically improved methods of growing, making and marketing wine, thereby setting the high standards for which the Rheingau is still famous.

Classic wine grapes

Although one of Germany's smaller wine regions (3274 hectares/8090 acres) the Rheingau boasts the highest percentage of Riesling (81 per cent). Late to ripen, this grape yields small quantities of high-quality wine prized for its fine bouquet, rich fruity flavour and pronounced acidity.

The other great wine grape of the region is the Spätburgunder, brought by monks from its home in Burgundy. It yields velvety red wines with a hint of blackberry aroma and a fruity, rather than tannic, acidity.

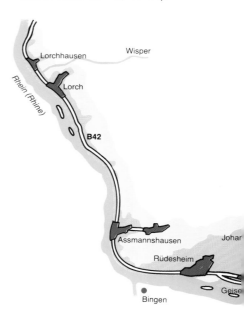

Rheingau vineyard area

From east to west, the Rheingau's vineyards become increasingly steep and the soil structure changes from deep, rich soils to cliffs of quartzite and clayish slate. Wines grown on the gentle slopes (from Hochheim to Hattenheim) tend to show a rounder fruitiness and milder acidity than the firm, piquant wines from the steep sites closer to Rüdesheim or on the hillsides some distance from the river (Rauenthal, Steinberg, Schloss Vollrads and Johannisberg).

All of the special attributes, or *Prädikats*, associated with German wines of superior quality originated in the Rheingau.

Documents dating from 1728 (Schloss Vollrads) and 1730 (Kloster Eberbach) show that some growers distinguished exceptional qualities and vintages from average growths by separately storing a few select wines in a special 'Cabinet' cellar. 'Cabinet', synonymous with the finest, is the forerunner of today's *Kabinett* wine.

Schloss Johannisberg is credited with recognizing the value of harvesting at various stages of ripeness or overripeness, in spite of the risks in delaying the harvest. *Spätlese* (literally 'late harvest') dates from 1775; *Auslese* (separating very ripe from normally ripe bunches) from 1787.

RHEINGAUER RÖMER
The typical wine glass of the region, the *Römer*, is prominent in the signs that mark the scenic driving, hiking and cycling routes.

RHEINGAUER RIESLING ROUTE
is a 70km (43 miles) autoroute through the entire region, from Wicker to Lorchhausen. Follow green signs with the *Römer* logo in white.

RHEINGAUER RIESLING PFAD
is a hiking trail (about 100km/62 miles) from Wicker to Lorchhausen. It winds through forests and vineyards, past monuments and wine estates, with excellent panoramic views from the hilltops. Follow green signs with the *Römer* logo in gold.

RHEINGAUER RIESLING RADWANDERWEG
is a cycling route through the vineyards and along the Rhine. Signs bear the *Römer* and a bicycle. Note: hiking and cycling trails also extend to Kaub.

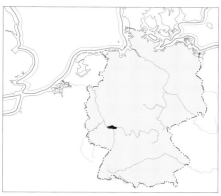

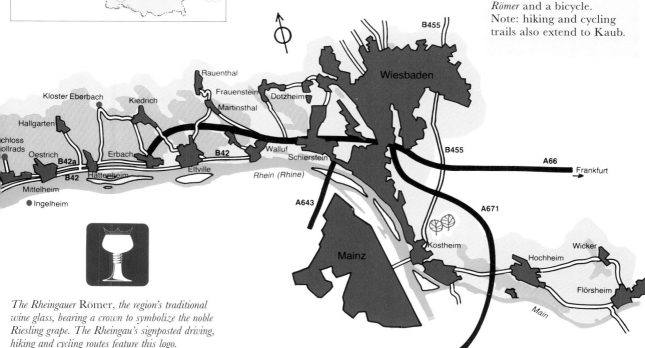

The Rheingauer Römer, *the region's traditional wine glass, bearing a crown to symbolize the noble Riesling grape. The Rheingau's signposted driving, hiking and cycling routes feature this logo.*

The Gateway to the Rheingau

WICKER
Flörsheimer Warte
In the vineyards between Flörsheim and Wicker via the path Steinmühlenweg. Tel: 06145/7686. Apr-Sep, Sat from 1500, Sun from 1130. Large selection of wines from Wicker and Flörsheim. Historic (1496) watch-tower. Idyllic setting.
Weingut Joachim Flick
Rheingaustr. 1. Mar-May and Sep-Oct, Fri-Sat from 1600, Sun from 1500.
HOCHHEIM
Haus Schönborn
Aichgasse 3 (Old Town). Tel: 06146/4075. Fax: 06146/2976. 1200-2200 May-Oct, from 1800 Nov-Apr. Closed Mon.
Riesling Stuben
Wintergasse 9 (Old Town). Tel: 06146/83310. Fax: 06146/833166. Daily from 1800. Very picturesque.
WIESBADEN
Bobbeschänkelche
Röderstr. 39. From 1700 Mon-Fri, from 1800 Sat. Cosy, inviting. Garden.
Weinkeller Altes Rathaus Marktstr. 16. From 1600 Tue-Fri, from 1200 Sat. In cellar of old town hall (1610). Diverse selection. Also *Sekt*.
Schlossweinstube
Rheingaustr. 140 (in Biebrich palace on banks of Rhine). 1400-2300 (except Mon).

The easternmost wine villages of the Rheingau are about 30km (18 miles) west of Frankfurt, near the confluence of the Main and Rhine rivers. The Riesling grape may have originated in this area. The oldest reference to it is in an invoice for delivery of Riesling vines from the Klaus Kleinfisch winery to Rüsselsheim castle in 1435.

Wicker, Flörsheim and Kostheim

Wicker is the *Tor zum Rheingau* (Gateway to the Rheingau) and the start of the *Rheingauer Riesling Route*. On the western edge of town, the König-Wilhelm-Säule (monument to King – later Emperor – Wilhelm) overlooks the vineyard bearing his name.

A pruning knife found in a Roman villa unearthed near Flörsheim supports the assumption that the Romans grew grapes in the area. There is also an interesting Baroque church on the river bank.

Kostheim was once an important woodworking centre and harbour for rafts laden with timber from the Franconian forests along the Main.

Franconian Rheingauers

The Main river flows through the heart of the Franken region (see pages 94-105) which is celebrated for its powerful, earthy wines and Baroque architecture. Perhaps for these reasons, the Rheingau villages along the Main are reminiscent of Franken. Their wines can have a distinctive earthy tone and are sometimes referred to as Franconian Rheingauers.

Hochheim's Riesling wines rank among the finest of the Rheingau. The vineyards are on gentle slopes of deep chalky soils. Their proximity to the river and a good microclimate enable vines to ripen a week or two earlier than elsewhere in the region. The wines are stylish and full-bodied, with a balanced acidity. Their earthy quality sets them apart from other Rheingauers. Spätburgunder is also grown here.

The best site, Domdechaney, was created in the early 18th century by the *Domdechanten* (deans) of Mainz Cathedral, who had the swampy lowlands near Hochheim's church (see photograph opposite) filled with earth and then planted with vines.

Queen Victoria and 'Hock'

Queen Victoria is said to have recovered from an illness after drinking the wine here. Her enthusiasm for Hochheimer wines reinforced the popularity of the nickname 'Hock', the generic term for all Rhine wines. The neo-Gothic (1854) monument dedicated to her stands in the middle of the riverside vineyard renamed Königin Victoriaberg.

Old Hochheim has charming half-timbered houses and cobbled alleyways. Two Baroque works of art are of interest – the statue Madonna auf dem Plan on the market square and the parish church overlooking the vineyards. The wine festival takes place in early July in the courtyards of the wine estates in Old Town.

Wiesbaden

Capital of Hesse and the largest town in the Rheingau, Wiesbaden is more famous for its waters than for its wine. The inscription *Aquis Mattiacis* above the Kurhaus refers to the Mattiaci tribe who settled here in pre-Roman times and the hot mineral springs discovered in AD 1. Charlemagne is said to have taken the waters in *Wisibada*, 'the baths in the meadows'.

Today, Wiesbaden is an elegant spa, with lush parks, tree-lined boulevards and magnificent turn-of-the-century villas. Wiesbaden's only vineyard, the Neroberg, is overlooked by the gilded onion domes of the Greek Chapel.

Schierstein, Dotzheim, Frauenstein

In the Middle Ages, these Wiesbaden suburbs were important wine towns. Today, the wines are enjoyed locally. Interesting buildings include Schierstein's Baroque parish church with its Rococo interior, and in neighbouring Biebrich, the Baroque palace on the banks of the Rhine.

Visit Frauenstein in the spring, when the hills are covered with cherry trees in blossom. There is a good view from the Goethe monument overlooking the Herrnberg vineyard. In the town, the Baroque altar in the church is particularly fine.

For a pleasant walk through the vineyards of Hochheim, take the path from the St Peter and Paul Church (below) in the Old Town to the Queen Victoria monument in the vineyard renamed in her honour in 1850 (see the label above).

WIESBADEN
Die Ente vom Lehel
(Hotel Nassauer Hof) Tel: 0611/133666. Fax: 0611/133632. 1800-2300 (except Sun-Mon). Superb cuisine, world-class wine list. Less extravagant fare at **Bistro**. Tue-Sat 1200-1500, 1800-2300. Both closed Jul-Aug.
L'Orangerie (Hotel Nassauer Hof) Tel: 0611/133633. Fax: (see above). 1200-1500, 1800-2300. Elegant interior. Terrace.
Käfer's (Kurhaus) Tel: 0611/536200. Fax: 0611/536222. Daily, 1130-2300. Lively. Terrace.
WALLUF
Weingut J. Becker's *Im Weingarten* Rheinstr. 6. May-Sep from 1700; Sat-Sun from 1500. Outdoor riverside pub serving snacks, or bring a picnic. Excellent wines (reds, too).

Wiesbaden to Kloster Eberbach

The 12th-century monastery church at Kloster Eberbach is one of the finest examples of Romanesque architecture in Germany. A row of Gothic chapels was added in the 14th century. The basilica has notable Gothic and Renaissance tombstones, including works by the important Rhenish sculptor Hans Backoffen.

BREAD AND WINE
Brot und Wein is the State Wine Domain's open-air wine pub in the Steinberg vineyard. From Kloster Eberbach take the road to Hattenheim; watch for the sign on the right. May-Sep, Sat-Sun, 1100-1900.

RHEINGAU MUSIK FESTIVAL
Historic buildings, wine estates and riverboats are the settings for over 100 musical events (Jun-Aug). For details contact: Rheingau Musik Festival, Zehntenhofstr. 5b, 65201 Wiesbaden. Tel: 0611/20099. Fax: 0611/260465.

Exit from the A66 at Frauenstein, take the B42 (towards Rüdesheim) to Walluf, and then turn left to reach the heart of the town, on the banks of the Rhine.

Viticulture in the Rheingau was first documented in a deed of gift in AD 779, when two vineyards in Walluf were presented to Kloster Lorsch (Bergstrasse). Today, very good Riesling and Spätburgunder wines are produced from the deep, chalky, loess soils. Walk along the old towpath next to the river (the tasting stand is located here). Driving on the B42 from Walluf towards Eltville, take the first right to reach Ober-Walluf and follow the signs to Martinsthal.

The vine-covered hills get steeper with the approach to the town and the Nonnenberg villa peers down from the hill on the left. The vineyard below it actually belongs to Rauenthal and is called Nonnenberg, after the *Nonnen* (nuns) who once owned the property. Martinsthal's best-known vineyard is *Wildsau* (wild sow). The name refers to the wild beasts who loved to eat the ripe grapes. Drive past the traffic light and turn left to reach Rauenthal, high on a hill. The tower of the 15th-century St Antonius church is visible for a considerable distance. Inside, a late Gothic Madonna lovingly hands the Christ-child a bunch of grapes.

Rauenthal's steep Riesling vineyards are among the best of the region. Baiken is a site of world class. The phyllite soils, with some loess and loam, yield elegant, racy wines with a spicy tone. Steely in character when young, they are long-lived and age well.

Gothic gem of the Rheingau
Return to Martinsthal, follow the signs to Eltville and, from there, take the right-hand turn to Kiedrich.

Near the town, the ruins of the Scharfenstein fortress appear on the right, as well as the spires of the Gothic pilgrimage church St Valentine's (1420) with its Gothic and Renaissance altars; Kiedricher Madonna (1330); richly carved pews with grape motifs; and star vaulting with original ceiling paintings. The 15th-century organ is the oldest in Germany and can be heard at Sunday mass (10:15 am) when the male choir sings Gregorian chants. St Michael's chapel (1434-44) is next door.

There is a Renaissance town hall opposite the church and half-timbered manor houses on the side streets.

Kiedrich's Riesling wines have a fine, piquant acidity. In warm years, they are spicy and full-flavoured.

Kloster Eberbach
Leave Kiedrich at the northern end of town and follow the signs to Kloster Eberbach (monastery) founded in 1135 by Bernhard of Clairvaux.

The Cistercian monks built Kloster Eberbach into one of the largest and most successful viticultural enterprises of the Middle Ages. At its height, the monastery received income and produce from more than 200 towns and estates and had its own fleet of ships on the Rhine.

Despite the setbacks of wars, secularization (1803) and changes in ownership, the tradition of viticulture at Kloster Eberbach has continued uninterrupted since the 12th century. Today, the Steinberg vineyard, planted adjacent to the monastery over 700 years ago by the monks, is one of the greatest names in German wine. The wines are powerful, with pronounced, fruity acidity and great depth of flavour.

Kloster Eberbach is the cultural wine centre of the Rheingau. Home of the German Wine Academy (see panel on the right), it is the site of prestigious auctions and wine tastings. There is a museum devoted to the history of the Cistercians, and concerts are held in the basilica.

The Romanesque and Gothic buildings, collection of historic wine presses and lovely gardens are well worth a visit (Apr-Sep 1000-1800; Oct-Mar 1000-1600 Mon-Fri and 1100-1600 Sat-Sun.) You can sample the wines in the historic Kloster-Schänke and the other restaurant in the grounds, or at the shop where wines and *Sekt* from the State Wine Domain (top vineyard sites throughout the Rheingau) are sold.

The Lay Brothers' Refectory at Kloster Eberbach today houses historic wine presses, the oldest of which dates from 1668. These were used by the Cistercians.

GUEST ROOMS AT KLOSTER EBERBACH
Am Saugraben.
Tel: 06723/9930. Fax: 06723/993100.

GERMAN WINE ACADEMY
Six-day study trip through Germany's wine country with lectures and tastings conducted by experts (in English). Visit wine estates in seven regions. Sep-Oct. Contact: German Wine Academy, PO Box 1660, 55006 Mainz. Tel: 06131/28290. Fax: 06131/282950.

Eltville to Rüdesheim

The Rhine promenade at Eltville, with a view of the Prince Elector's castle.

Eltville

From Kloster Eberbach, return to Kiedrich and follow the road towards the Rhine. As you enter Eltville, turn left on Bertholdstrasse and left again on Schwalbacher Strasse to visit the *Jugendstil* press house (now a tasting room and shop) of the State Wine Domain, nos.56-62 on the left. The historic part of the town is near the river, south of the B42.

Eltville's origins date from Roman times (*alta villa*) but its days of glory were in the 14th and 15th centuries. A favourite residence of the Archbishops of Mainz, Eltville was first in the Rheingau to receive town rights (1332). In the tower of the Prince Elector's castle there is a memorial to Johannes Gutenberg, the inventor of movable-type printing, who lived here in the 15th century. There are fine works of art and wall paintings in the late Gothic Church of St Peter and St Paul. Renaissance manors line the side streets, and there is a tasting stand on the river front.

The vineyards are on gentle slopes of rich loess which yield softer and rounder wines than the steep hillside sites. Several *Sekt* (sparkling wine) producers have cellars in Eltville, immortalized by Thomas Mann's *Felix Krull*. The *Sektfest* is in July.

Erbach, Hattenheim and Hallgarten

Drive west on the B42 past the last traffic light and out of town. Turn right (off the B42) towards Erbach. On the left is 12th-century Klosterhof Drais, a noble wine estate once owned by Kloster Eberbach. The regional wine-growers' co-operative is on the right, as is the late Gothic St Markus-Kirche, a church named after the village's patron saint. The road continues past half-timbered houses in the market square and Schloss Reinhartshausen, a wine estate once owned by the Princes of Prussia (now also a hotel and gourmet restaurant).

The sloping vineyard from here to Hattenheim is the world-famous Marcobrunn. There is a sandstone

TRADITIONAL WINE PUBS

MARTINSTHAL
Weingut Diefenhardt
Hauptstr. 11. From 1700
Tue-Sat. Mid-Apr to mid-Oct.

KIEDRICH
Schloss Groenesteyn
Oberstr. 36-37. From 1700.
Closed Mon, Tue and Jan.

ELTVILLE
Gelbes Haus Burgstr. 3.
From 1600. Closed Wed and Jan.

ERBACH
Weingut Oetinger
Rheinallee 2. From 1430
Tue-Sat, from 1100 Sun.
Closed Jan, Feb.

Weingut D.v. Oetinger
Rheinallee 1-3. From 1430
(except Tue), from 1100
Sat-Sun. Closed Jan, Sep.

HATTENHEIM
Zum Krug Hauptstr. 34.
Tel: 06723/99680. Fax:
06723/996825. 1200-1400,
1800-2200. Closed Sun eve,
Mon and Jan. Cosy hotel.

WINKEL
Weingut Jacob Hamm
Hauptstr. 60. From 1800
(except Wed, Thu) and
from 1600 Sun (1200 Sun
Jul-Aug). Easter-Nov.

Weingut J. Ohlig
Hauptstr. 68. Open Jan-Apr, Oct only. From 1630
(except Mon, Tue), from
1530 Sun.

Weingut Basting-Gimbel Hauptstr. 70-72.
From 1130-1400, 1730-2300 (except Wed) and
1130-2300 Sun. May-Sep.

GEISENHEIM
Weingut Schumann-Nägler Nothgottesstr. 28.
From 1600 Wed-Sat, from
1500 Sun. Easter-Oct.

monument at St Mark's well (*Brunn[en]*), from which the vineyard may take its name. Others say the name refers to the well's location at the boundary (*Mark*) between Erbach and Hattenheim – both towns coveted the rights to this exceptional site. Year after year, the clayish marl soils yield elegant Riesling wines. There are fine Gothic crucifixes and shrines in the cemetery and vineyards. The *Erdbeerfest*, a celebration of strawberries and wine, is in June.

The road continues to Hattenheim, which also has its *Brunnen* sites: Nussbrunnen and Wisselbrunnen, both producing high-quality wines of great finesse and delicacy. The intricate designs on the houses in the market square are remarkable. Try a glass of Hattenheimer wine at the *Burg* (castle) at the wine festival in August or at the tasting stand on the banks of the river, in the three huge barrels opposite the Shell petrol station on the B42.

Leave Hattenheim on the road which runs through the town (not the B42). Near the railway crossing, watch for the right turn to Hallgarten, set back in the hills below the forest. As the slopes steepen, the wines become racier, more pronounced in acidity and fuller-bodied.

In the Maria-Himmelfahrt Church, look for the Madonna with the Christ-child holding a bunch of grapes (1420). For a panoramic view of the Rhine valley, visit the tasting stand at the edge of the new part of town, on the road leading into the forest.

Oestrich, Mittelheim and Winkel

Return to the B42 and drive west to Oestrich, which has more vineyards than any other town in the Rheingau. The 18th-century crane on the left was the start of the journey to Rotterdam for many a barrel of wine. The half-timbered façade of the Hotel Schwan is on the right. Lenchen and Doosberg are the town's best-known sites, yielding round, hearty wines.

At Mittelheim, the Rhine is at its widest (1 km, just over half a mile) and resembles a huge lake. Turn off the B42 at the first exit for Winkel. There is a tasting stand here and, nearby, the restaurant Graues Haus, in Germany's oldest (probably AD 850) stone house.

While walking along Hauptstrasse you will see 16th- and 18th-century houses, many of which are estates with wine pubs in the courtyards, and are usually open in the evenings and at weekends. In 1814, Goethe found inspiration in the Rheingau's landscape and legendary 1811 vintage during his stay with the Brentano family. You can see the rooms where Goethe worked (by appointment: Brentanohaus, Am Lindenplatz 2, 65375 Oestrich-Winkel. Tel: 06723/2068. Fax 06723/87792.).

From Hauptstrasse, follow signs to Schloss Vollrads, one of the greatest names in German wine.

Banners displayed throughout the region indicate where wine is for sale – here, at the open-air wine tasting stand in Oestrich.

GOURMET DINING

ERBACH
Marcobrunn Hauptstr. 43 (Schloss Reinhartshausen). Tel: 06123/676432. Fax: 06123/676400. Wed-Sat 1800-2300, Sun 1200-1500. Closed Jan. Elegant hotel.
Pan zu Erbach Eberbacher Str. 44. Tel: 06123/63538. Fax: 06123/4209. 1800-2200 (except Wed). Also 1130-1400 Sun.
HATTENHEIM
Kronenschlösschen Rheinallee. Tel: 06723/640. Fax: 06723/7663. 1900-2200. Closed Feb. **Bistro** 1200-1400, 1900-2200 all year. Charming hotel.

The Gutsausschank (wine pub) at Schloss Vollrads is a pleasant setting for sampling the estate's wines and regional specialities.

HISTORIC SETTINGS

SCHLOSS VOLLRADS
Gutsausschank. Tel: 06723/5270. Fax: 06723/6666. May-Oct 1200-2200 (Mon, from 1700). Nov-Apr closed Wed, Thu.
WINKEL
Graues Haus
Graugasse 10. Tel: 06723/2619. Fax: 06723/4739. 1800-2200 May-Oct (except Tue); Nov-Apr (except Mon-Tue). Sat-Sun also 1200-1400. Closed Jan-Feb. Gourmet restaurant with garden.
Brentanohaus Am Lindenplatz 2. Mon-Fri from 1700, Sat-Sun from 1200. Closed Thu, Jan, Feb. Idyllic garden.
JOHANNISBERG
Gutsausschank in the grounds of the Schloss. Tel: 06722/96090. Fax: 06722/7392. Daily, 1130-1400, 1730-2130.

Schloss Vollrads

The earliest documented sales of Vollrads wines date from 1211. In 1330, the Greiffenclau family moved from their ancestral home in the Graues Haus to the moated castle tower situated in the hills behind Winkel, at the edge of the Taunus forest. For 27 generations, members of the founding family ran the estate and lived in the 17th-century Baroque palace in the estate grounds.

The wines of Schloss Vollrads are elegant, fruity and piquant. Like most classic Rheingau Riesling wines, they improve with bottle age. You can try the wines at the *Gutsausschank* (wine pub) in the estate grounds. The 'Lucullan Wine Tastings' conducted in the historic period rooms of the palace are truly memorable. (For details, contact: Schloss Vollrads, 65375 Oestrich-Winkel. Tel: 06723/660. Fax: 06723/6666.)

Schloss Johannisberg

Return to Kirchstrasse; turn right on Greiffenclaustrasse and watch for signs to Schloss Johannisberg, on the next hillside to the west. Drive through the vineyards, via Winkelerstrasse. The turning to the palace is marked, on the left.

Another of Germany's great traditional estates, Schloss Johannisberg was founded by Benedictines who established a monastery here in 1100. The earliest cellars date from this time.

Under the ownership of the Abbey of Fulda in the 18th century, the palace and extensive cellars were built, the planting of Riesling was made mandatory and estate bottling (a novelty at the time) was begun.

It was during this time that the benefits of a late harvest were recognized, albeit by chance. In 1775, so the story goes, the courier sent from Johannisberg to Fulda to obtain permission to begin the harvest was delayed. Meanwhile, the grapes had started to rot, yet the monks decided to salvage what they could. To their surprise (and delight) the resultant wine was delicious. The monument to the delayed courier, the 'Spätlese Rider', in the estate's courtyard is a tribute to quality-oriented growers, then and now.

After secularization (1802) the estate changed hands several times, until it was presented to Chancellor Metternich (1816), ancestor of the present owners.

The cellars, among the most impressive in the world, house the *Bibliotheca Subterranea* (underground library), with rarities dating from 1748. (Cellar visits by appointment only. Contact: Schloss Johannisberg, 65366 Geisenheim-Johannisberg. Tel: 06722/700935. Fax: 06722/700933.)

The wines of Schloss Johannisberg are full and rich, with a spicy fruitiness and marked acidity. Sample them at the *Gutsausschank* or prior to purchase in the shop, both in the estate grounds. The view from the terrace is outstanding. Markers show where the 50th degree of latitude runs through the vineyards.

Johannisberg and Geisenheim

Depart through the tree-lined alley; turn left and follow the road downhill and left, through the village of Johannisberg. On this road, the Grund, there are several fine estates. Look for the green banners with the regional logo. *Weinverkauf* signs indicate that wine is for sale.

Turn right into the Industriestrasse to drive to Geisenheim. Lime trees, noble manor houses, half-timbered houses and ancient fountains make a delightful setting. The late Gothic Rheingauer Dom (church), with its two red neo-Gothic spires, has fine altars and tombs. The peace treaty to end the Thirty Years' War was drafted in the Schönborner Hof.

Geisenheim's international reputation derives from its State Research Institute and School of Oenology. It was here, in 1882, that Dr Müller from Thurgau in Switzerland created the grape variety named after him by crossing Riesling and Gutedel grapes. The institute is Germany's major supplier of resistant rootstock clones; it operates experimental vineyards, a modern winery and a shop where you can sample the wines (Mon-Thu 0800-1200, 1300-1700, Fri 0800-1300).

Institutions such as this carry on the tradition of quality-oriented viticulture established by the Church and aristocracy in the Middle Ages.

Geisenheim's wines are full, round, and sometimes earthy in taste. The soils of the sloping vineyards are deep, partly stony, loamy-loess over a stratum of quartzite.

From Geisenheim, drive for two minutes on the B42 to Rüdesheim. On the hillside to the right is St Hildegard, a Benedictine nunnery in the midst of the Klosterberg vineyard, named after the medieval mystic, the Abbess St Hildegard of Bingen.

THREE CLASSIC ESTATES
Germany's great wine tradition owes much to these three classic wine estates, which have served as models of quality viticulture for centuries. The origin of the Prädikats (special attributes) that denote German wines of superior quality can be traced to them. Kloster Eberbach is open to the public; the cellars of Schloss Vollrads and Schloss Johannisberg may be visited by appointment.

Schloss Johannisberg majestically overlooks some of the world's greatest Riesling vineyards. From the Gutsausschank (wine pub) or the terrace there is a fabulous panorama of the Rheingau.

Rüdesheim

The Niederwald-Denkmal affords an excellent view of Rüdesheim and the Rhine valley. The statue of Germania (about 12m/40ft high) is visible for miles.

Rüdesheim is one of the best-known wine villages of Germany, not least because of its pub-lined Drosselgasse (Thrush Alley) and other attractions which draw thousands of tourists every year.

Rüdesheim has been settled since Roman times, as evidenced by pruning knives found in the vineyards, but it was during the Middle Ages that it became an important commercial centre, thanks to its location at the end of an important trade route to circumvent the unnavigable waters of Binger Loch. It is still a centre of wine, *Sekt* (sparkling wine) and brandy production.

Some of the medieval townscape still exists, such as the Adlerturm, a late Gothic defence tower which was part of the 15th-century town wall,

St Jakobuskirche with its fine sandstone altar and tombs, Brömserburg fortress (now a wine museum) and patrician houses near the market square, on the Steinstrasse and Oberstrasse.

Museums

The terrace of the wine museum in Brömserburg fortress, Rheinstrasse 2, affords a good view of the Rhine. Weather permitting, you can enjoy a glass of wine here, weekends. Among its exhibits is a collection of glassware dating from Roman times, and historic artifacts related to wine-growing. (Open daily, 0900-1800, mid-Mar to mid-Nov.)

There is an unusual collection of automatic musical instruments from the 18th-20th centuries at Siegfried's Mechanical Music Cabinet in the Brömserhof, Oberstrasse 29. (Open daily, 1000-2200, mid-Mar to mid-Nov.)

RÜDESHEIM
Rüdesheimer Schloss
Drosselgasse. Tel: 06722/90500. Fax: 06722/47960. Daily, 1200-1430, 1800-2200. Closed Xmas-Feb. Lively, but cosy, indoors; tree-shaded courtyard. Hotel (entrance on Steingasse 10, street parallel to Drosselgasse).
Bistro Berg Schlossberg
Grabenstr. 8. Tel/Fax: 06722/1026. 1800-2200 Mon-Sat, also 1200-1400 Mon-Fri. Vinothek (wine shop) of owner, Weingut Georg Breuer, is next door.
Jagdschloss Niederwald
Auf dem Niederwald 1. Tel: 06722/1004. Fax: 06722/47970. Hotel in former hunting palace near the *Denkmal* (monument) above (N of) Rüdesheim. 1130-1400, 1830-2130 mid-Mar to mid-Nov. From mid-Nov to mid-Mar lunch Sat-Sun, dinner Wed-Sun. Fine food and wine in a peaceful, forested setting.

LORCH
Hilchenhaus Rheinstr. 48. Tel: 06726/2060. Fax: 06726/1043. Apr-Oct 1200-1400, 1730-2130 (except Thu). Feb-Mar, Nov-Dec from 1800. Closed Jan. Cosy, vaulted cellar and in good weather, outdoor seating on the terrace (view) upstairs.
Weingut Friedrich Altenkirch Binger Weg 2 (E edge of town). From 1600 Fri-Sun, Sep-Nov. Friendly.
Weingut Troitzsch-Pusinelli Bächergrund 12. From 1600 Fri-Sun, Jun-Aug. Spectacular panorama from the heights of this wine pub.

Schlossberg, Berg Rottland, Berg Roseneck, Bischofsberg, Klosterberg. You can sample the wines at the tasting stand near the river, east of the Adlerturm, or at one of the dozens of pubs on or near the Drosselgasse. The Rüdesheimer Schloss, in the historic *Zehnthof* (tithe court) has one of the most extensive wine lists of the region, featuring nearly 300 Rheingau wines from 1929 to the present. Older rarities are available on request.

Excursions

Germania, the statue visible from miles away, is part of the Niederwald-Denkmal (monument) built in 1883 to commemorate the re-establishment of the German Empire after the Franco-Prussian War. From the terrace you can see the Rheingau, Rheinhessen and Nahe wine regions. Hike, drive or ride up the hill by cable car. (Departs from Oberstrasse, daily 0930-1700. Closed Nov-Easter.)

An enjoyable vineyard walk starts at Ringmauer (near the car park north of the town centre) and follows Panorama Weg to the Brömserburg.

At Rüdesheim the Rhine narrows, turns sharply and resumes its south-north course. The vineyards become increasingly steep around the bend, as the ruins of Burg Ehrenfels come into view. Once a customs fortress and refuge for the treasures of Mainz Cathedral in time of war, Ehrenfels(er) is known today as a white grape variety (crossing of Riesling and Silvaner) bred at Geisenheim in 1929.

The wines

The vineyards on the weathered quartzite and slate cliffs produce some of the region's finest wines, concentrated in flavour, flowery in bouquet. Riesling ripens well here, even in cool or rainy years, when it struggles to ripen elsewhere.

The best sites have *Berg* (hill) in their names, for example Berg

65

Rüdesheim to Lorchhausen

The steep vineyards of Assmannshausen are renowned for velvety, fruity red wine from the Spätburgunder (Pinot Noir) grape. It is a superb partner to regional specialities, such as Wild (game).

ASSMANNSHAUSEN
Hotel Krone
Rheinuferstrasse 10. Tel: 06722/4030. Fax: 06722/ 3049. Mar-Dec 1200-1430, 1830-2130 daily. Jan-Feb Fri-Sat 1800-2130, Sat-Sun 1200-1400. Elegant restaurant with terrace overlooking the Rhine. The wine list features the owner's (and other) estate wines.

Assmannshausen
This town has been synonymous with the red wine grape Spätburgunder for centuries. The vines ripen well on the blue-red phyllite slate, yielding velvety, fruity red wine with a fine, blackberry tone. They are lighter,

leaner and less tannic than their counterparts of Burgundy. Höllenberg is the classic site. Riesling is the main white grape variety.

For a view of the town, its vineyards and the castles on the opposite side of the Rhine, take the chairlift up to the Niederwald. (Departs from near the Heiligkreuzkirche daily 1000-1700. Closed Nov-Easter.)

Lorch and Lorchhausen
From the B42, one would never expect to find an historic wine village hidden behind the railway embankment at Lorch. Park alongside the river and walk into the town through an underpass to discover the ancient buildings of Lorch.

RHEINGAU RIESLING

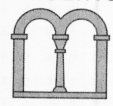

CHARTA
is a group of quality-oriented Rheingau wine estates founded in 1984 to promote Riesling wine in the classical Rheingau style. Quality standards are rigorous and only specially-selected wines may be bottled in the Charta's tall, slim bottles embossed with a double Romanesque arch, the logo which also appears on the labels and capsules.

'THE RHINE IN FLAMES'
Spectacular fireworks displays on the Rhine, 1st Sat Jul, from Rüdesheim to Assmannshausen.

From its Roman and Frankish origins, Lorch developed into a powerful and prosperous town in the Middle Ages. Thanks to its situation at the mouth of the Wisper river, the start of the important overland trade route to Rüdesheim, Lorch was settled by clerics and aristocrats who profited from the revenues of the town's dyers, vintners, weavers, and merchants.

At the stone bridge crossing the Wisper there are remnants of the town fortifications which once extended as far as Burg Nollig (11th century, now in ruins). The *Heimatmuseum* (local history museum with valuable art treasures) is next door to the town hall. St Martins-Kirche is an important Gothic church overlooking the Rhine. It is famous for its richly carved high altar (1483) and choir stalls (13th century).

Walk down the ancient stone steps from the church terrace (view) to the Rheinstrasse. The house of the Knight Hans von Hilchen (no.48), a gem of Renaissance architecture (1546), is now a wine restaurant belonging to a noble wine estate.

Riesling hiking paths
Continue walking east, to the Bahnhof (railway station), to the start of a *Riesling-Wanderweg*, a 7km (4 mile) trail through vineyards, from Kapellenberg to Bodental-Steinberg. It is signposted with information about grape varieties and work in the vineyards, and there are fine views.

At the other end of town, en route to Lorchhausen, you can walk up to Burg Nollig, which towers over the Schlossberg vineyard, for a view of the Rhine valley and Bacharach on the opposite shore. A path through the vineyards leads to Lorchhausen, at the border of Hesse and the end of the Rheingau.

Wars, the Plague and engineering on the Rhine to make the Binger Loch passable all contributed to Lorch's decline as a commercial centre. But the tradition of viticulture, dating from at least the 11th century, successfully weathered the storms.

Lorch and its suburb, Lorchhausen, have a large vineyard area, planted primarily with Riesling and Spätburgunder grapes. The quartzite and weathered slate cliffs are extremely labour-intensive, but yield fresh, lively wines with lots of fruit. Slate brings out the fruity acidity of the Riesling and often imparts a slight *spritz* or natural sparkle to the wine.

The Wisper valley
For a scenic ride through beautiful forests and past castle ruins, drive through the Wispertal (Wisper valley), famous for its fresh and smoked trout. The road starts at the stone bridge in Lorch and ends in the pretty spa of Bad Schwalbach.

Lorch viewed from the fortress ruins of Burg Nollig, near the border with the romantic Mittelrhein region.

Rheinhessen

Rheinhessenwein.
DER WEIN DER WINZER.

The region's slogan is 'Rheinhessen Wine – the Vintners' Choice'.

Rheinhessen is Germany's largest wine-growing region as well as the home of Liebfraumilch, internationally the best-known Rhine wine. Rheinhessen's gentle, rolling hills lie within the large elbow formed by the Rhine river as it flows from Worms to its sweeping bend around Mainz and west to its next turn at Bingen. This is spacious, fertile farmland carpeted with fields of grain and vegetables, orchards and vineyards and patches of forest. Mainz, an important centre of the wine trade, has many historic and cultural sights.

It is also worthwhile exploring the small wine villages, appealing in their simplicity and unexpectedly rich in artistic detail, from beautifully carved courtyard portals to treasures in the parish churches. From *Hoffeste* (festivals in vintners' courtyards) to festive *Wanderungen* (hikes) through the vineyards, there are hundreds of events at which to sample Rheinhessen's immense variety of wines.

The region is situated in a basin ringed by forests and mountains that check cold winds and excessive rainfall. This temperate climate and the fertile soils provide ideal growing conditions for grapes, a fact recognized by the Romans more than 2000 years ago when they settled the area and planted the first vines.

During the rule of the Frankish kings, viticulture expanded to meet the increased demand for wine by the Church and the court. Charlemagne, in particular, fostered improvements in growing and making the wine and is credited as an initiator of the *Strausswirtschaft* (the right for a grower to sell his wine in his home for a few months of the year). The Church also promoted quality wine-growing and, as owner of many vineyards, exerted considerable influence on the region's viticultural development.

The largest of Germany's wine regions (26,428 hectares/65,304 acres), Rheinhessen holds the world record for area planted with the ancient white grape variety Silvaner (3418 hectares/8446 acres). Müller-Thurgau, the main variety, and several aromatic new crossings make for great variety among Rheinhessen's white wines. Portugieser and Spätburgunder are the principal red varieties, traditionally grown near Ingelheim, but today, throughout the region. Relatively small quantities of Riesling are cultivated and sold usually as estate-bottled wines, rather than in bulk to be bottled elsewhere. Plantings of Grauburgunder and Weissburgunder (Pinot Gris and Pinot Blanc) are increasing.

Except for a few steep sites near Bingen and along the Rhein Terrasse, the vineyards are on gentle slopes or flatlands and the grapes can be harvested with modern machinery.

Loess and weathered, heavy clay soil (loam and chalky marl) predominate in most parts of Rheinhessen except near Bingen (slate) and near Nackenheim and Nierstein, where bright red soil called *Rotliegendes* (a mixture of red slate and sandy clay) prevails.

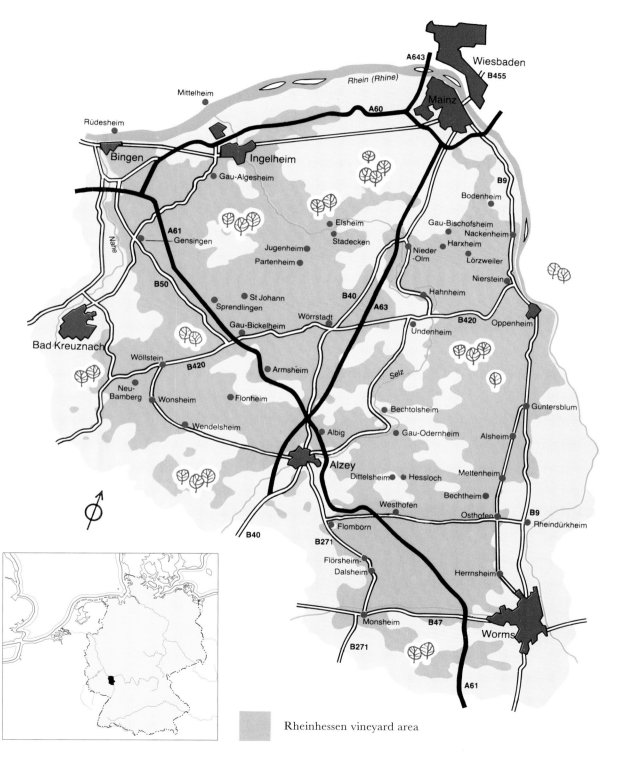

Rheinhessen vineyard area

Mainz

Drei Lilien Ballplatz 2.
Tel: 06131/225068. Fax:
06131/237723. 1200-1400,
1800-2230. Closed Sun,
Mon. Inviting and friendly.

Gebert's Weinstube
Frauenlobstr. 94 (north of
Kaiserstr.). Tel: 06131/
611619. Fax: 06131/
611662. Mon-Fri 1130-
1345,1800-2200, Sun
1800-2200. Traditional
wine restaurant.

Haus des Weines
Gutenbergplatz 3 (next to
the theatre). Tel: 06131/
228676. Daily, from 1100.
Large selection of German
wines (also by the glass).

Am Bassenheimer Hof
Acker 10 (nr Schillerplatz).
Tel: 06131/237357.
Restaurant from 1830,
bistro from 1800. Closed
Sun. Lively and cosy.

TYPICAL WINE PUBS

Alt Deutsche Weinstube
Liebfrauenplatz 7 (near the
Gutenberg Museum). From
1600. Closed Sun.

Augustiner Keller
Augustinerstr. 26. From
1700 Mon-Fri, from 1200
Sat-Sun.

Dr Flotte Kirschgarten
21. From 1100 Mon-Sat.

Hottum Grebenstr. 3
(near Augustiner Str.)
From 1600.

Weinhaus Michel
Jakobsbergstr. 8 (near the
Augustiner Str.). From
1600. Closed Sun.

Weinhaus Rote Kopf
Fischergasse 3. From 1500.
Closed Sat.

Weinhaus Schreiner
Rheinstr. 38. From 1700
Mon-Fri, from 1130 Sat.

Weinhaus Wilhelmi
Rheinstr. 51. From 1700.

Zum Spiegel Leichhof 1
(behind the Dom, near the
Augustiner Str.). From 1600
Mon-Fri, from 1200 Sat.

Mainz is situated on the Rhine,
opposite the mouth of the Main.
From a citadel built by Roman
legionaries in 38 BC, *Moguntiacum*
developed into the most important
military town of the region and was
made capital of the Roman province
Germania Superior in AD 297. There
is a wealth of Roman artifacts (some
related to wine) at the Römisch-
Germanisches Zentralmuseum and
the Mittelrheinisches Landesmuseum,
and at the Museum für Antike
Schiffahrt you can see 4th-century
Roman ships (museums all closed Mon).

St Boniface and St Willigis

Mainz declined in importance when
the Romans departed in the 5th
century, but blossomed again in the
8th century, when the Pope sent
Boniface to evangelize the Germans.
Mainz became an archbishopric and
developed into the most important
centre of Christianity north of the
Alps. In AD 975, Willigis was named
Archbishop and work was started on
the cathedral. As Chancellors of the
empire and Electors, the Archbishops
of Mainz wielded power for centuries,
far beyond the borders of Mainz. The
art treasures in the cathedral museum
(closed Sun) are testimony of their
wealth and are well worth seeing.

Mainz's most famous son

By the 13th century, Mainz was a
prosperous, free imperial city known
as *Aurea Moguntia* (Golden Mainz).
Johannes Gutenberg set up his
famous printing press with movable
type in Mainz in about 1450.
Gutenberg's revolutionary invention
is demonstrated daily, on a replica
press in the Gutenberg Museum. The
university of Mainz, founded in 1477,
was renamed in his honour in 1946.

Palaces and mansions

After great destruction in the 17th
century (the Thirty Years' War and
Louis XIV's rampage through the
Rhineland), 18th-century Mainz
enjoyed another period of glory, when
Prince Electors and noble families
built splendid palaces and mansions.
Several are located on Schillerplatz
and Schillerstrasse; Weihergarten (see
the courtyard of house no.5); and
opposite the Theodor-Heuss-Brücke,
along the street parallel to the Rhine.

Mainz and wine

Given its situation at the intersection
of important trade routes and its
location in the heart of Germany's
winelands, it is not surprising that
Mainz developed into a major wine
centre. Today, no barrels of wine are
loaded on to boats here, nor are vines
grown within Mainz proper.

Nevertheless, as the capital of
Rheinland-Pfalz, which includes six
of the thirteen German wine regions,
Mainz is an important administrative
centre for wine and the site of trade
fairs. *Weinforum Rheinhessen*, an annual
presentation of the region's finest
wines (last weekend Oct), is but one of
many wine events that take place here.

Celebrations with wine

Johannisnacht (late June) and *Weinmarkt*
(late Aug) are the major wine festivals
of Mainz. The greatest celebration of
all, though, is the carnival season,
from 11:11 am on 11 November to
Ash Wednesday when wine flows
freely at costume balls and parties,
and during the huge parade through
Mainz on Rose Monday (*Rosenmontag*
– the German name for the Monday
before Lent. The name comes from
dialect, which roughly translates as
'Wild Monday').

A walk through Mainz
The market square is a good place to begin a walking tour of this 2000-year-old town. From 0600 to 1400 (Tue, Fri, Sat) the farmers' market fills the square with fresh flowers and vegetables from nearby fields. In the midst of the colourful stands is Germany's oldest (1576) Renaissance fountain and the entrance to St Martin's, one of the three (Mainz, Worms and Speyer) spectacular Rhenish imperial cathedrals.

To see historic books with illuminated letters and the Gutenberg Bible, walk in the direction of the Rhine to the Gutenberg Museum (except Mon and Jan) on Liebfrauenplatz. Mainz's Old Town lies along Augustiner Strasse and its side alleys behind the Dom (cathedral). The beautiful half-timbered houses are now boutiques and wine pubs, very lively at night.

From the Dom, walk along Ludwigsstrasse to Schillerplatz, ringed by Baroque palaces, to see the modern fountain devoted to Mainz's famous carnival festivities. Turn left to walk up the Gaustrasse to St Stephan's Church, worth visiting for its stained glass windows by Chagall.

WINE SHOP
Weincabinet Leichhofstr. 10. Mon-Fri 1000-1830, Sat 1000-1600. Outstanding selection of German wines.

The Mainzer Dom (cathedral). The interior, with its wealth of sculptures from the 13th-19th centuries, is as splendid as the exterior.

The Rhein Terrasse

Superb vineyards of the Rhein Terrasse at Nierstein.

BODENHEIM
Weingut Kühling-Gillot 'Am Pavillon'
Oelmühlstr. 25. Mid-Jun to early Sep from 1700 Fri-Sun. Wine pub in garden.
GAU-BISCHOFSHEIM
Weingut Nack Pfarr-Str. 13. Tel: 06135/3043. Fax: 06135/8382. From 1800 (except Tue). Sun also 1200-1400. Gourmet wine restaurant.
HARXHEIM
Harxheimer Weinstube
Enggasse 1. Daily from 1800. Wine pub in quaint half-timbered house.
ZORNHEIM
Zornheimer Weinstube
Röhrbrunnenplatz 1. Wed-Sat from 1700. Sun from 1130. Charming, cosy pub.
NACKENHEIM
Weinrestaurant Gunderloch Carl-Gunderloch-Platz 1. Tel: 06135/2341. Fax: 06135/2431. Wed-Sat 1600-2200. Sun 1200-2200. Gourmet wine restaurant. Garden.
Landhotel St. Gereon
Carl-Zuckmayer-Platz 3. Tel: 06135/92990. Fax: 06135/929992. Restaurant Tue-Fri and Sun 1130-1400, Tue-Sat 1800-2200, wine pub in vaulted cellar Fri-Mon from 1800. Cosy, friendly country inn.

Schaufenster Rheinhessens (showcase of Rheinhessen) is the slogan on signs of the Rhein Terrasse's wine towns. This is one of Germany's classic Rhine wine areas. Our route, from Mainz via the B9 (parallel to the Rhine) to Mettenheim, is known as the *Liebfrauenstrasse*. (Follow the signs for Worms as you leave Mainz.)

St Alban
This is the collective name for the vineyards from the southern end of Mainz to Bodenheim. The name comes from the St Alban monastery in Mainz, a medieval vineyard owner.

In Bodenheim, the St Alban coat of arms is on the oriel of the town hall (1608), one of Rheinhessen's finest half-timbered buildings. If your visit is in early June, you can attend the St Alban wine festival in vineyards near the saint's shrine.

The ancient wine towns of Gau-Bischofsheim, Harxheim, Zornheim and Lörzweiler are in the hills some way from the Rhine, yet justify a detour to see the historic buildings and sculptures in the churches. From Lörzweiler, the road leads to Nackenheim on the Rhine.

At the edge of town, it is worth stopping to see the interior of the Baroque St Gereon's Church. A bust of Nackenheim's favourite son, writer Carl Zuckmayer (1896-1977), adorns the half-timbered town hall. He dubbed Rheinhessen wine 'the wine of laughter ... charming and appealing'.

Here and in nearby Nierstein, the vineyards are on steep slopes of *Rotliegendes* (bright red soil) which gives the wines a light earthy tone.

Nierstein
En route to Nierstein, you pass some of Germany's most famous vineyards (Rehbach, Auflangen and Spiegelberg) and St Kilian's Church, set in Glöck, possibly Germany's oldest recorded vineyard (742 AD). Turn right at Breitgasse to reach the market square.

With nearly 1100 hectares (2700 acres) of vineyards, Nierstein is the largest wine-growing village on the Rhine. Its wine festival (first weekend in August), with a parade in medieval dress, is a great tasting opportunity.

For an outstanding view, walk or drive into the vineyards *am roten Hang* (on the red slope) from Karolinger-strasse. From the *Wartturm* (watch tower) turn right and continue towards the Rhine, to the lookout stand at Brudersberg. Vintners set up wine stands along this path in mid-June – a delightful setting for a tasting.

Oppenheim and Guntersblum

The Church of St Katherine is the most important Gothic church between Cologne and Strasbourg. From the intricately carved exterior to the magnificent 14th-century stained glass windows inside, it is well worth a visit. Other historic buildings are grouped around the medieval town hall on the market square. Here, too, is a sparkling wine pub, Gillot Haus.

Guntersblum is famous for its Kellerweg, an alley lined with some 100 cellars and press houses of the town's wine-growers since c.1600.

Rheinblick

This means 'view of the Rhine' and is the name both of Alsheim's best-known vineyard and of its wine festival in mid-June. In September (third Sunday), wine stands are set up along a scenic marked path between Alsheim and Hangen-Wahlheim.

Mettenheim, the southern gate to the Rhein Terrasse, has a Baroque church and a lovely town hall. Twenty Mettenheimer vintners operate a wine pub at 'Sandhof' (weekends, May-Aug). From the B9 drive towards Eich near the Rhine. Watch for the right turn after one kilometre (half a mile).

NIERSTEIN
Winzergenossenschaft Karolingerstr. 6. Wine shop. Mon-Fri 0900-1200, 1300-1800. Sat 0900-1700.
OPPENHEIM
UNDERGROUND TOURS *Untergrundführungen* of the town's ancient cellars. Contact: Sektkellerei Gillot, Wormser Str. 84. Tel: 06133/3239. Fax: 06133/2046. Or inquire at Gillot Haus (Merianstr. 1-3).
MUSEUM OF VITICULTURE Deutsches Weinbau-museum Wormser Str. 49. Apr-Oct 1300-1700 (except Mon). History of wine-growing and production in Germany from Roman times to the present.

Oppenheim's market square during the wine festival in mid-August.

Worms

Worms is one of Germany's oldest cities. It was the capital of a large Celtic settlement and an important Roman garrison town before becoming the short-lived capital of Gunther's Burgundian kingdom (AD 413). Its destruction by the Huns (AD 436) is retold in the *Song of the Nibelungs*.

Golden era

During its golden era, the free and imperial town of Worms was the site of more than 100 imperial diets (synods), including that of 1521 at which Martin Luther refused to revoke his writings. After this significant event, Worms' political importance declined as the German emperors lost their authority.

Although much of the town was devastated during the Thirty Years' War, the War of the Palatinate Succession and World War II, there are still many historic treasures.

St Peter's Cathedral

One of Germany's three great Rhenish imperial cathedrals, St Peter's was built in the 11th-12th centuries on the site of the old Roman forum. The ornate exterior is worth seeing before viewing the works of art inside, including the Baroque high altar by Balthasar Neumann and the Rococo choir stalls.

Jewish culture

Europe's oldest surviving Jewish cemetery, with tombstones dating from the 11th century, is on Andreasring. Germany's oldest synagogue (1034) and the Rashi House, a museum devoted to the history of Worms' Jewish community, are located on Judengasse, once the heart of the Jewish quarter.

The Liebfrauenstift-Kirchenstück vineyard surrounding the Liebfrauenkirche (Church of Our Lady) in Worms. Capuchin monks first planted vines here in 1450.

Liebfraumilch

Centuries ago, Rhine wines from the vineyards surrounding the Gothic Liebfrauenkirche (Church of Our Lady) were named Liebfraumilch, literally 'Milk of the Blessed Mother'.

As demand increased, the term Liebfraumilch became a broad regional appellation for the world's most popular German Rhine wine.

Liebfraumilch is a blend of Germany's classic white grape varieties. It is a soft, easy-to-drink wine. Both quality and price are directly related to the quality-consciousness of the producer named on the label.

DITTELSHEIM-HESSLOCH
Restaurant Weinkastell Auf dem Kloppberg (east of Alzey, via Framersheim, at top of the hillside). Wed-Fri 1800-2400, Sat-Sun from1100 (Nov-Mar, Sat from 1800). Country inn with panoramic view.

FLÖRSHEIM-DALSHEIM
Weingut Schales Alzeyer Strasse 160. Tel: 06243/7003. Fax: 06243/5230. By appointment, wine tastings are held in the family's wine museum; collection of historic tools, glasses and wine artifacts worth seeing.

Alzey and the Countryside

The Schloss (castle) is just one of many historic buildings in the pleasant town of Alzey. The tourist office in the Rathaus (town hall) has brochures in English describing a 90-minute circular walk of Alzey.

The wine-growing area between Worms and Alzey is known as the Wonnegau (land of bliss). As in the other rural areas of Rheinhessen, grapes are usually not the only agricultural product. Grapes or wines are often sold in bulk (rather than bottled) to large wineries or co-operatives. The small growers supply the components used to make Liebfraumilch, for example.

Unexpected artistic details

In many of the villages, even simple structures often have artistic details, such as a beautiful portal or a carved cellar door. Peep into the courtyards.

Unique to the Wonnegau are the *Trulli* (see the label above), cone- or dome-shaped vintners' huts used as tool sheds and shelters for vineyard workers. These huts, similar to those in Apulia, are in the vineyards south-east and north-west of Alzey.

Country wine villages

Leave Worms from the north-west and drive via Herrnsheim – worth a stop to see the Schloss (palace) and its English gardens – to the old wine villages of Osthofen, Bechtheim, Westhofen and Bermersheim.

Flörsheim-Dalsheim is surrounded by an unusual *Fleckenmauer* (notched stone wall), while in Monsheim you can see a Stone Age monolith, the Hinkelstein, in the Schlosshof (castle courtyard). From here it is only minutes to Alzey via the B271.

Alzey

Along the side streets of Obermarkt (market square) there are many beautiful half-timbered houses. The Renaissance town hall on Fischmarkt and the fountains and historic buildings on Rossmarkt are also worth seeing, as are the 12th-century Schloss (castle) and remnants of the town's fortifications. On the outskirts of town is the grape breeding institute where Georg Scheu (pronounced 'Shoy') bred many of the aromatic new crossings planted in this region.

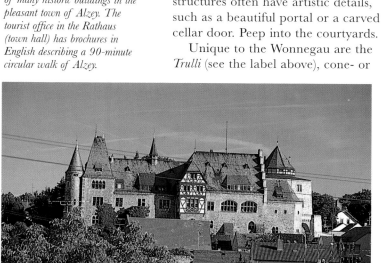

Bingen and its Environs

Neu-Bamberg in the heart of the scenic hilly countryside of 'Rheinhessen's Switzerland'.

BINGEN
Brunnenkeller
Vorstadt 60. Tel/Fax:
06721/16133. Mon-Thu
1200-1400, Mon-Sat 1800-
2300. Gourmet restaurant in
historic cellar.

HACKENHEIM
Metzlers Gasthof
Hauptstr. 69. Tel: 0671/
65312. Fax: 0671/65310.
Gourmet restaurant: 1900-
2200 (except Mon). Also Sun
1200-1400. Weinstube:
1200-1400, 1800-2230
(except Mon). Terrace.

SAULHEIM
La Maison de Marie
Weedengasse 8. Tel: 06732/
3331. Fax: 06732/8076.
1830-2130 (except Thu).
Also Sun 1200-1400.
Creative, contemporary
cuisine, excellent wine list.

FOR FURTHER INFORMATION
Contact the regional wine
promotion board:
Rheinhessenwein
An der Brunnenstube 33-35,
55120 Mainz.
Tel: 06131/99680.
Fax: 06131/682701.

**FOR TOURIST INFORMATION
AND CALENDAR OF EVENTS**
Rheinhessen-Information
Wilhelm-v-Erlanger-Str. 100,
55218 Ingelheim.
Tel: 06132/787565.
Fax: 06132/787560.

The western part of Rheinhessen has three main areas of interest: Bingen, with the region's only quartzite-slate soils and its steep Scharlachberg site (Riesling is a speciality); Ingelheim, a centre of red wine production; and the attractive hills not far from the Nahe known as 'Rheinhessen's Switzerland'.

Bingen

Bingen's strategic position at the confluence of the Nahe and Rhine rivers was enhanced when the Roman Drusus built the first bridge, the foundations of which still support Bingen's oldest bridge (c.10th century) across the Nahe. Medieval Bingen was an important conduit for goods and armies between Mainz, Koblenz and Trier and it is still a centre of the wine trade.

St Martin's Basilica, near the ancient Drusus bridge, is a Gothic church with an 11th-century crypt, beautiful vaulting and medieval sculptures.

Panoramic views

Since Celtic times, Klopp hill in the centre of Bingen has been the site of fortresses which have been burned down, blown up and bombed through the centuries. Today, the town hall and an interesting history museum (open from Easter to Oct, closed Mon) are in the reconstructed Klopp fortress. From its tower you have a sweeping view of the area.

The St Rochus Kapelle is a hillside chapel with an impressive altar and crucifix outside. Perched atop the Rochusberg, it is visible for miles, especially when it is illuminated at night.

Ingelheim

Charlemagne had a *Pfalz* (palace) here. One winter's day, it is said, he noted that the snow had already melted on the opposite side of the Rhine (today the site of Schloss Johannisberg) and ordered vines to be planted there.

You can visit the remains of the Pfalz and its Saalkirche (church). Also worth seeing is the Burgkirche, unusual in that both it and its cemetery are encircled by a stone wall.

Ingelheim's chalky clay soils yield some of the region's finest Spätburgunder and Portugieser red wines, celebrated at the *Rotweinfest*, a huge wine festival in late September.

If you visit in May or June you can enjoy famous Ingelheimer asparagus and attend 'International Days', six weeks of art exhibitions, cultural events and wine tastings. (For details, contact the sponsor: Boehringer, Internationale Tage, Binger Str. 173, 55218 Ingelheim. Tel: 06132/774336. Fax: 06132/774456.)

'Rheinhessen's Switzerland'
From Ingelheim, drive south via Jugenheim, Partenheim and St Johann (all have treasures in their churches) to Sprendlingen.

To take in the sights of the splendid countryside, begin at Gau-Bickelheim and drive a circular route through Wöllstein, Neu-Bamberg, Wonsheim, Wendelsheim, Flonheim and Armsheim. From here it is an easy drive back to Bingen via the A61.

On the road from Wendelsheim to Nack watch for the sign to the Teufelsrutsch (Devil's Slide) vantage-point for a stunning view.

There are also several *Trulli*, or vintners' huts, to see in the vineyards between Wendelsheim and Flonheim.

Ancient, vaulted cellars of a traditional family estate in Ingelheim, known for its red wines. Here, the cellar-master is tasting a sample from the cask. To extract wines from the barrel, he inserts the tube into the opening at the top of the cask and sucks on it. He frequently has to check the wine's development in order to decide when it is ready to be bottled. He must also regularly 'top up' the barrels (add wine to compensate for evaporation) to keep the casks completely full, so that the wine is not exposed to air (oxidation) – which could result in vinegar if left unchecked.

The Pfalz

'Cheers! The Pfalz.' is the region's slogan – a harbinger of the warm hospitality that awaits visitors to this region, often called the Tuscany of Germany.

'The Three B's of the Pfalz' – Bassermann, Bürklin and Buhl – great, traditional wine estates that have contributed to Germany's international reputation for fine wine.

The Pfalz is bordered by Rheinhessen to the north and France to the south and west. For nearly 80km (50 miles), a thick ribbon of vineyards runs parallel to the foothills of the forested Haardt Mountains. To become acquainted with the landscape and picturesque wine villages from Bockenheim to Schweigen, you can drive the *Deutsche Weinstrasse* (German Wine Road) or walk the marked *Wanderweg* (hiking trail).

Not only grapes, but also figs, lemons, sweet chestnuts and almonds thrive in this exceptionally warm, sunny climate. Pfälzer hospitality is as inviting as the climate. These people are legendary for their ability to 'eat, drink and be merry'. Thus it is not surprising that the world's largest wine festival is held here, or that the region's typical wine glass, the *Schoppen*, holds half a litre (about a pint) of wine. Share a *Schoppen* in a wine pub or at one of the Pfalz's wine festivals.

The word Pfalz derives from the Latin *palatium*, meaning palace. (The imperial residence in Ancient Rome was on the Palatine Hill.) *Kaiserpfalz*, for example, is an imperial palace. Other derivations include palatine, a lord with royal privileges, and palatinate, the territory he ruled. The English form 'Palatinate' is often used in reference to the Pfalz, meaning the Rhine territory formerly ruled by the counts palatine.

The Pfalz owes its German heritage to its 'wealth of wine', for when the Carolingian Empire was divided in AD 843 (Treaty of Verdun), the Pfalz was ceded to Louis the German to ensure the eastern territory's supply of Communion wine.

Roman origins

The great tradition of wine-growing in the Pfalz dates from Roman times. Of the many Roman wine artifacts unearthed throughout the region, three finds are particularly exciting. Two Roman farms where grapes were

also cultivated were discovered in the 1980s when the vineyards east of Wachenheim and north of Ungstein were reorganized. Both sites, the *Villa rustica* and the *Römerkelter*, are worth seeing. Near Speyer, wine was found in a glass amphora dating from c.AD 300, sealed airtight under a layer of resin and oil, thus enabling the wine to survive more than 16 centuries. You can see this rarity in the Speyer wine museum.

Zum Wohl. Cheers!

The Pfalz is Germany's second largest wine region (23,720 hectares/58,612 acres) but it often has a larger crop than Rheinhessen. Most of the best vineyards are on slopes at the foot of the Haardt Mountains.

There are many soil types in a region this large. Loam soils predominate, in a variety of mixtures with coloured sandstone, chalk, loess, clay and sand. Riesling, Müller-Thurgau, Kerner and Silvaner are the leading white grape varieties. Morio-Muskat, Scheurebe and small amounts of the ancient specialities Gewürztraminer and Muskateller, as well as the more neutral Grauburgunder and Weissburgunder, are all grown in the Pfalz. Red wine production is increasing. Portugieser, Dornfelder and Spätburgunder are the main red grapes planted here.

Cobbled streets full of flower boxes and vine-clad houses, delicious wine and food and friendly, outgoing people make the Pfalz especially inviting. The best time to enjoy this ambience is between March, when the almond trees blossom, and the end of the harvest in mid-November.

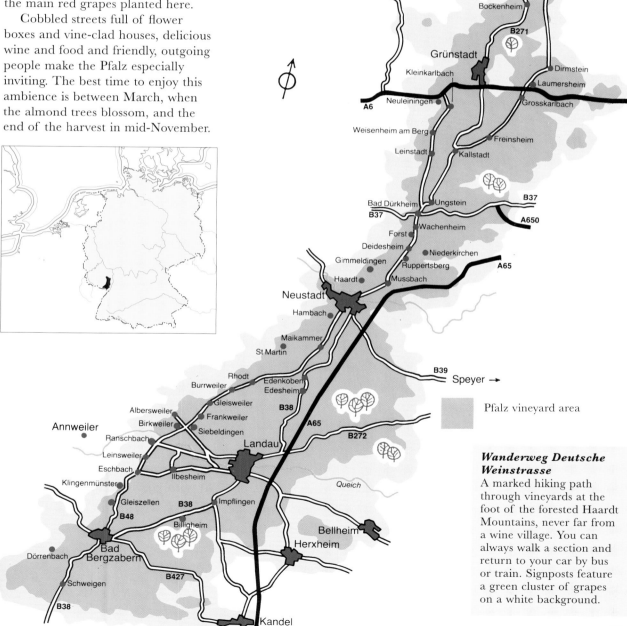

Pfalz vineyard area

Wanderweg Deutsche Weinstrasse

A marked hiking path through vineyards at the foot of the forested Haardt Mountains, never far from a wine village. You can always walk a section and return to your car by bus or train. Signposts feature a green cluster of grapes on a white background.

Bockenheim to Bad Dürkheim

Neuleiningen, perched high above the vineyards, is ringed by its 13th-century walls.

BOCKENHEIM
Haus der deutschen Weinstrasse Weinstr. 91. Tel: 06359/94330. Fax: 06359/943325. Daily, from 1100. Showcase for Pfälzer wine and food. Good view.

NEULEININGEN
Alte Pfarrey Untergasse 54. Tel: 06359/86066. Fax: 86060. 1200-1330, 1800-2130 (except Mon; Tue dinner only). Charming restaurant and hotel.
Liz' Stuben Am Goldberg 2. Tel: 06359/5341. From 1900, Tue-Sat. Only by reservation. Very cosy, in the Gissels' pretty house.

GROSSKARLBACH
Karlbacher Hauptstr. 57. Tel: 06238/3737. Fax: 06238/4535. 1200-1330, 1800-2130 (except Mon, Tue). Lovely courtyard.

FREINSHEIM
Luther Hauptstr. 29. Tel: 06353/2021. Fax 06353/8388. 1800-2130 (except Sun). Gourmet restaurant, excellent wine list. Hotel.
Von-Busch-Hof Buschhof 5. Tel: 06353/7705. Fax: 06353/3741. Restaurant: from 1800 Wed-Sat, from 1100 Sun. 13th-century Weinkeller: from 1700 Thu-Sun. Both closed mid-Jan to mid-Feb.

KALLSTADT
Hotel Weincastell Zum Weissen Ross Weinstr. 80-82. Tel: 06322/5033. Fax: 06322/8640. Wed-Sun 1200-1430, from 1800. Closed mid-Jan to mid-Feb. Half-timbered inn (1488). Fine regional fare, superb Koehler-Ruprecht wines.
Henninger Weinstr. 93. 1200-1400, 1800-2130 (except Mon). Cosy pub.

The *Deutsche Weinstrasse* (German Wine Road) begins in Bockenheim and ends some 80km (50 miles) south at Schweigen on the French border. It corresponds mainly to the B271.

The *Wanderweg Deutsche Weinstrasse* (German hiking trail) also begins in Bockenheim, to the right of Leininger Ring and opposite St Martin's Church. St Lambert's Church, further south on the right, has a notable Madonna and Christ-child with a cluster of grapes.

Leiningerland
From 1100 to the French Revolution, the Counts of Leiningen ruled the area surrounding Grünstadt, where they built their residence after their fortresses in Neuleiningen and Altleiningen were destroyed. All three places are worth a visit, particularly the romantic medieval town of Neuleiningen. Remains of the fortress crown tiers of winding alleys lined with half-timbered houses, all of which are encircled by the ancient town walls. There are wonderful views from all levels.

From here, follow the road parallel to the Eckbach (stream) from Kleinkarlbach to Grosskarlbach, a traditional wine village with Renaissance manors built around spacious courtyards. Explore the town on foot to see the beautifully carved portals, old mills and art treasures in both churches. Historic Kändelgasse, a picturesque lane along the stream, is the site of a typical wine festival in late July or early August.

If time permits, make a small detour north via Laumersheim to Dirmstein, where noble mansions (Marktstrasse, Obertor and Metzgergasse) and a church designed by Balthasar Neumann are all worth seeing.

Take the country road through the vineyards from Dirmstein and Grosskarlbach to Freinsheim, another medieval gem, surrounded by town walls and tower gates. The best walking tour is along the winding alley

Visitors can walk along Freinsheim's medieval town walls, which are punctuated at intervals by watchtowers and gateways.

a tasty Pfälzer speciality made of minced pork, potatoes, spices, etc, cooked in a casing (sow's stomach). At the wine festival in early September, you can enjoy 'Saumagen twice' – in your glass and on your plate.

Vineyard heights

The country road from Kleinkarlbach to Bad Dürkheim via Weisenheim am Berg and Leistadt is especially pretty, not least because of its height, overlooking the wine road and Rhine plain. Travelling this road gives you a feel for the 'layers' of vineyards in this section of the Pfalz. The Bismarck-Turm (tower) provides a good view.

A Roman wine estate

This was discovered in the Weilberg site near Ungstein when the vineyards were uprooted in 1981 as part of the vineyard reorganization programme. The owners of the site generously agreed to forfeit their vineyards to enable archeologists to continue excavation and restoration work.

While it is interesting to view Roman artifacts in a museum, it is even better to see the origins of German viticulture on site, a reminder that even 2000 years ago these sunny hillsides were favoured locations for growing grapes.

Ungstein borders Bad Dürkheim, home of the *Wurstmarkt*, the world's largest wine festival. It takes place in mid-September on the grounds near the *Dürkheimer Riesenfass*, the 1,700,000-litre cask near the entrance to the town (at other times of the year, a good place to park). You can sample the local wine and tasty regional specialities in the restaurant inside the cask (daily from 1100). Try a *Leberknödel* (liver dumpling) or *Pfälzer Rumpsteak* (roast beef with onions).

next to the old walls, starting from the Baroque town hall and Gothic church at the heart of town. The walls are also the unique setting for the *Stadtmauerfest* (wine festival) in mid-July.

'Saumagen twice'

Kallstadt is renowned for elegant Riesling and stylish Silvaner wines. Saumagen (sow's stomach) is the name both of its best vineyard and of

Bad Dürkheim to Neustadt

Bad Dürkheim's Riesenfass *(giant cask) contains a wine restaurant.*

This portion of the German Wine Road includes some of Germany's most famous wine villages. The classical vineyards on the hillsides yield big, ripe wines full of character. Here, as throughout the Pfalz, there are traditional family estates, large and small, and very good local co-operatives producing wines from numerous red and white varieties. The area's fame, however, derives from its Riesling wines and from the 'three B's of the Pfalz': Bassermann, Bürklin and Buhl – far-sighted estate owners who were staunch supporters and models of quality wine-growing at the turn of this century.

Wine, water and woods

The picturesque forests of the Haardt Mountains frame Bad Dürkheim, as popular today for its wine, woods and saline springs as it was in Roman times. The spa facilities and casino are in an attractive park near the giant cask. At harvest time you can try a *Traubenkur* (grape juice cure).

Dürkheim is well known for its *Wurstmarkt* (sausage market), a festival dating from the 14th century, when thousands of pilgrims stopped here every autumn en route to Spain. The hospitable natives provided wine, sausages and bread. Wheelbarrows tipped upright served as 'stands', a cask of wine fitting neatly between the handles. Today, half a million *Schoppen* of wine, 60,000 chickens and 180,000 kg (400,000 lbs) of sausage are consumed at the eight-day festival every year.

The surrounding woods are not only beautiful, but also rich in historic sites: the Heidenmauer, a Celtic bulwark; a Roman quarry; ruins of both the Gothic Limburg Abbey and the mighty Hardenburg fortress.

Wachenheim, Forst and Deidesheim

Panoplies of vines – green in summer and brilliant golden red in autumn – adorn aristocratic manors along the narrow streets of these wine villages.

DEIDESHEIM
MUSEUM OF WINE CULTURE
Museum für Weinkultur
(in the historic town hall).
Wed-Sun 1600-1800.
Closed Jan-Feb. Wine
articles of cultural-
historical significance.
NEUSTADT
Haus des Weines
Rathausstr. 6 (in a Gothic
house from 1276). Apr-Oct:
Mon-Fri 1000-1300, 1430-
1830; Sat 0930-1500; Sun
1400-1700. Nov-Mar:
closed Sun and Mon; Sat
0930-1400. Showcase for
Neustadt wines and grape-
based products, with 30
wines to taste by the glass.

*Neustadt's fountain depicts the
fabled Elwetritschen (creatures).
Anyone needing an alibi has been
'hunting Elwetritschen'.*

Wachenheim's hillside landmark, the Wachtenburg, affords a good view and a chance to sample the local wine (the pub is open all year, Sat after 1200, Sun after 1000; May-Oct also Wed-Fri after 1600). To see the *Villa rustica* (Roman farm, c.AD 20) drive towards Friedelsheim (east of the B271).

The drive from Wachenheim to Forst is scarcely a kilometre (half a mile), but to see the beautiful Renaissance houses and historic wine estates of Forst, you must bear to the right at the fork in the road just before the town or you will miss 'old' Forst completely. The Baroque statue of the Madonna in the vineyards overlooking the town is the namesake of the Mariengarten site.

The market square in Deidesheim, with the 16th-century town hall and Gothic church of St Ulrich, is among the prettiest in the Pfalz. This is the site of the annual *Geisbockversteigerung* (goat auction) on Pentecost Tuesday, a custom dating from the Middle Ages, when neighbouring Lambrecht paid tribute to Deidesheim for grazing rights.

A stroll along romantic Feigengasse, Deichelgasse or Heumarktstrasse is delightful. Or enjoy a glass of wine in Schloss Deidesheim or in its idyllic garden (Mar-Oct, Sat from 1200, Sun from 1500, Mon-Wed from 1700).

Co-operative wineries
In nearly every village, these offer well-made wines of exceptionally good value. Deidesheim's Winzerverein was the first (1898) in the Pfalz. All have shops where you can sample the wines prior to purchase and many have wine restaurants next door.

Neustadt
With some 1800 hectares (4500 acres) of wines, Neustadt and its wine suburbs comprise the largest wine-growing community in Germany.

In late September, Neustadt hosts a major wine event, the *Deutsche Weinlesefest* (German wine harvest festival). The ten-day celebration includes a colourful parade and the coronation of the German Wine Queen.

The market square, the centre of the Old Town, is dominated by the Baroque town hall and the Gothic Liebfrauenkirche (church), with a decor rich in sculptural details.

Historic residential buildings of interest are on the streets near the market square, such as Metzgergasse, Rathausstrasse and Hauptstrasse. From May to Oct you can travel on the 'Kuckucksbähnel' (historic trains) from Neustadt to Elmstein, for a scenic ride through the beautiful Pfälzer forest.

Speyer

BAD DÜRKHEIM
Hotel Fronmühle
Salinenstr. 15. Tel: 06322/
94090. Fax: 06322/940940.
1200-1430, 1800-2130
(except Mon). Garden.
Weinstube Bach-Mayer
Gerberstr. 13. Tel: 06322/
8611. Mon-Sat from 1700.
Try a *Pfälzer Teller*, hearty
regional fare.
WACHENHEIM
Gerümpelstube
Hintergasse 4. Tel: 06322/
8550. Fri-Tue from 1600.
Sun from 1200. Closed Aug.
Restaurant Luginsland
Weinstr. 2 (next to co-op).
1130-1400, 1700-2200.
FORST
**Gutsausschank Acham-
Magin** Weinstr. 67. Tel:
06326/315. Wed-Sat from
1600. Closed Jan, Feb.
**Gutsausschank
Spindler** Weinstr. 44. Tel:
06326/280. Tue-Sat 1130-
2130. Closed Jan.
Zum Schockelgaul
Weinstr. 96. Tel: 06326/
5669. Wed-Sun from 1700.
Sun also 1200-1400.
DEIDESHEIM
Deidesheimer Hof Am
Marktplatz. Tel: 06326/
96870. Fax: 06326/7685.
For gourmets **Schwarzer
Hahn** Tue-Sat from 1900.
Regional fare at **St Urban**
from 1200 daily. Outdoor
seating. Pretty hotel.
Gasthaus zur Kanne
Weinstr. 31. Tel: 06326/
966012. Fax: 06326/966096.
Restaurant 1730-2200.
Rustic fare in the
Weinstube from 1730
daily. Oldest inn of the Pfalz
(1160), inviting courtyard.
NEUSTADT
Altstadtkeller
Kunigundenstr. 2. Tel:
06321/32320. Fax: 06321/
7280. 1130-1400, 1800-2230
Tue-Sat,1730-2100 Sun.

Speyer Cathedral, the epitome of Romanesque architecture in Europe, was erected by the Emperor Konrad II in 1030. Much of the architectural detail was inspired by northern Italy (which was part of the German Empire at the time).

Multiple towers and the innovative use of vaulting are echoed in the cathedrals of Worms and Mainz. The crypt, the largest and most beautiful i Germany, is the burial place of four emperors, three empresses, four kings and five bishops.

Speyer is situated on the Rhine some 25km (15 miles) east of Neustadt. Its origins date from settlements during the Stone, Bronze and Iron Ages. In Roman times, it was an important military and commercial centre of the upper Rhine, and in the 11th century Speyer was named capital of the German Empire.

The magnificent Kaiserdom (imperial cathedral) testifies to Speyer's importance as a centre of temporal and ecclesiastical power during the Middle Ages. The Historisches Museum der Pfalz has excellent displays recounting Speyer's 5000 years of history, and it houses the *Domschatz*, the original art and historic treasures of the cathedral. (Domplatz, open 1000-1800 except Mon).

Speyer was a bishopric as early as the 4th century. The bishops were the heads of Church and State until 1294, when they renounced their secular authority and Speyer was declared a free imperial city. Henceforth, the 'border' between the spiritual and worldly realms was symbolized in front of the cathedral by the *Domnapf* (basin), which was traditionally filled with wine (1500 litres) for the populace whenever a new bishop was consecrated.

Historic sights

Not far from the cathedral, on the Judengasse, is the former centre of Jewish culture in Speyer. The 11th-century synagogue is gone, but you can visit the women's baths, which are underground – the oldest and largest of their kind in present-day Germany.

Town fortifications were built during the 13th century. Two of the original 68 towers are intact: Altpörtal, the impressive western gate on Maximilianstrasse, and Heidentürmchen, a two-storey defence tower in the garden behind the cathedral.

Baroque enthusiasts will enjoy the rich decor of the Dreifaltigkeitskirche (Church of the Holy Trinity) and the archive and chambers of the town hall. The neo-Gothic Gedächtniskirche (Memorial Church) commemorates those who protested at the edict of the Diet of Speyer in 1529 which rejected Luther's theses (hence the name Protestants).

The cathedral

In 1027, Konrad II was crowned Emperor by the Pope. Three years later, he laid the cornerstone of Germany's supreme work of Romanesque architecture. The cathedral is remarkable for its innovative vaulted bays, probably the earliest use of extensive groined vaulting in Europe.

During the second period of construction (1082-1125), the flat wooden ceiling of the nave was replaced with vaulting, the Kaisergruft (crypt) was enlarged and decorative dwarf galleries and towers were added to the exterior. (Apr-Oct: Mon-Sat 0900-1900, Sun 1330-1900. Nov-Mar: Mon-Sat 0900-1700, Sun 1330-1700.)

Speyer and wine

Although there are no longer any vineyards in Speyer, it has a long tradition of wine culture. The Bishops of Speyer were the most important vineyard owners in the Pfalz from 1100 until Napoleon secularized church properties in 1803. The wine museum in the Historisches Museum der Pfalz chronicles 2000 years of viticulture with historic and cultural objects related to wine, including the world's oldest bottle of wine.

NEUSTADT-MUSSBACH
Weinstube Eselsburg Kurpfalzstr. 62. Tel: 06321/66984. Wed-Sat from 1700. Closed mid-Dec – mid-Jan.
Schüle Erben Kurpfalzstr. 49. Tel: 06321/6118. Fri-Tue from 1700.
NEUSTADT-HAMBACH
Winzergaststätte Weinstr. 110, and **Maxburg** Weinstr. 179. Both open 1200-1400, 1700-2200. Pubs of the Hambach co-op.
SPEYER
Backmulde Karmeliterstr. 11-13. Tel: 06232/71577. Fax: 06232/629474. Tue-Sat 1130-1430, 1900-2100. Creative, excellent wine list.
Hotel Goldener Engel Mühlturmstr. 1a. Tel: 06232/13260. Fax: 06232/132695. From 1800 (except Sun). Vaulted stone cellar.
Kutscherhaus Fischmarkt 5a. Tel: 06232/70592. Fax: 06232/620922. 1130-1400 and from 1800 (except Wed). Guest rooms.

The Southern Wine Road

Hambacher Schloss, where 30,000 people demonstrated for freedom and unity in 1832, raising the German colours (black, red and gold) for the first time.

ST MARTIN
Winzerhof Maikammerer Str. 22. Tel: 06323/94440. Fax: 06323/944455. 1130-1400, 1730-2130 (except Wed, Thu and Jan). Terrace. Guest rooms.
EDENKOBEN
Zur alten Kanzlei Weinstr. 120. Wed-Sun from 1700. Tel: 06323/3983. Cosy wine pub in vaulted cellar. Guest rooms.
EDESHEIM
Weincastell Staatsstr. 21. Tel: 06323/2392. Fax: 06323/81676. Wed-Sun 1130-1400, 1730- 2200. Closed 4 weeks Jan-Feb. Guest rooms.
Weingut W. Anselmann Staatsstr. 58-60. Mid-May to mid-Sep from 1100. A typical *Strausswirtschaft*.
RHODT
Rietburg-Weinstube Theresienstr. 87. From 1800 Thu, Sat and Sun. Sep-Oct, daily from 1800 (except Mon). Delightful atmosphere. Music on Sun.
BURRWEILER
Burrweiler Mühle (in the old mill). Wed-Sat from 1500, Sun from 1200. Closed mid-Dec to mid-Jan.
FRANKWEILER
Robichon-Frankenburg Orensfelsstr. 31. Tel: 06345/3268. Fax: 06345/8529. 1200-1400, 1800-2200 (except Mon eve and Tue). Gourmet restaurant.
BIRKWEILER
St Laurentius Hof Hauptstr. 21. Tel: 06345/8945. Fax: 06345/8946. Wed-Sun 1130-1400, Tue-Sun 1800-2200. Closed Jan. Cosy. Guest rooms.

The large wine-growing area from Neustadt to the French border at Schweigen is known as the *Südliche Weinstrasse* (Southern Wine Road). The B38 leads directly to Landau, the commercial centre of the wine trade. It is better, however, to use the parallel road to the west, which is the continuation of the German Wine Road and is less crowded with traffic.

The southern Pfalz has enjoyed a renaissance during the past 25 years. Local pride abounds. Historic buildings have been lovingly restored and richly adorned with flowers. Individual houses and entire villages compete to be named the 'prettiest' in contests.

Pride is also manifested in the improved quality of the wines. The co-operatives have been instrumental in raising standards and implementing marketing strategies to polish the area's image. And the distinctive wines of five dynamic growers known as 'Fünf Freunde aus der Südpfalz', have won the southern Pfalz international

acclaim. (Details: Weingut Friedrich Becker, Hauptstr. 29, 76889 Schweigen. Tel: 06342/290. Fax: 06342/6148.)

Neustadt's wine suburbs

Neustadt's wine suburbs, at the gateway to the Southern Wine Road, deserve mention. The important viticultural teaching and research institute of Mussbach owns the Pfalz's oldest (8th century) wine estate, Johannitergut. Within its ancient stone walls there is a pretty courtyard and medieval garden (always open) and a wine museum in the Herrenhof (by appointment, Tel/Fax: 06321/66772). Eselshaut (donkey's hide) is the name of Mussbach's best-known vineyard.

The Hambacher Schloss, known as the cradle of German democracy, also merits a visit (Mar-Nov 0900-1830). Two restaurants offer wine and a view.

The Panorama Weg between Königsbach and Gimmeldingen and the Leopold-Reitz-Weg (from the co-op parking lot in Haardt) are nice walks.

Maikammer to St Martin

The Kalmit, highest summit (673m/ 2208ft) of the *Pfälzer* woods, is the backdrop of the wine villages Maikammer and Alsterweiler. To the east, a veritable sea of vineyards stretches from the forest's edge well into the Rhine plain. Maikammer has cheerful half-timbered houses and in the Alsterweiler Kapelle (chapel) there is a remarkable Gothic triptych. The scenery along the road to St Martin via the Kalmit is worth the slight detour from the wine road.

St Martin, a romantic little wine village, is considered by many to be the prettiest in the Pfalz. The town's patron saint and namesake is honoured with a parade and festival on 11 November. You can enjoy a good view over a glass of wine at the Kropsburg fortress above the town.

Edenkoben to Rhodt

Edenkoben is a charming wine town known for Silvaner wines. A *Weinlehrpfad* (educational wine trail) through the vineyards leads to Schloss Ludwigshöhe, a palace built (c.1850) in the style of a Pompeian villa by King Ludwig I of Bavaria. The period rooms and art gallery with works of the leading German impressionist, Max Slevogt (1868-1932), are worth a visit (0900-1215, 1400-1615 except Mon and Dec).

From here, take the Rietburgbahn (chairlift, daily, Easter-Oct, 0900-1700) further uphill to the Rietburg fortress ruins for a spectacular panorama extending to Heidelberg, Worms and Speyer on a clear day.

In Rhodt, you can see Germany's oldest productive vines, a plot of Traminer more than 350 years old, in the Rosengarten site opposite the co-operative. Historic sights include St

Georgs-Kirche, Baroque houses, a town hall dating from 1606 and the 18th-century Schlössl (little palace) at the northern edge of town.

The names of the next few wine villages end with *weiler*, the German word for hamlet. Much of their appeal lies in the natural beauty of their surroundings. In Burrweiler there is an unusually ornate sandstone portal carved with animal symbols (near the corner of Hauptstrasse and Weinstrasse). Gleisweiler is a health resort with a subtropical park near the Kurhaus (clinic). On Bergstrasse you can see works of the local artist Herbert Lorenz in a sculpture garden in front of his home.

Schloss Ludwigshöhe, the summer residence of King Ludwig I of Bavaria, who called this part of the Pfalz 'the most beautiful square mile of my realm'. Ludwigshöhe is also the name of the vineyards on the hills overlooking Edenkoben.

LANDAU-NUSSDORF
Landhaus Herrenberg
Lindenbergstr. 72. Tel:
06341/60205. Fax: 06341/
60709. From 1700 (except
Thu). Wine estate's lovely
hotel and wine restaurant.
HERXHEIM-HAYNA
Hotel Krone Hauptstr.
62 (10km/6 miles SE of
Landau). Tel: 07276/5080.
Fax: 07276/50814.
Gourmet restaurant: Wed-
Sun 1800-2030. Rustic
Pfälzer Stube Wed-Mon
1200-1330, 1800-2030.
First-class cuisine, wines.
SCHWEIGEN
Deutsches Weintor
Wine shop of co-operative.
Mar-Dec 0900-1700 daily.
Jan-Feb closed Mon, Tue.

FOR FURTHER INFORMATION
Contact the regional wine
promotion board:
Pfalzwein, Chemnitzer Str.
3, 67433 Neustadt.
Tel: 06321/912328.
Fax: 06321/12881.

*Theresienstrasse is the premier
attraction of Rhodt. Vines and fig
trees embellish the façades of
growers' houses on this lane.*

Geilweilerhof in Siebeldingen

Many new grape varieties have been
bred here. The spicy Morio-Muskat,
a popular white wine grape in the
southern Pfalz, was developed here
in the 1950s. It is named after its
breeder, Peter Morio, who was born
in nearby Ranschbach. The wine shop
at the grape breeding institute affords
a unique opportunity to sample wines
made from experimental varieties
(Mon-Fri 0830-1130 and 1230-1430).

Annweiler and Burg Trifels

To visit one of Germany's most
impressive fortresses, Burg Trifels,
drive west from Siebeldingen via
Albersweiler to Annweiler, a quaint
little resort. On Wassergasse,
Quodgasse and Schipkapass, you can
see the historic houses and a paddle-
wheel picturesquely situated along the
stream running through the town.

Burg Trifels, a former imperial
residence, is built into a rocky cliff in
the Pfälzer woods. The crown jewels
were stored in the chapel during the
12th and 13th centuries (copies are on
display here; the originals are in
Vienna). Richard the Lionheart was

imprisoned here from 1193 to 1194.
Burg Trifels was never captured, but
was damaged by lightning in 1662. It
has been rebuilt in neo-Romanesque
style over the past 50 years.

Landau and suburbs

Landau, the wine capital of the
southern Pfalz, was under French rule
from 1648 until the early 19th century.
After a devastating fire in 1689, Louis
XIV sent his military engineer Vauban
to rebuild Landau into the 'mightiest
fortified town of Christendom'.

The French Gate and the German
Gate are well preserved. The rest of
the extensive ramparts and moats have
been turned into beautiful gardens.

One of Germany's oldest (1540)
folk festivals, the *Purcelmarkt*, is held in
Billigheim in mid-September. There is
a parade featuring historical costumes,
followed by an afternoon of horse
races and medieval games, including a
Purcel (somersault) race. Wine stands
are set up in growers' courtyards and
on the market square.

You can return to the wine road via
Ilbesheim, which has a notable Gothic
town hall, half-timbered houses and
an important regional co-operative.

Leinsweiler

The town is situated at the foot of the
Slevogthof, Slevogt's hillside summer
home, which he decorated with
remarkable frescoes depicting scenes
from operas by Mozart and Wagner
(The rooms are open Mar-Oct, Mon-
Wed, 1115 and 1330, also 1600 Sat-
Sun; restaurant from 1030-1800).

Eschbach to Bad Bergzabern

Viewed from Eschbach, the ruins of
the 11th-century Madenburg fortress
look like a miniature city on top of
the hill. It affords a good view and

Winzergasse (Growers' Alley) in Gleiszellen, a wine village typical of the southern Pfalz. Muskateller wines are a speciality here.

has interesting details, such as Renaissance portals and tower staircases. Klingenmünster and Gleiszellen (on Winzergasse) have pretty half-timbered houses.

Bad Bergzabern is a spa with notable buildings on its market square. On Königstrasse 45, you can dine in the most magnificent Renaissance house of the Pfalz, the Gasthaus zum Engel (except Tue). Down the street, have a look inside the courtyard of the 16th-century ducal palace.

Dörrenbach to Schweigen

Idyllically set in a side valley is the wine village of Dörrenbach. An awe-inspiring fortified church is an interesting counterpoint to the half-timbered houses it overlooks.

Vineyards and orchards line both sides of the wine road as it winds past steep hills toward Schweigen.

From the platform of the monumental Deutsches Weintor (German Wine Gate), you have a good view of the vineyards, German to the north and French to the south. Near the gate there are arrows to the *Weinlehrpfad* – Germany's first educational wine path – a pleasant walk through the vineyards and lined with historic objects and sculptures. The Weintor marks the end of the wine road, and of our journey through the Pfalz.

DEUTSCHE WEINSTRASSE
The German Wine Road (1935), the first of its kind in Germany, is a route that runs the length of the Pfalz. The last Sunday in August it is the site of a huge wine and folk festival, *Erlebnistag*, with all kinds of activities and tasting stands en route.

The Bergstrasse

The old Roman trade route *strada montana* (mountain road) runs parallel to the Rhine in the foothills of the Odenwald (Oden Forest). It extends some 70km (45 miles) from Darmstadt to Wiesloch, south of Heidelberg. The Bergstrasse is known as the spring garden of Germany, for its fruit and almond trees are among the earliest to blossom. At harvest time the slopes shimmer with the golden leaves of the vines.

It is an attractive landscape, with castle ruins on many summits and traditional vintners' huts sprinkled between the orchards and hillside vineyards. The medieval town centres are picturesque and several historic buildings house restaurants or wine pubs. You can also sample the wines at festivals from late April through September, or on May Day, when tasting stands are set up in the vineyards for the annual *Weinlagen-Wanderung* (vineyard walk).

Market day in Bensheim, when the market square comes alive with the colours and aromas of fresh produce and flowers. Bensheim was granted the right to hold a market in AD 956.

There is an 'island of vines' near Gross-Umstadt (east of Darmstadt), but the heart of the small region known as the Hessische Bergstrasse (465 hectares/1150 acres) is between Zwingenberg, Bensheim and Heppenheim. The vineyards further south are part of the Baden region. Nearly all the vineyards are hilly parcels of land, and thus labour-intensive. The Staatsweingut (State Wine Domain) in Bensheim is the largest private estate (36 hectares/90 acres), but most growers are 'hobby vintners' and belong to co-operatives.

Bergstrasse wines are primarily white. Riesling is the premier grape variety; Müller-Thurgau, Silvaner and Grauburgunder (Pinot Gris) are also grown. The wines are hearty, with a lively, fruity acidity. A high proportion of the wines are dry or medium dry in style.

The traditional everyday wine glass is called a *Halber* – the name refers not to a 'half' litre, but rather to a quarter litre.

The Odenwald's 'Island of Wine'

About 50 hectares (124 acres) of vines are planted near Gross-Umstadt, the northern gateway to the Oden Forest. The quartz and porphyry soils yield earthy Müller-Thurgau and Silvaner wines, similar to their Franconian counterparts. Riesling is cultivated here, too.

The Renaissance buildings in the market square in Gross-Umstadt are worth seeing. Visit in late August, when the co-operative has 'open house' or in mid-September, for the annual wine festival and parade.

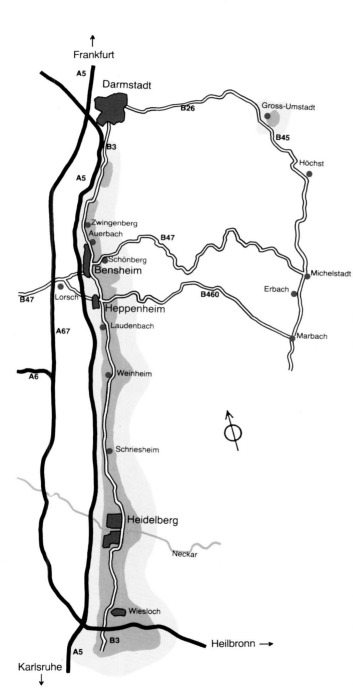

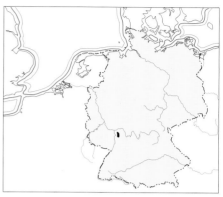

Hessische Bergstrasse

From Darmstadt, drive south on the B3 to Zwingenberg, the oldest town on the Bergstrasse. Watch for the right turn into the *historische Scheuergasse*, a lane with historic *Scheuer* or *Scheier* (barns) that were built outside the town walls due to the risk of fire. Here, and in the market square near Obertor (east of the B3), many of the beautiful half-timbered houses are shops and pubs.

From the B3 turn left into the Ernst-Ludwig-Promenade to visit the Auerbacher Schloss ruins, a good vantage-point (with a terrace café). A walk through Auerbach's Fürstenlager park (via Bachgasse) is recommended. It has exotic plants, Germany's tallest sequoia, a porcelain museum (closed Nov-Feb and Mon) and a lovely café and restaurant in the Herrenhaus.

Bergstrasse vineyard area

The ancient Starkenburg fortress ruins overlooking Heppenheim's steep vineyards. The fortress tower (open Sundays and holidays 1400-1800) and the café-restaurant Burgschänke (Tue-Fri from 1400, weekends from 1100) afford a panoramic view.

GROSS-UMSTADT
Weingut Brücke-Ohl
Georg-Aug.-Zinn-Str. 23.
1130-1400 (except Sat) and
1800-2200. Closed Mon.
ZWINGENBERG
Café Piano Obertor 6.
From 1700, Sun from 1100
(closed Thu and Nov).
Wine and asparagus estate.
Weinstube Rebscheier
Scheuergasse 12. Daily
from 1000. Try the local
cheese speciality, *Kochkäse*.
AUERBACH
Blauer Aff Kappengasse
2 (nr Weidgasse). From
1700 (except Mon). Cosy.
Parkhotel Herrenhaus
(Fürstenlager Staatspark).
Tel: 06251/72272. Fax:
06251/78473. Daily 1130-
1430. By reservation only,
dinner. Lovely restaurant
and hotel. Historic site.
BENSHEIM
Walderdorffer Hof
Obergasse 30. Mon-Sat
from 1800, Sun 1130-1430
and from 1630. Oldest
half-timbered house in
south Hessen; indoor and
garden seating.
Weingut Josef Mohr
Grieselstr. 51-59. Mon-Fri
after 1600 (pub).

Bensheim

Between Zwingenberg and Bensheim
the soils are loess-loam and weathered
granite, an important building
material in Roman times. East of the
B3 (towards Lautertal-Riechenbach)
you can visit the geological site known
as the Felsenmeer, testimony to the
Romans' skill as stonemasons.

The Old Town of Bensheim is very
picturesque. Between the Marktplatz
and the Rinnentor-Turm (once a
town gate) on Neumarkt are many
historic houses and fountains. Via the
Kalkgasse near the Stadtpark there is
a scenic path through the vineyards to
the Kirchberghäuschen. The terrace
is perfect for a glass of wine with a
view (from 1100, except Mon).

Heppenheim

The most splendid view of the Rhine
valley is from Starkenburg fortress
ruins (1065) overlooking charming
Heppenheim (a short drive plus a ten-
minute walk or 30 minutes on foot).

Sights include the 16th-century
town hall, complete with a
Glockenspiel; the neo-Gothic Church
of St Peter, called the Cathedral of
the Bergstrasse; and half-timbered
houses on the market square.

The co-operative in Heppenheim,
Bergsträsser Winzer, produces about
64 per cent of the region's wine.
Their shop is on the B3 and offers a
vast selection of wines that you can
sample prior to purchase (Mon-Fri
0800-1830; Mar-Dec also Sat 0830-
1600). Yellow sandstone, as well as
loess and loam, are the soil types of
Heppenheim's vineyards.

Badische Bergstrasse

The southern part of the Bergstrasse
belongs to the Baden wine-growing
region. The wines are similar to those
of the Hessische Bergstrasse, but take
on more body and volume near
Wiesloch, where the soils are a chalky
mix of keuper and loam.

Weinheim's historic buildings are
worth a visit. They are on the market
square; in the Gerberviertel (tanners'
quarter) near Stadtmühlgasse – watch
for signs for footpaths to the castle
ruins of Wachenburg and Windeck
(good views); and in the palace
grounds next to the Schlosspark.

Vine-covered slopes come into view
again near Schriesheim, beneath the
ruins of Strahlenburg fortress (terrace
restaurant). The historic wine and folk
festival *Mathaise-Markt*, dating from
1579, takes place in early March.

A wine town since the 12th
century, Wiesloch, at the southern
border of the Bergstrasse, has retained
much of its medieval character. The
co-operative, Winzerkeller Wiesloch, is
the largest producer. Their large shop,
the Weinpavillon, is at Bögnerweg 3
(Mon-Fri 0900-1730, Sat 0900-1300).

A statue of the Virgin Mary adorns the fountain in Heppenheim's fine market square.

You can visit the Carolingian *Torhalle* (gatehouse) at the former Abbey of Lorsch, founded in AD 764 and important during the reign of Charlemagne. Most of the castles along the Bergstrasse were built to defend the Abbey, whose Codex documents viticulture in many of the villages from the 8th century.

From here, two scenic routes run at right angles to the Bergstrasse: the *Siegfriedstrasse* (B460) and the *Nibelungenstrasse* (B47). Both lead to Michelstadt, with its town hall dating from 1484 and its picturesque market square; Steinbach, with the superb Carolingian Einhardsbasilika dating from AD 800 (the church is named after Charlemagne's biographer); and Erbach, with its museum of ivory carving – about one hour's drive from Bensheim or Heppenheim.

For hiking enthusiasts, Bergstrasse-Odenwald Nature Park has more than 700km (420 miles) of marked trails.

BENSHEIM
Staatsweingut Bergstrasse Grieselstr. 34-36. Mon-Fri 0800-1200, 1330-1700; Sat 1000-1200. State Wine Domain shop.
HEPPENHEIM
Winzerkeller Amtsgasse 5 (historic Amtshof). Daily 1100-1400 and 1700-2300.
SCHRIESHEIM
Strahlenberger Hof Kirchstr. 2. Tel: 06203/63076. Fax: 06203/68590. 1830-2100 (except Sun and holidays). Gourmet dining.
WIESLOCH
Weinrestaurant Freihof Freihofstr. 2. Tel: 06222/2517. Fax: 06222/51634. 1200-1400 and 1800-2200 (closed Tue). Historic, gourmet restaurant.
La Chandelle (in Hotel Mondial) Schwetzinger Str. 123. Tel: 06222/5760. Fax: 06222/576333. Mon-Sat 1830-2130. Gourmet fare and excellent wine list.
Langen's Turmstube Höllgasse 32. 1130-1400 and 1730-2200 (except Wed). Historic setting.

FOR FURTHER INFORMATION
Contact the regional wine promotion board: Weinbauverband Hessische Bergstrasse, Kettelerstr. 29, 64646 Heppenheim. Tel: 06252/75654. Fax: 06252/788256.

Franken

Franken, the hill region east of Frankfurt, lies between the Spessart Hills and the Steiger Forest. Most of the vineyards follow the zig-zag of the Main river through a countryside rich in art treasures, from simple wayside shrines and chapels to churches and palaces within the towered gates of medieval wine villages. Würzburg is both the wine and cultural centre of Franken.

Franken is best known for dry, powerful, earthy wine bottled in a distinctive round flagon called a *Bocksbeutel*. You can enjoy the wine with local specialities (fish, sausages, sauerkraut, potato dumplings) in an atmospheric country inn or at a colourful wine festival. Wine tastings take place in the historic Marienberg fortress in Würzburg. You can also sample wine at local co-operative wineries or Würzburg's three major estates, or family estates throughout the region.

The region was settled by and named after a Germanic tribe, the Franks. Christianity came with the Irish missionaries in the 7th century. St Kilian, the most famous of these, became patron saint of the region's wine-growers. By the 8th century, the monasteries were spreading viticulture throughout the land.

Würzburg's charitable hospitals
Franken was Germany's largest wine-growing area (40,000 hectares/ 98,800 acres) in the Middle Ages, when the vineyards and the wine trade were principally in the hands of the monasteries and the aristocracy. The Church and the nobility, however, were not the only ones to benefit from wine. For centuries, revenues from two of Franken's renowned wine estates in Würzburg have funded charitable foundations for the sick, the poor and the elderly: Bürgerspital (1319) and Juliusspital (1576).

From the 16th century to the 19th, viticulture declined as a result of wars and secularization. The demand for wine decreased as coffee and tea became available. At the turn of this century, new pests and diseases attacked the vines.

During the past 40 years, the vineyards have been reorganized to improve working conditions and efficiency. Degenerate vines have been replaced by vigorous, virus-resistant new plants.

Nevertheless, the supply of Franken wine is limited, for the vines in this continental climate are more subject to frost damage than vines grown in the milder Mosel and Rhine growing areas.

Grape varieties
Franken's 6114 hectares (15,108 acres) of vineyards are planted mostly with Müller-Thurgau and Silvaner grapes. Other white varieties include new crossings, such as Bacchus, Kerner, Scheurebe, Perle and Rieslaner (a local speciality). Riesling is grown only in very warm sites, such as Würzburg's famous vineyards Stein and Innere Leiste. A small amount of red wine (Spätburgunder, Portugieser) is produced, primarily in the west, near Miltenberg.

FOR FURTHER INFORMATION
Contact the regional wine promotion board:
Frankenwein-Frankenland
Haus des Frankenweins,
Kranenkai,
97070 Würzburg.
Tel: 0931/390110.
Fax: 0931/3901155.

Haus des Frankenweins
features wines from all of Franken. Apr-Oct, Mon-Fri 1000-1800. Nov-Mar, 1000-1700. Sat (all year), 1000-1300.

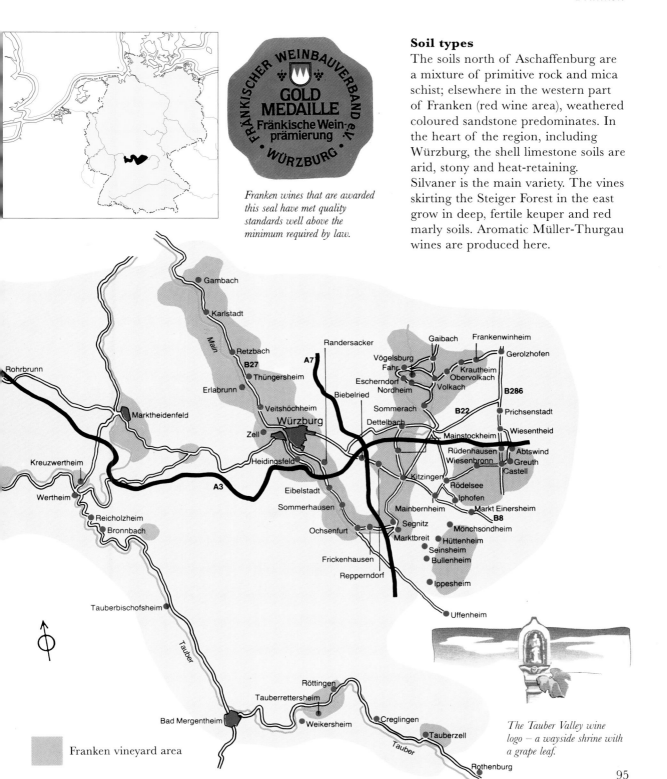

GOLD MEDAILLE
Fränkische Wein-prämierung
FRÄNKISCHER WEINBAUVERBAND e.V.
WÜRZBURG

Franken wines that are awarded this seal have met quality standards well above the minimum required by law.

Soil types

The soils north of Aschaffenburg are a mixture of primitive rock and mica schist; elsewhere in the western part of Franken (red wine area), weathered coloured sandstone predominates. In the heart of the region, including Würzburg, the shell limestone soils are arid, stony and heat-retaining. Silvaner is the main variety. The vines skirting the Steiger Forest in the east grow in deep, fertile keuper and red marly soils. Aromatic Müller-Thurgau wines are produced here.

The Tauber Valley wine logo – a wayside shrine with a grape leaf.

Franken vineyard area

Würzburg

Würzburg is a classic wine city on the Main river. From a Celtic fort on the hilltop site of today's Marienberg and a small village of fishermen and raftsmen, the town developed into a centre of European culture under the rule of bishops and prince bishops (1030-1802). They left a legacy of Gothic and Baroque masterpieces and world-famous wine estates.

The vineyards

Baroque sandstone statues of rulers and saints line the 15th-century Alte Mainbrücke (stone bridge). From here there is a fine view of Würzburg's landmark, the Marienberg fortress, majestically overlooking the Schlossberg vineyard. The Riesling site of Innere Leiste is on the steep slope below the fortress which faces south (around to the left).

The Stein vineyard

The famed site of Stein is an expanse of some 85 hectares (210 acres) of Riesling and Silvaner vines covering

St Kilian on the Alte Mainbrücke (old bridge over the river Main) and the Marienberg fortress.

the chalky hills north of town. Stein-Harfe is a small vineyard within Stein.

The Silvaners are rich in bouquet, full-bodied and mild; the Rieslings have a fine fruitiness, piquant acidity and full, long-lasting flavour.

Walk along the *Stein-Wein-Pfad* – an educational path through the vineyards – with ancient and modern open-air sculptures. (Allow 2½ hours for the entire route; 1-1½ hours for a shorter walk, from near the railway station to the castle hotel Schloss Steinburg [restaurant open daily], overlooking the vineyards and town.)

Famous historic estates

Staatlicher Hofkeller in the Residence, and the charitable institutions, Bürgerspital and Juliusspital, are among the greatest historic wine estates of Germany, founded in 1128, 1319 and 1576 respectively. All have beautiful vaulted cellars with richly

Three world-class estates
The Staatlicher Hofkeller, Bürgerspital zum Heiligen Geist and Juliusspital are among the largest and finest wine estates in Germany. Their vineyard holdings include top sites throughout Franken, as well as Würzburg's renowned vineyards, such as Stein. Each estate has a wine pub and shop in the grounds where the wines may be sampled. Their impressive, historic cellars, with their ornately carved casks, may be visited by appointment.

carved wooden casks. They own the majority of Würzburg's finest sites and have holdings in vineyards throughout the region. Each estate has a wine pub and wine shop (open Mon-Fri 0900-1730 and Sat 0900-1200) on the premises.

Wine festivals are held in the courtyard of the Bürgerspital (in June) and in the gardens of the Residence (early July). Juliusspital hosts concerts during 'Culture Days' (in May).

Marienberg fortress

The fortress complex dates from 1201 and served as the residence of the prince bishops from 1253 to 1719. Today, the Baroque armoury houses the Mainfränkisches Museum with a wine museum, Franconian folk art and works by the Gothic sculptor Tilman Riemenschneider. A gala culinary wine tasting is held in the *Kelterhalle* (hall with wine presses) in autumn. You can also visit the Marienkirche (originally a rotunda) and the palace gardens. (Open Apr-Oct 1000-1700; Nov-Mar 1000-1600. Closed Mon. Restaurant 1000-2400. Closed Mon.)

The Residence

The prince bishops' palace built between 1720 and 1744 according to plans by Balthasar Neumann ranks as one of the finest Baroque structures in Europe. Frescoes by Tiepolo decorate the Imperial Hall and the cupola above the magnificent staircase.

Don't miss the richly adorned court church, the palace gardens and the Rococo wrought-iron gates. (Open Apr-Oct 0900-1700 and Nov-Mar 1000-1600; closed Mon.)

Treasures of art history

The prince bishops (such as Julius Echter and members of the Schönborn family) were great patrons of the arts. The town has many historic fountains, monuments, churches and buildings in styles ranging from Romanesque to Rococo.

The Cathedral of St Kilian, Neumünster and Marienkapelle are highly recommended. Try to see the town hall and the old university as well as the beautiful Rococo façade of the Haus zum Falken (near the market square), where guided tours begin.

HISTORIC WINE PUBS
Bürgerspital-Weinstuben
Theaterstr. 19. 0900-2400 (except Tue). Closed Aug.
Gasthof Zur Stadt Mainz
Semmelstr. 39. 0700-2400 Mon-Sat, 0700-1500 Sun. Guest rooms.
Hofkeller-Weinstuben
(Residence, building on right) 1000-2400 (except Mon).
Juliusspital-Weinstuben
Juliuspromenade 19. 1000-2400 (except Wed). Closed Jul.
Weinhaus Zum Stachel
Gressengasse 1. 1100-0100 (except Sun).

HISTORIC HOUSE
Hotel Rebstock
Neubaustr. 7. Tel: 0931/ 30930. Fax: 0931/3093100.
Restaurant 1200-1400, 1830-2130 (except Sun).
Fränkische Weinstube
1630-2400 (except Mon and Aug).

CRUISE THE MAIN
by boat from Würzburg dock Alter Kranen (old crane) to Veitshöchheim (45 min) to visit the 17th to 18th century Schloss (palace) and its superb Rococo gardens. Palace open Apr-Oct 0900-1200, 1300-1700 (except Mon). Gardens open daily, all year, from 0800 to dusk.

MUSIC AND WINE
The Baroque Festival (May) and Mozart Festival (June) feature great orchestras and top wines of Franken in the magnificent Baroque Residence.

A festive wine tasting in the splendid vaulted cellars of the Staatlicher Hofkeller in Würzburg's Baroque Residence.

The Tauber Valley

One of the many wayside shrines in the beautiful Tauber valley.

KLINGENBERG
Zum alten Rentamt
Hauptstr. 25a. Tel: 09372/
2650. Fax: 09372/2977.
Wed-Sun 1800-2130. Also
1200-1330 Sat and Sun.
Gourmet restaurant.
MILTENBERG
Altes Bannhaus
Hauptstr. 211. Tel: 09371/
3061. Fax: 09371/68754.
1200-1400, 1800-2130
(except Thu; Jan). Hotel.
AMORBACH
Der Schafhof (Otterbach
valley). Tel: 09373/997330.
Fax: 09373/4120. Gourmet
fare at **Abtstube** (except
Mon, Tue), simpler fare at
Benediktinerstube
(except Wed, Thu), 1200-
1400, 1830-2100. Hotel.

This route is from Wertheim,
where the Tauber flows into the
Main, to medieval Rothenburg. From
Würzburg, drive west on the A3 to
the Wertheim exit. (Or, to visit the red
wine district, start from Frankfurt and
follow the Main.) Return to Würzburg
from Rothenburg via the A7.

Western Franken
The westernmost vineyards of
Franken are less than half an hour
east of Frankfurt, just north of
Aschaffenburg. The primitive rock
and mica schist soils yield hearty,
pithy Müller-Thurgau wines.

Aschaffenburg is notable for its
Romanesque cloisters and works of
art by Cranach and Grünewald in the
Stiftskirche St Peter and St Alexander
(Collegiate Church) and Schloss
Johannisburg, a Renaissance palace.

Red wine near Miltenberg
Upstream, a deep ribbon of coloured
sandstone provides excellent conditions
for producing ruby-red, velvety, full-
bodied Portugieser and Spätburgunder
wines near Rück, Erlenbach,
Klingenberg and Grossheubach,
then east of picturesque Miltenberg
from Bürgstadt to Kreuzwertheim.
Müller-Thurgau and Silvaner are the
main white varieties.

Miltenberg has very beautiful half-
timbered houses on the market square
and along the Hauptstrasse. Walk up
to the Mildenburg fortress for a good
view of the town and the Main valley.

From here, drive south on the
B469 to visit the former Benedictine
monastery in Amorbach with its
richly-furnished library, banqueting
hall and church (Stumm organ
recitals May-Oct, Tue-Sat 1500, also
1100 Sat). Then return to the road
along the Main to Wertheim.

Tauber valley wine
Historically, the Tauber valley is
part of Franken. Wars from the
16th century to the 19th caused
great suffering and poverty among
the peasants. After secularization, the
area north of the Main became part
of Bavaria, while the Tauber valley
and other land south of the Main was
ceded to Württemberg and the newly
created Grand Duchy of Baden.

Political boundaries were redrawn
after World War II. Today, most of
the Tauber valley's vineyards are part
of the Baden wine-growing region; a
few vineyards near Bad Mergentheim
belong to Württemberg; and three
wine towns are part of Franken. The
wines, however, all bear a strong
family resemblance and are typically
Franconian: robust, pithy and usually
dry. Most are bottled in the *Bocksbeutel*.
The soils are primarily shell-limestone.
Müller-Thurgau predominates.

Wertheim – 'Little Heidelberg'
The oldest parts of the town date
back to the 12th century. For the best
view, take the steps up to the Burg
Wertheim ruins, where you can also
enjoy a glass of wine at the restaurant
terrace (Easter-Oct).

Historic houses line Maingasse,
Münzgasse and the market square.
Opposite the Renaissance well at the
centre of the square are the Gothic
Stiftskirche, St Kilian's Chapel and an
interesting history museum (closed
Mon) in a group of buildings linked
by an unusual double winding
staircase. Its collection of costumes
(1800-1950), coins, silhouettes and
paintings is worth seeing.

Nearby, on Mühlenstrasse 24, the
Glasmuseum chronicles glass-making
from Egyptian times to present
(closed Mon; Nov and Jan-Mar).

Reicholzheim and Bronnbach

Germany's largest collection of red sandstone crucifixes, wayside shrines and a Baroque church are worth seeing in Reicholzheim. To sample wines from many of the villages, visit the co-operative Tauberfränkischer Bocksbeutelkeller (Mon-Fri 0900-1200, 1300-1700, Sat 0900-1200).

In 1151, Cistercian monks founded Bronnbach monastery. The cloisters, Baroque Josephssaal and church (Rococo choir stalls) are the settings for concerts and can be seen during tours (Apr-Oct, Mon-Sat 0915-1200, 1400-1700; Sun 1230-1700).

Tauberbischofsheim

This medieval town has fine half-timbered houses on its market square and along the Hauptstrasse, which leads to the Schlossplatz, the site of an impressive tower and Kurmainz castle. Inside you can see fascinating old household items and antique furniture (Apr-Oct, Tue-Sun 1430-1630, also 1000-1200 Sun) and there are wine tastings in the Schlosskeller (1st and 3rd Wed, 1400-1800).

Lauda and Beckstein

Although not always visible from the main road, there are many vineyards in the side valleys. The co-operative (Mon-Fri 0800-1800, Sat 0900-1300) and its restaurant (1000-2200, except Wed, Jan) in Beckstein are good places to taste the wines. A vineyard path with nice views begins near the co-op.

The Klosterkirche in Gerlachsheim (east of Lauda) is truly stunning, with its pastel walls and ceilings, ornate stucco work and gilded Rococo pulpit.

Bad Mergentheim

This spa was the residence of the Teutonic Knights. Exhibits in the 16th-century Deutschordensschloss depict the Order's history. To get a feel for the town, walk along the Marktplatz, Gänsmarkt and the alleys near Johanniterhof, then through the lush Schlosspark and Kurpark.

The famous Madonna altar by the Gothic painter Grünewald is in the St Maria church in Stuppach, only 6km (4 miles) south-west via the B19.

Markelsheim and Weikersheim

Vineyards surround the typical, rural wine village of Markelsheim. Several charming pubs and the co-operative's wine shop offer a wide range of wines (Mon-Fri 0800-1200, 1300-1700, Sat 0800-1200). Near Weikersheim's market square is the Princes of Hohenlohe's Renaissance hunting palace, with an exquisite collection of china, furniture and tapestries. The Rittersaal (Knights' Hall) has a unique painted ceiling (Apr-Oct 0900-1800, Nov-Mar 1000-1200 and 1330-1630). The Baroque gardens, Orangery and Dorfmuseum are also worth a visit.

The scenic drive to Niederstetten via Laudenbach affords views of the ancient *Steinriegel*, vertical mounds of stone and soil built in the vineyards to check cold winds and, at night, to release heat absorbed during the day. Then return to the *Romantische Strasse* (Romantic Road) and turn right.

Tauberrettersheim

The stone bridge was designed by Balthasar Neumann in 1733 to replace the wooden one destroyed in a flood. St Nepomuk, the statue on the bridge, is the saint who guards against such disasters. Röttingen (whose town hall has an exhibition of folklore) and Tauberzell, the other Franconian wine village on the Tauber, are only minutes away from Rothenburg.

BÜRGSTADT
Weinhaus-Hotel Stern Hauptstr. 23. Tel: 09371/2676. Fax: 09371/65154. Fri-Tue 1830-2200, Sat-Sun also 1200-1330. Cosy inn.
WERTHEIM-BETTINGEN
Schweizer Stuben Geiselbrunnweg 11. Tel: 09342/3070. Fax: 09342/307155. 1900-2200 Wed-Mon. Also 1200-1400 Sun. Top gourmet restaurant. Also: **Schober** for regional fare. Fri-Tue 1200-1400, 1800-2200. Both closed Jan. Luxurious country inn.
MARKTHEIDENFELD
Weinhaus Anker Obertorstr. 13. Tel: 09391/1736. Fax: 09391/1742. 1130-1400, 1800-2200 (except Mon, Tue lunch). Fine regional cuisine. Also: rustic **Weinstube** (hours as above), and cellar pub 'Schöpple' from 1800 (except Tue). Hotel.
LAUDA
Ratskeller Josef-Schmitt-Str. 17. Tel: 09343/62070. Fax: 09343/2820. Tue-Sun 1130-1400, Mon-Sat 1730-2200. Try the tasty dishes made with *Grünkern* (grain spelt, harvested while still 'green' or unripe). Guest rooms.
BAD MERGENTHEIM
Hotel Victoria Poststr. 2. Tel: 07931/5930. Fax: 07931/593500. Gourmet restaurant **Zirbelstuben** Tue-Sat 1800-2200 (closed Aug) or **Vinothek** (less formal) daily 1200-1400, 1800-2200. Elegant hotel.
NIEDERSTETTEN
Hotel Krone Marktplatz 3. Tel: 07932/8990. Fax: 07932/89960. Daily 1130-1400, 1730-2130. Good country cooking, local wine. *Ferkelmarkt* (piglet market) Mon 1000-1200.

The Bocksbeutel *Route*

This route follows the Main river through several important wine villages south of Würzburg. Depart on the B13 and return on the B8.

The wine routes in Franken are not actually signposted. If Bavaria ever grants permission to mark them, the signs will doubtless depict Franken's wine logo, the *Bocksbeutel*.

Most of the wine villages have a medieval townscape, with all or part of a town wall, gateways and defence towers. Gabled Renaissance town halls, often with carved balustrades, are typical of the area. Elaborate statues of the Virgin Mary are frequent, as are statuettes adorning façades or corner niches of houses.

The wines
Nearly all the vineyards are on steep or sloping south-facing hills of shell-limestone soils. Silvaner and Müller-Thurgau are the main grape varieties. The wines are aromatic and hearty with a powerful fruity flavour. They are usually very dry.

Randersacker to Ochsenfurt
The first vineyards outside Würzburg are Randersacker's Teufelskeller and Pfülben. The latter is remarkable for its Riesling. Look for the late Romanesque tower of St Stephen's

Church as a starting point for a walk through the Old Town.

Within the town walls of Eibelstadt are the Baroque town hall and ornate statue (1660) of the Virgin Mary on the market square.

The ancient towers of Sommerhausen, the next wine village, have become home to an artists' colony and a well-known theatre in the Würzburger Tor (tower gate).

Among the historic buildings on the main street are the 16th-century town hall with pinnacled gables and a Renaissance castle.

Cross the Main on a 550-year-old stone bridge to Ochsenfurt, a town with lovely half-timbered houses and picturesque wrought-iron signs. The 'new' town hall (c.1500) has a Glockenspiel (1560) with symbolic figures, including two oxen (Ochsenfurt means 'oxen ford') and the figure of Death turning an hour glass, alluding to the thousands killed during the Peasants' Revolt (1525).

Also of note are the painted Renaissance ceilings of the Ratssaal (council chambers) inside the town hall. A Riemenschneider statue and lavish tracery in the St Andreas Church are worth seeing.

Around a loop of the Main
Frickenhausen is a restored medieval town. The Valentiuskapelle is a Baroque chapel overlooking the Kapellenberg vineyard, the town and the Main valley. At the other end of the loop, the towers, historic buildings and old crane of Marktbreit form a romantic silhouette. The town hall, built into the old town wall, is part of an interesting ensemble of Renaissance buildings. Sulzfeld also has medieval towers, gates and half-timbered houses.

FRANKEN
E. und W. Haßold

EHERIEDER MÜHLE

1996er Kitzinger Eherieder Berg
Bacchus

11% vol   Qualitätswein   750 ml
A. P. Nr. 4420-001-97
Abfüller: E. und W. Haßold - D-97318 Kitzingen

Kitzingen and Repperndorf

Kitzingen, which had a bridge across the Main by the 13th century, was an important medieval trading centre. There are many old buildings near the market square, including a splendid three-storey town hall with patterned gables; St Johannis Church, with 15th-century choir stalls and

wall paintings; and the parish church in Italian Baroque style. To see carnival masks and costumes, visit the museum in the Falterturm (Apr-Nov, Sat and Sun 1400-1700). Also worth seeing is Balthasar Neumann's Heilig-Kreuz Church in the suburb of Etwashausen. From here, continue on the B8.

Repperndorf is the headquarters of the Gebietswinzergenossenschaft, the region's large, modern co-operative, which accounts for about a quarter of Franken's wine production and has some 2600 members in 100 towns. (Wine shop and museum open Mon-Fri 0800-1800, Sat 0800-1400).

In Biebelried, the Riemenschneider sculpture in the parish church merits a visit before returning to Würzburg.

CYCLING PATHS
There are excellent cycling paths throughout Franken and many places to rent bicycles. For details about the M-T-F 'Radachter' ('double-wheel' circular path through the Tauber valley and part of the *Bocksbeutel* Route), contact the Touristikgemeinschaft Liebliches Taubertal, PO Box 1254, 97932 Tauber-bischofsheim. Tel: 09341/82294. Fax: 09341/82366. Their maps suggest routes and give sightseeing tips.

Church spires and watchtowers dot the medieval townscape of Ochsenfurt on the river Main. The town hall's tower boasts an allegorical Glockenspiel.

The Steigerwald

The Weinstall, a wine restaurant in the former Stall (stables) of the Fürstlich Castell'sches Domänenamt. The white grape variety Rieslaner is a speciality of the estate.

This route includes Franken's easternmost wine towns on the foothills of the Steiger Forest. Leave Würzburg on the A3; exit at Schweinfurt Süd/Wiesentheid and drive south to Rüdenhausen. Return to Würzburg from Gollhofen on the A7 or B13 (the *Bocksbeutel* Route – see pages 100-101) via Ochsenfurt.

The wines

In this rural countryside, vineyards are scattered on sloping hillsides capped by protective forests. Mineral-rich, heavy gypsum keuper soils give the wines great substance. The Müller-Thurgaus are particularly aromatic, with a fine flowery bouquet. The Silvaners are full-bodied, mouth-filling wines with a distinctive bouquet sometimes described as earthy. In addition to these classic varieties, try the new crossings (white) as well as some of the red wines produced here.

Castell

From the Autobahn exit drive via Rüdenhausen to reach Castell, where the family of the same name have grown vines since at least 1258. For centuries, they have set high standards of quality in the area.

The cellars, a wine shop and a wine pub are in the grounds of the family's late 17th-century castle in the village.

The classical interior of the Schlosskirche is decorated with local alabaster and comes as a surprise after its Baroque exterior.

The Kirchberg vineyard is on the slope rising toward the church, while the Schlossberg, named after the ruins of the Castell's ancestral Schloss (castle) at the top of the slope, sweeps around the adjacent hill. From Wiesenbronn there is a good view of Castell and its vineyards.

The Schwanberg

'Swan Hill' is covered with a vast expanse of superb vineyards near the towns of Rödelsee and Iphofen. From Rödelsee, walk (half an hour) or drive (5 minutes) to Schloss Schwanberg at the top of the hill to enjoy the views over a glass of wine from the Küchenmeister or Schwanleite sites (Turmcafé open Apr-Oct 1100-1800 except Mon).

Drive via Mainbernheim, ringed with a massive 15th-century stone wall and 18 towers, to Iphofen, an ancient wine town seemingly untouched by time. Its medieval townscape is authentic, with intact walls, towers and one of Germany's most picturesque town gates, the Rödelseer Tor. A walk through the winding streets takes you past half-timbered houses, which contrast with the Baroque town hall. In the Gothic St Veit's Church look for the sculpture of St John by Riemenschneider.

The vineyards Kalb, Kronsberg and Julius-Echter-Berg (remarkable for its Riesling vines) have been famous for centuries. Iphöfer wines graced the tables of Queen Elizabeth II at her coronation and the Pope

ABTSWIND
Waldschänke Schloss Friedrichsberg (in the forest, en route to Rehweiler). 1100-2200 (except Tue and Nov). Outstanding view. A *Weinlehrpfad* (marked vineyard path) is nearby.

CASTELL
Weinstall Schlossplatz 3. Tel: 09325/463. Fax: 09325/6832. 1100-2200 (except Thu, Fri and Jan). Regional cuisine, wines from the Castell estate. Cosy indoors, nice terrace.

RÖDELSEE
Winzergenossenschaft Schloss Str. 2 in Schloss Crailsheim (1696). Mon-Fri 0800-1200, 1300-1700; Sat 0800-1200. Lovely setting for co-op's wine shop.

IPHOFEN
Zehntkeller Bahnhofstr. 12. Tel: 09323/3062. Fax: 09323/1519. Daily 1130-1400, 1830-2130. Closed Jan. Pleasant wine restaurant and hotel in historic tithe cellars.

IPPESHEIM
Schlosskeller Hauptstr. 1. Tel/Fax: 09339/740. Wed-Mon 1100-1400, 1800-2130 (wine, light fare 1400-2130). Garden.

MUSEUMS
IPHOFEN
Knauf Museum Am Marktplatz. Apr-Oct, Tue-Sun 1400-1800. Tue, Sun also 1000-1200. Unusual display of plaster copies of major works of antiquity.

MÖNCHSONDHEIM
Handwerker- und Bauernmuseum (in the Kirchenburg, 17th-century fortified church). Mid-Mar to Nov, Tue-Sat 1330-1800; Sun 1100-1800. Collection of historic rural decorative arts and crafts.

during his visit to Germany in the 1980s.

Ancient walls and town gates
The southern part of this route winds through forests and ancient wine towns unknown outside their borders. Fortified churches are an interesting feature of this area. They often provided the only refuge for peasants during the centuries of war which plagued the region.

From Iphofen, drive east on the B8 to Markt Einersheim, where the town hall and church are part of the fortifications. Then turn south to Mönchsondheim and follow the

country roads to the wine towns of Hüttenheim, Seinsheim, Bullenheim and Ippesheim. The medieval town of Uffenheim, no longer part of today's wine country, is nevertheless worth a visit. Finally, return to Würzburg.

The picturesque Rödelseer Tor, one of Iphofen's three 15th-century town gates.

POMMERSFELDEN
Schloss Weissenstein
18th-century Schönborn palace near Bamberg (east on the A3, exit no.79). An architectural gem with an art gallery, rich furnishings and a porcelain collection. Tours Apr-Oct 0900-1200, 1400-1700 (except Mon).
Schlosshotel (in the palace). Tel: 09548/680. Fax: 09548/68100. 1100-1400, 1800-2100. Outdoor restaurant with a terrace.

The Mainschleife

Schleife means 'loop'. This route includes the wine towns on the Main river, north-east of Würzburg. Drive east on the A3; exit at Schweinfurt Süd/Wiesentheid. Return to Würzburg on the B22 via Dettelbach.

The wines
The vine-covered slopes of the broad river valley from Volkach to Sommerach form the largest area of contiguous vineyards in Franken. Shell-limestone is the main soil type. Robust, full-flavoured wines are produced from Müller-Thurgau and Silvaner grapes; new crossings offer a variety of tastes and aromas.

To Volkach via the medieval towns
From the Autobahn exit, drive north on the B286 to Prichsenstadt, a picturesque wine town ringed by a moated stone wall. Enter at the gateway tower to view the half-timbered houses and town hall on the Hauptstrasse.

You can see historic buildings on Gerolzhofen's market square, which is also the site of a huge wine festival in mid-July. From here drive to Volkach, in the heart of the Mainschleife.

Volkacher Ratsherr
In Volkach, Ratsherr (councillor) is not only the name of the town's large vineyard (150 hectares/370 acres), but also the town's 'ambassador of wine' who dresses in medieval costume for festivals and tastings.

See the Renaissance town hall (1544) and beautiful fountain in the market square.

In the midst of the vineyards north-west of town is one of Riemenschneider's most famous Madonnas, in the Gothic pilgrimage

Ancient half-timbered and gabled façades are part of the medieval charm of Prichsenstadt, a typical Franconian wine village.

church, Maria im Weingarten. (Open Mon-Sat 0930-1145 and 1300-1700, Sun 1100-1200 and 1300-1700.)

Vogelsburg to Escherndorf
The best panoramic view of the Main loop and its wine towns is from the top of the Vogelsburg (Bird Castle) west of Volkach.

On the path through the vineyards from Vogelsburg to Escherndorf there is a beautifully carved stone statue of Christ bearing the Cross.

At *Weinherbst*, wine festivals that take place every weekend, September to November, you can try wines from the famous vineyard Lump.

The Madonna fountain in front of Volkach's Renaissance town hall, notable for its double open staircase and half-timbered oriel.

CRUISE THE MAIN
by boat on a Mainschleifen-Rundfahrt (round trip) in 1.5 hours from Volkach.

VOLKACH
Gasthof zur Schwane
Hauptstr. 12. Tel: 09381/ 80660. Fax: 09381/806666. 1200-1400, 1800-2130 (except Mon and Jan). Historic (1404) hotel and wine restaurant. Courtyard.
VOGELSBURG
Splendid view from the wine estate run by Augustinian nuns on top of the hill. Spicy Traminer wines are the speciality. Wine pub open daily 0900-2000 (except Mon). Closed Dec-Feb.
NORDHEIM
Zehnthof Hauptstr. 2. Tel: 09381/1702. Fax: 09381/4379. 1130-1430, 1730-2100 (except Mon). Historic tithe court of a former monastery.
SCHLOSS HALLBURG
Weinstuben (between Volkach and Nordheim). Tel: 09381/2340. Fax: 09381/2568. May-Sep from 1100. Closed Mon in Apr, Oct; closed Mon-Tue in Nov, Dec, Feb, Mar. Closed Jan. Live music and events with Schönborn estate wines. Lovely garden.
DETTELBACH
Himmelstoss Bamberger Str. 3. Tel: 09324/4776. Fax: 09324/4969. Wed-Sun 1130-1400, 1800-2300. Closed Jan. Creative cuisine. Cheerful indoors, vine-covered courtyard.

Nordheim and Sommerach

From Escherndorf, cross the Main to Nordheim, where viticulture has been documented from AD 892. Its sites of Vögelein and Kreuzberg cover some 400 hectares (1000 acres). Two Renaissance buildings are of particular interest: the St Laurentius Church, with its beautiful sculptures, and the *Zehnthof* (tithe court), now a restaurant that serves the local co-operative's wines.

Drive to Sommerach via Schloss Hallburg (towards Volkach), where you can enjoy art exhibits, brunch, and all kinds of music (classical, 'oldies' and jazz) with the local wines in the restaurant and its garden.

Sommerach, the other wine town on the 'island' between the Main river and Rhein-Main-Donau canal, has retained its medieval look and has many half-timbered houses and Baroque mansions. Franken's oldest co-operative (1901) produces most of the town's wine, from the Katzenkopf and Rosenberg sites. From late April to 24 June, try the Mainschleife's other delicious speciality, asparagus.

Dettelbach via Schwarzach

See the intricately-carved wayside shrine Graue Marter (1511, Riemenschneider school) en route to Dettelbach, the last medieval wine village on the route and well worth a visit. Also try to see the Rococo interior of the pilgrimage church Maria im Sand east of the town. Return to Würzburg on the B22.

Württemberg

'Connoisseurs drink wine from Württemberg' is the region's motto.

FOR FURTHER INFORMATION
Contact the regional wine promotion board:
Werbegemeinschaft Württembergischer Weingärtnergenossenschaften
Raiffeisenstr. 6,
71696 Möglingen.
Tel: 07141/24460.
Fax: 07141/244620.

Although most of Württemberg's wine is made by co-operatives, there are several noble families that have been outstanding winemakers for centuries.

Württemberg is a rural area of considerable natural beauty between the foothills of the Swabian Jura and the Tauber river valley. Stuttgart and Heilbronn are the region's major cities; both are rich in history and culture. But it is in the countryside and villages which line the valleys of the Neckar river and its tributaries that the character of Württemberg really comes alive. The *Schwäbische Weinstrasse* (auto route) and the signposted *Radweg* (bicycle trail) show the way as they wind across the region from Weikersheim to Metzingen.

The Swabians are known for their hospitality, hearty country cooking and delicious red and white wines served in the *Viertele* – a round, quarter-litre glass with a handle – difficult to tip over. 'Broomstick Inns' (*Besenwirtschaften*) in vintners' homes serve the local wines. Look for a birch-broom or wreath over the doorway.

Viticulture in Württemberg dates back at least to the 8th century. It was probably introduced by monks from Burgundy when they established monasteries in the region. Today, most of the 16,500 *Weingärtner* or *Wengerter* are part-time vintners with less than half a hectare (one acre) of vines. The majority of 'Neckar wines' are produced and marketed by well-equipped local co-operatives.

This is the fifth largest wine-growing region of Germany (11,187 hectares/27,643 acres). It is planted with slightly more red than white grape varieties. The countryside is a patchwork of fields and forests with vineyards and orchards scattered throughout – but not at random: they are planted only on warm, south-facing slopes, usually along river valleys.

Most of the vineyards were originally terraced with stone walls by the growers to prevent erosion, retain and reflect heat and serve as property boundaries. During the past 40 years, the vineyards have been 'modernized' and most of the walls removed to improve efficiency. However, a few sites still retain their original character, notably those near the Felsengärten (cliff gardens) above the bends of the Neckar river between Mundelsheim and Hessigheim and Besigheim.

Regional specialities
Ruby-red, fruity Trollinger wine is the regional favourite and seldom found outside Württemberg. Often, it is blended with another red variety, Lemberger, which on its own yields deep red, powerful wine with a lingering aftertaste. Elegant, aromatic red wines are also produced from members of the Burgundy (Pinot) family: Spätburgunder (Pinot Noir), Schwarzriesling (Pinot Meunier), Clevner and Samtrot.

Riesling is the most important white variety, but hearty, earthy white wines are also produced from Silvaner and Müller-Thurgau grapes. Kerner, a crossing of Trollinger and Riesling, was bred in Württemberg and is named after the physician and poet Justinus Kerner. Typical Kerner wines are full-bodied, with a rich bouquet and fine acidity.

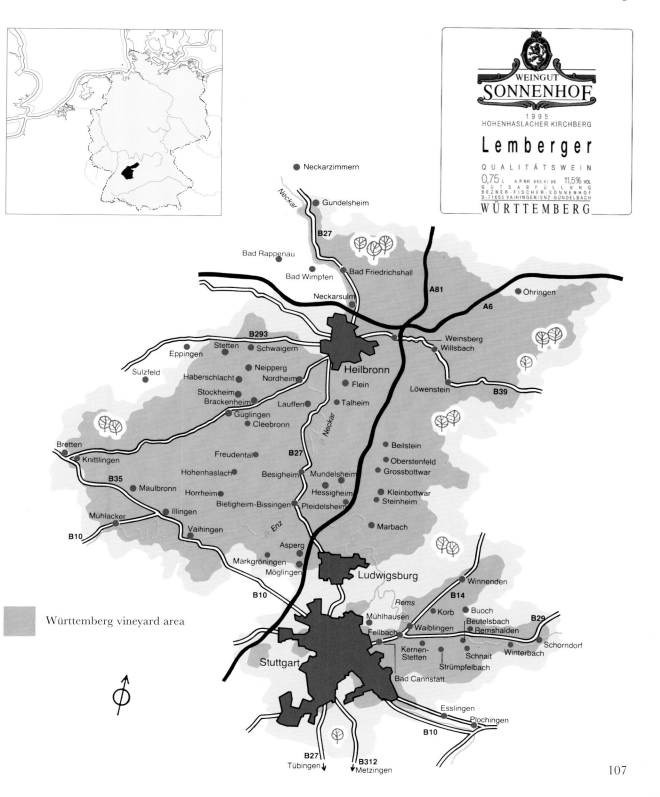

WEINGUT
SONNENHOF
1995
HOHENHASLACHER KIRCHBERG
Lemberger
QUALITÄTSWEIN
0,75 L   A.P.NR. 665 41 96   11,5% VOL
G U T S A B F Ü L L U N G
BEZNER-FISCHER-SONNENHOF
D-71665 VAIHINGEN/ENZ-GÜNDELBACH
WÜRTTEMBERG

Neckarzimmern
Neckar
Gundelsheim
B27
Bad Rappenau
Bad Wimpfen
Bad Friedrichshall
A81
Öhringen
Neckarsulm
A6
Weinsberg
B293
Willsbach
Stetten
Schwaigern
Eppingen
Heilbronn
Neipperg
Sulzfeld
Flein
Haberschlacht
Nordheim
Löwenstein
B39
Stockheim
Brackenheim
Lauffen
Talheim
Güglingen
Cleebronn
Bretten
R. Neckar
Beilstein
Knittlingen
Freudental
B27
Oberstenfeld
Grossbottwar
B35
Hohenhaslach
Besigheim
Mundelsheim
Maulbronn
Horrheim
Hessigheim
Kleinbottwar
Steinheim
Mühlacker
Bietigheim-Bissingen
Pleidelsheim
R. Enz
B10
Vaihingen
Marbach
Asperg
Markgröningen
Möglingen
Ludwigsburg
Winnenden
B10
Rems
B14
Buoch
Mühlhausen
Korb
Beutelsbach
B29
Fellbach
Waiblingen
Remshalden
Schorndorf
Kernen-
Stetten
Schnait
Winterbach
Stuttgart
Strümpfelbach
Bad Cannstatt
Esslingen
Plochingen
B10
B27
B312
Tübingen↓
↓Metzingen

Württemberg vineyard area

Stuttgart

CRUISE THE NECKAR
Float by scenic vineyard country on an 'NPS' boat, departing from Wilhelma dock in Bad Cannstatt. Daily round trips, Mar-Oct, to Ludwigsburg, Marbach, Felsengärten and Lauffen.

PANORAMIC VIEW
For a view extending all the way to the hills of the Swabian Jura, ascend the *Fernsehturm* (television tower) in the suburb of Degerloch. Total height: 217m (712ft). Observation platforms at 150m (492ft).

GOURMET DINING
Hotel am Schlossgarten
Schillerstr. 23. Tel: 0711/ 20260. Fax: 0711/2026888.
Restaurant 1200-1400, 1800-2200. **Zirbelstube** (same hours except Sat and Mon no lunch; closed Sun).
Skyline Restaurant (in the TV tower). Tel: 0711/ 246104. Fax: 0711/ 2360633. Tue-Sun 1200-1430, 1800-2200. Lighter fare at the **Turm Bistro**, daily, 1000-2330.
Speisemeisterei Am Schloss Hohenheim (in the suburb Hohenheim). Tel: 0711/4560037. Fax: 0711/ 4560038. Sun 1200-1300, Tue-Sat 1830-2100.
Top Air (Terminal 1, 4th floor, Airport). Tel: 0711/ 9482137. Fax: 0711/ 7979210. Sat from 1800, Sun-Fri 1145-1400, 1745-2200. Reserve a *Fenstertisch* (window table) for a view.
Vinothek Delice
Hauptstätter Str. 61. Tel: 0711/6403222. Mon-Fri 1830-2400. Top wine list.
Wielandshöhe Alte Weinsteige 71 (Degerloch). Tel: 0711/6408848. Fax: 0711/6409408. Tue-Sat 1200-1400, 1830-2100.

Stuttgart, the capital of Baden-Württemberg, is situated in a wooded basin on the Neckar river. Full of gardens and parks, it also has about 40 hectares (100 acres) of vineyards within the city limits. Greater Stuttgart boasts nearly 400 hectares (1000 acres) of red vines and five local co-operatives. The annual *Weindorf am Marktplatz* (wine festival in late August and early September) attracts up to 100,000 people daily.

Stuttgart is the home of Porsche (museum in Zuffenhausen, a suburb, open daily 0900-1600) and Daimler-Benz, whose famous 'Mercedes' first appeared in 1901. An important publishing centre, Stuttgart is also well known for the production of optical, photographic and electrical equipment. Its ballet, theatre, concerts and museums are as famous as its historic and contemporary buildings.

Stuttgart's wine suburbs

Bad Cannstatt, just across the Neckar river, is a town of wine and water. Its mineral springs, dating from Roman times, produce 22 million litres (between 4 and 5 million gallons) daily and are the most productive in Europe. Red and white grapes grow on the steep shell-limestone slopes surrounding the town. A scenic trail through the vineyards starts near the street Roter Stich in Burgholzhof.

The next wine town along the Neckar is Unterürkheim. You can visit the Daimler-Benz Museum in the factory grounds (Mercedesstrasse 136, open Tue-Sun 0900-1700).

On the hillside above is the village of Rotenberg, where there is a mausoleum containing the graves of Queen Katharina and King Wilhelm I built on the site of the House of Württemberg's ancestral castle. The town's vineyard is named Schlossberg (Castle Hill). From here to Uhlbach there is a marked vineyard path.

The region's largest wine museum is on Uhlbacher Platz 4, in a restored press house (open Apr-Oct, Sat-Sun 1400-1800, Sun also 1000-1200). Then drive to Obertürkheim and follow the Neckar river road to Esslingen.

A WALK THROUGH STUTTGART
From the main railway station, walk along the elegant Königsstrasse. To the left is the beautiful Oberer Schlossgarten (palace garden) with the Staatstheater and Staatsgalerie (art museum; famous Picasso collection). The Neues Schloss on Schlossplatz is modelled on Versailles. The Altes Schloss (old castle) on Schillerplatz was built in 1320 as a moated castle and 'modernized' in the 16th century in Renaissance style. In the summer concerts are held in the courtyard with its three-storeyed arcade. Today, it is the Württemberg Landesmuseum with historical exhibits and art treasures (open Tue 1000-1300, Wed-Sun 1000-1700).

Also on Schillerplatz, see the Stiftskirche (Collegiate Church), a late Gothic hall church with impressive 16th-century sculpted tombs of the Counts of Württemberg. Nearby are the Markthalle (market hall) and Marktplatz (market square).

Stuttgart is also known for its elegant shops, from Klett Passage (arcade) near the main station and along Königsstrasse and its side streets, including Calwerstrasse and the famous Calwer Passage.

Esslingen

Esslingen is an important wine centre and is where the great trade route from Flanders to Venice crossed the Neckar. The former free imperial town can look back on 1200 years of viticulture and is the home of Kessler Sekt, the oldest sparkling wine producers of Germany (1826).

The market square is a good starting place for a walking tour. Visit the Church of St Denis, a Gothic basilica with exquisite stained glass windows and two Romanesque towers that are linked by a footbridge. Just opposite the Rococo-style Neues Rathaus (new town hall) is the Renaissance façade of the former town hall, with a two-storeyed belfry and a Glockenspiel. There are many splendid half-timbered houses near the Innere Brücke, one of the oldest post-Roman bridges of Europe. If you walk up to the Burg (fortress), you can enjoy the views in the restaurant in the historic tower Dicker Turm (1130-1400, 1730-2200; Sun, brunch only).

From here, continue to Plochingen, which has 17th-century half-timbered houses on the market square and a Gothic fortified church. Cross the Neckar and travel south on the B313.

The Upper Neckar valley

The southernmost vineyards of the region are scattered along the Neckar river at the edge of the Swabian Jura. The Swabian Wine Road begins at Metzingen, remarkable for its seven ancient presses (Kelterplatz) and wine museum in the Herrschaftskelter (Apr-Oct, Sun 1000-1700). Follow signs to Neuffen to see the ruins of Hohenneuffen fortress (1100) that rise above the town's medieval centre.

Continue on the scenic road to Nürtingen and then back to Esslingen and Stuttgart.

Greater Stuttgart's vineyard area is larger than that of Sachsen.

THE 'ONIONS' OF ESSLINGEN
The town's 9-day wine festival in August is called the *Zwiebelfest* (Onion Festival). Why the people of Esslingen are nicknamed 'onions' is open to debate. Is it due to the large quantities grown nearby – or the huge number used to make *Zwiebelkuchen* (onion quiche), a favourite food served in autumn with the new wine?

Legend has it that the devil once gleefully walked through the town unrecognized by its proud citizens. At the market, he tried to beguile a vendor into giving him an apple: she obliged with an onion. Enraged, the devil ran from town, crying that henceforth its 'sharp' citizens should be called 'onions'.

East of the Neckar

The scenic vineyards near Hessigheim get their name from the Felsengärten (cliff gardens).

PLOCHINGEN
Stumpenhof (in suburb Stumpenhof). Tel: 07153/ 22425. Fax: 07153/76375. Wed-Sun 1200-1400, 1800-2130. Fine regional cooking.
METZINGEN
Hotel Schwanen (next to St Martin's). Tel: 07123/ 9460. Fax: 07123/946100. 1200-1400, 1800-2200.
LUDWIGSBURG
A beautifully designed town full of historic buildings and palaces. Visit Germany's largest Baroque Schloss (tours daily) and the palace gardens, 'Baroque in Bloom' (daily Apr-Oct, 0730-2030). Walk through the adjoining nature and wildlife park to the palace and hunting lodge Favorite. The Duke of Württemberg's wine estate at Schloss Monrepos is a 45-minute walk from the town.
Schlosshotel Monrepos Tel: 07141/3020. Fax: 07141/302200. 1200-2200.
ASPERG (nr Ludwigsburg) **Hotel Adler** Stuttgarter Str. 2. Tel: 07141/26600. Fax: 07141/266060. 1200-1430, 1830-2200. Friendly atmosphere, nice garden.

From Ludwigsburg drive north on the B27 to the fortified town of Besigheim. The market square is ringed with 15th-century houses. The parish church contains a late Gothic altar carved by the Master of Urach.

From here, the road to Hessigheim, Mundelsheim and Pleidelsheim follows the course of the Neckar as it cuts through steep shell-limestone hills to form a series of spectacular loops. The terraced vineyards rising from the banks of the river are named Käsberg, Felsengarten and Wurmberg. Trollinger and Riesling are the primary grape varieties. The local co-operative in Hessigheim, the Felsengartenkellerei, is a good vantage point as well as a good place to sample and purchase wine.

In Marbach, you can visit Schiller's birthplace in the Old Town and the museum named after him in a palace just outside the village. (Schiller National Museum is open daily 0900-1700; exhibits on Schiller, Kerner, Rilke and other German writers.)

The Bottwar valley

Further north along the Swabian Wine Road, there are a series of small villages with vineyards scattered throughout the hillsides. Here, too, Trollinger and Riesling are the main grape varieties. Steinheim made headlines in 1933, when the skull of a primitive man (250,000 years old) was discovered. You can see it and other historic exhibits in the Urmensch Museum just off the market square and left of the fountain (open Tue-Sun 1000-1200 and 1400-1600).

Half-timbered houses and the Romanesque St Georgskirche, with its 9th-century frescoes are worth seeing in Kleinbottwar. The hillside castle above the town, Schloss Schaubeck, is the home of one of the region's noble families and renowned wine estates. Grossbottwar has a beautiful half-timbered town hall (1526) with a clock where a stork strikes the hour. The Schiefes Haus is a curiously slanting vintner's home from the 16th century.

Ruins with a view

Travel along the scenic road to Oberstenfeld and watch for the turning to the 13th-century Burg Lichtenberg (fortress) for a view of the entire Bottwar valley. The ruins of Burg Hohenbeilstein ('Langhans' fortress) overlook the village of Beilstein, and there is a falconry. From Löwenstein and Willsbach follow the road to Weinsberg, site of Germany's oldest oenological school (1868) and Württemberg's largest wine estate. The Justinus Kerner House is now a museum.

Nearby, you can walk the extensive wine trail on the Schemelsberg and visit the ruins of the Weibertreu fortress (273m/896ft high).

The harvest near Obersulm-Willsbach (east of Weinsberg). The hand-picked grapes are loaded into the container on the picker's back. He then carries them to a larger collection vat.

Women and wine

Weibertreu refers to the town's 'faithful wives' who outwitted the Hohenstaufen Emperor Conrad III in 1140, when he besieged the town. He offered them safe conduct out of town and permission to take their dearest possessions with them. They went through the town gate carrying their husbands on their backs!

Heilbronn was immortalized in Heinrich von Kleist's play *Käthchen von Heilbronn* (1808). Kathy is a symbol of female beauty, virtue and devotion and is still a key figure in the town's activities. The town hall's astronomical clock and Kilianskirche (St Kilian's Church) with its Gothic high altar and ornate Renaissance tower are worth seeing. The annual *Weindorf* (huge wine festival, mid-September) is among the region's most popular. Try the red wines, particularly the Lemberger. Ascend the Wartberg for a view of the medieval town and surroundings.

Two villages just south of Heilbronn, Flein (known for its Riesling wines) and Talheim (which specializes in red wines from the Schwarzriesling, or Pinot Meunier) are also important wine centres.

Hohenlohe: Kocher, Jagst and Tauber river valleys

Named after the Hohenlohe dynasty, this north-eastern part of the region extends as far as Weikersheim. The wines are predominantly white and as earthy and robust as their Franconian cousins. (See pages 98-99.) All three valleys are very scenic and have many castles that are interesting to visit.

111

West of the Neckar

From Ludwigsburg, follow the signs to Möglingen, home of Württemberg's *Zentralgenossenschaft* (central cellars), the umbrella organization of the entire region's local co-operatives. Their shop offers a vast selection of wines (in the *Gewerbegebiet*, industrial park, Mon-Fri 0800-1700). Stop at the former free imperial town of Markgröningen, with its fine market square. Rich in historic buildings from the 15th century to the 17th, it has one of the most skilfully crafted half-timbered town halls in Germany. The *Schäferlauf* (Shepherds' Festival) takes place in late August.

Stromberg and Heuchelberg

The vineyards and wine towns are scattered throughout the countryside and to follow the Swabian Wine Road means some backtracking. Castles dot many of the summits and the oldest sections of the villages (usually the market squares) have retained their medieval character.

Here is a fairly direct route which gives you a flavour of the area. Travel from Vaihingen, notable for its steep terraced vineyards on the slopes beneath Schloss Kaltenstein (castle), to Horrheim. The town's old press house, now a wine museum, has a massive old press made from a 10.5m/34ft 6in tree trunk (open 1 May and at festivals).

At Hohenhaslach follow the signs to Freudental, Cleebronn and Brackenheim, birthplace of the Federal Republic's first president, Theodor Heuss. Turn west and drive to Stockheim and Haberschlacht, a very attractive stretch. Schloss Stocksberg towers above and provides the best view of the countryside.

Continue north to Neipperg, a village in the shadow of the double-towered Romanesque castle of the noble family of the same name, and to Schwaigern. The Rococo Neipperg Schloss is the heart of a group of historic buildings, including a famous wine estate, a restaurant, the town hall, and the 12th-century Stadtkirche with its elaborate altars and furnishings.

This is the viticultural heart of the area, where the slopes of the wide valleys are thick with vineyards. One third of production is hearty, steely white wine, but the area is especially known for its powerful, full-bodied red wine. Lemberger, Trollinger, Schwarzriesling and Spätburgunder thrive on the keuper and marl soils. They are excellent with fresh game from the forests and fields nearby.

Right: The Rathaus (town hall) in Markgröningen's market square is one of the finest half-timbered buildings in Germany.
Below: To the right of Bietigheim's Renaissance town hall is the Hornmoldhaus which houses the city museum. The fountain commemorates Duke Ulrich of Württemberg.

Lauffen

From Schwaigern, travel the country road via Nordheim to Lauffen, situated on a loop of the Neckar. With nearly 600 hectares (1500 acres) of vines, many still terraced in the classical manner, Lauffen is one of the most important wine-growing centres of the region.

The Schwarzriesling is the main grape variety, but Trollinger and a small amount of white grapes are also grown. The town traces its origins to the 3rd century and excavations have unearthed a Roman farm. It is a typical medieval townscape and the poet Hölderlin was born here.

Bietigheim-Bissingen

Travel south on the B27 to Bietigheim-Bissingen, where the Enz and Metter rivers join. The 1200-year-old town of Bietigheim has many beautiful buildings, notably the Hornmoldhaus (next to the town hall), remarkable for the 16th-century Renaissance paintings that decorate the walls and ceilings of the interior. Most of the town's wine is produced at the Felsengartenkellerei and sold under the collective vineyard name Schalkstein. Return to Ludwigsburg to complete the circular tour.

Excursions west of Vaihingen

Visit the former Cistercian monastery Kloster Maulbronn with its well-preserved Romanesque and Gothic buildings (Mar-Oct daily 0900-1730; Nov-Feb 0900-1700 except Mon.)

In Knittlingen, you can visit the museum devoted to the alchemist and magician Dr Faust (closed Mon).

Pforzheim's Schmuckmuseum has splendid jewelry from 5000 years ago to the present (Tue-Sun 1000-1700).

EAST OF THE NECKAR
OBERSTENFELD (NE of Grossbottwar) **Hotel Zum Oxen** Grossbottwarer Str. 31. Tel:07062/9390. Fax: 07062/939444. 1200-1400, 1800-2200 (except Tue and Jan). Pretty pavilion.
ÖHRINGEN-ZWEIFLINGEN
Wald- und Schlosshotel Friedrichsruhe
(lkm/half a mile south of Zweiflingen, in a forest). Tel: 07941/60870. Fax: 07941/61468. **Restaurant** (classic gourmet fare) and rustic **Jägerstube** 1200-1400, 1845-2200. One of Germany's top addresses, with elegant hotel and renowned wine estate.

WEST OF THE NECKAR
OCHSENBACH (between Hohenhaslach/Güglingen) **Zum Schwanen** Dorfstr. 47. Tel: 07046/2135. Fax: 07046/2729. 1130-1430, 1730-2200 (except Mon).
GÜGLINGEN
(nr Brackenheim)
Herzogskelter Deutscher Hof 1. Tel: 07135/1770. Fax: 07135/17777. 1200-1400, 1800-2200 (except Mon). Historic press house. Guest rooms.
SCHWAIGERN
Zum Alten Rentamt
Schloss Strasse 6. Tel: 07138/5258. Fax: 07138/1325. Daily 1200-1400, 1800-2300. Historic house. Guest rooms. Wine estate next door: Schlosskellerei Graf von Neipperg.
BIETIGHEIM
Zum Schiller Marktplatz 5. Tel: 07142/41018. Fax: 07142/46058. Mon from 1800, Tue-Sat 1200-1400, 1800-2200. Closed 3 weeks at Pentecost. Superb wine list, excellent cuisine. Very friendly hotel-restaurant.

The Rems Valley

STETTEN (nr Kernen)
Weinstube Bayer
Gartenstr. 5. Tel: 07151/
45252. Fax: 07151/43380.
Tue-Sat 1200-1400, 1800-
2130. Sun 1200-1330. Huge
wine list, contemporary
cuisine. Garden seating.
Zum Ochsen Kirchstr. 15.
Tel: 07151/94360. Fax:
07151/943619. 1200-1415,
1730-2130 (except Wed).
Swabian fare. Hotel.
**Weinstube-Hotel Idler-
Zur Linde** Dinkelstr. 1. Tel:
07151/949130. Fax: 07151/
9491341. Wed-Sun 1200-
1400, Tue-Sun 1800-2200.
STRÜMPFELBACH
Zum Lamm Hindenburg
Str. 16. Tel: 07151/967636.
Fax: 07151/967638. Wed-
Sun 1200-1400, 1800-2100.
Guest rooms.

*A Württemberg tradition: a wine-
grower enjoying a* Viertele *of*
Schillerwein.

This part of Württemberg is
especially beautiful in spring, when
the cherry trees blossom, and in
autumn, when the vineyards turn
golden and the aroma of new wine
and *Zwiebelkuchen* (onion quiche) is in
the air. The vineyards lie in the side
valleys of the Rems river.

There are dozens of tiny inns with
evocative signs hanging over their
doors, bearing names like *Ochsen*
(Oxen), *Lamm* (Lamb), and *Hirsch*
(Stag) or *Post* (referring to the old post
road stations), where you can sample
the local wine and dishes. Most of
the wines are produced by the local
co-operatives, but a few of the inns
offer their own (*Eigenbauweine*).
Trollinger and Riesling are the main
varieties. Compared to their
counterparts from the Middle and
Lower Neckar valley, the Rems wines
are generally lighter and livelier
thanks to their fruity acidity.

South of the Rems

Three side valleys south of the
Rems river, with the wine villages of
Kernen-Stetten, Strümpfelbach and
Schnait, are easily reached from
Stuttgart via Bad Cannstatt and
Fellbach (roads B14 and B29).

The marked hiking trail through
the vineyards of Fellbach begins near
the co-operative and leads up to the
Kappelberg, offering a good view of
the valley. Follow signs from the
suburb of Rommelshausen to
Kernen-Stetten, an old wine-growing
town with a 14th-century castle and a
hiking path round the ruins of the
Yburg fortress. Rather than returning
to the B29, follow the winding
country road south (towards
Esslingen). As the road ascends into
the forest, look back at the Yburg
ruins amidst the steep vineyards
lining the cone-shaped hills.

Watch for signs to Aichschiess and
Schanbach – this route brings you
into the next valley, to Strümpfelbach,
an idyllic village full of half-timbered
houses. Now return to the B29 to
reach Beutelsbach, the heart of
viticulture in the Rems valley. At
the Remstalkellerei (regional co-
operative) you can sample and
purchase wines from all of the
villages on this route. Follow the signs
to Schnait, where you can see the
altar in the Church of St Wendelin
and the Silcher Museum (in 1837
Silcher wrote the music to Heine's
Song of Loreley).

Return to the B29 and cross the
Rems at Winterbach.

North of the Rems

Remshalden is a pretty town with
colourful half-timbered houses and an
old watch tower. The scenery from
nearby Grunbach, north to Buoch

A typical house in the peaceful wine village of Strümpfelbach in the Rems valley.

and Winnenden is very attractive. There is a wonderful view of the old-style vineyards with their stone walls and terraces just as the forest clears and you descend into the valley at Winnenden.

From Winnenden, drive south to Korb and Waiblingen, with its pretty market square and two churches of interest, the Nonnenkirche (1496) and St Michael's (1480). To complete our loop through the Rems valley, return to the B29 at Fellbach.

Hearty Swabian cooking

Maultaschen a spicy mixture of meat, spinach, onions in pasta squares; served in clear broth or *geschmälzt*, with melted butter and fried onions on top.
Spätzle handmade noodles. Mixed with cheese, they're *Kässpätzle*.
Gaisburger Marsch rich stew of beef, potatoes and *Spätzle*.
Schwäbischer Rostbraten Swabian roast beef topped with fried onions.
Saure Kutteln pickled tripe.
Saure Nieren pickled kidneys.
Schupfnudeln potato dough noodles.
Hausgemacht or *handgeschabt* refer to homemade or handmade food.

Schillerwein

This is a 300-year-old Württemberg speciality made by pressing and fermenting red and white grapes together and named after the play in colours (*schillern*) from red to pink to white of this fruity wine as it shimmers in a glass.

Baden

The region's slogan means 'Baden wine: kissed by the sun'.

FOR FURTHER INFORMATION
contact the following
organizations:
Weinwerbezentrale
Badischer
Winzergenossenschaften
Kesslerstr. 5,
76185 Karlsruhe.
Tel: 0721/557028.
Fax: 0721/557020.

Badischer Weinbauverband
(Baden Wine-growers'
Association)
Merzhauser Str. 115,
79100 Freiburg.
Tel: 0761/459100.
Fax: 0761/408026.

Baden, the southernmost of Germany's wine regions, stretches some 400km (240 miles) along the Rhine from the Bodensee (Lake Constance) to the Bergstrasse. Most of the Tauber valley vineyards (see pages 98-99) are also part of Baden. The *Badische Weinstrasse* (Baden Wine Road), often corresponding to the B3, runs through Heidelberg, Baden-Baden, Freiburg and many picturesque Black Forest wine villages. Onion-domed churches and half-timbered chalets dot the landscape of vineyards, orchards and forests. The beautiful play of colours is best seen in spring or autumn.

The concentration of top German restaurants is highest in Baden. Simple country inns also offer exceptional food, wine and fruit brandies, a regional speciality. You can also try the wines at festivals, co-operatives and traditional wine estates.

A Gothic tribe, the Alemanni, expanded viticulture started by the Romans, but the Church provided the real impetus for the extensive development of wine-growing in Baden.

In the Middle Ages, landowners often bequeathed vineyards to quite distant monasteries. To encourage quality-consciousness among its tenant growers, the Church promulgated some of the first regulations governing work in the vineyards and cellars.

After the widespread destruction of the Thirty Years' War and the War of the Palatinate Succession in the 17th century, viticulture enjoyed a period of revival, only to be plagued by a series of natural, economic and political calamities in the late 19th and 20th centuries. By 1949, Baden's vineyard area had shrunk to an all-time low of 5862 hectares (14,485 acres).

Baden today
Baden has recovered during the past five decades and is now third in size after Rheinhessen and the Pfalz (16,224 hectares/40,090 acres).

Vineyards have been replanted and reorganized to improve efficiency.

Most of the region's 28,000 growers are members of co-operatives, where high quality standards and modern cellar technology yield wines that consistently win prizes at national wine competitions.

While some 85 per cent of Baden's wine is produced by co-operatives, there are also a number of traditional wine estates whose excellent wines are in such demand at home that they are scarcely known outside Baden.

Tradition of wine and food
One of the warmest wine regions of Germany, Baden is a popular holiday resort, not least because of its great tradition of wine and food, shared with nearby Alsace and Switzerland. Most of the classic Baden grape varieties are relatively neutral and mild in acidity and thus ideal for producing harmonious dry wines that go well with food.

Two of the oldest of all grape varieties are found in Baden: Gutedel, grown in Egypt for at least five thousand years, and Muskateller, dating from Roman times.

Each of Baden's nine districts is distinctive in terms of landscape and wine, yet they all share a sense of *joie de vivre*.

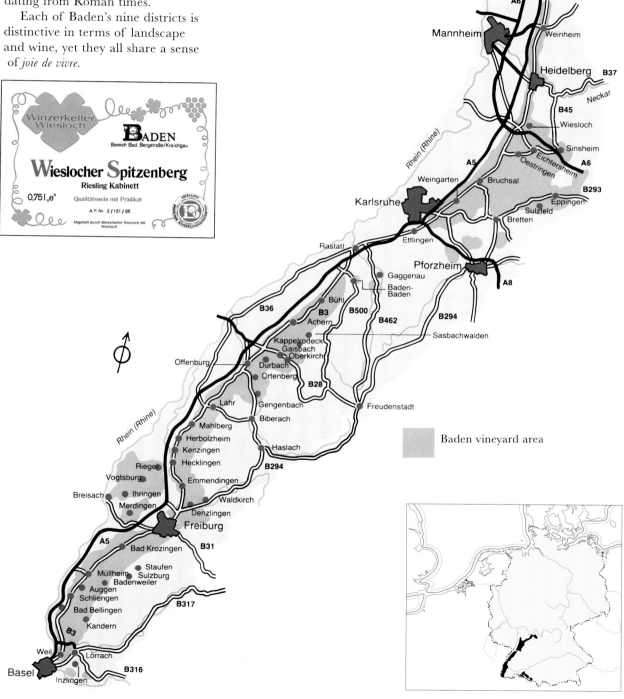

Baden vineyard area

Heidelberg and the Neckar Valley

Heidelberg lies at the foothills of the Oden Forest on the Neckar river, not far from its confluence with the Rhine. Its natural beauty and striking townscape, crowned by majestic castle ruins, made Heidelberg a favourite among writers and artists of the Romantic period.

There are excellent views of the town and the castle from the Heiligenberg (sacred hill) on the opposite side of the Neckar, site of a Celtic settlement and later a monastery, whose 9th-century ruins can still be visited. Today, Heiligenberg is the name of the vineyard nearby.

The castle and the university
Both owe their existence to the *Kurfürsten* (Prince Electors) of the Pfalz (Palatinate) who made Heidelberg their residence for 500 years.

Germany's oldest university, founded in 1386 by Kurfürst Ruprecht, remains one of Europe's most respected educational institutions. Its library houses a splendid collection of rare medieval manuscripts (displayed during exhibitions).

The castle is a complex of buildings, towers and gardens built by the Electors as their residence from the 14th century to the 17th. The Renaissance structures are among the finest in Germany. Despite the heavy damage in 1689 and 1693, during the War of the Palatinate Succession, there is still much to see (guided tours daily, Apr-Oct 0900-1700, Nov-Mar 0900-1600) and from the Great Terrace there is a fine view of Old Heidelberg.

Heidelberg's wine tradition
To appreciate Heidelberg's wine tradition, see the *Grosses Fass* (huge cask) in the castle, said to be the world's largest (220,000 litres or nearly 300,000 bottles of wine). It was built in 1751 to hold the Elector's tithe (tenth) of the Palatinate wine harvest. You can still enjoy a glass of wine at the castle, in the *Weinstube* in the grounds (from 1800, except Wed, Sun).

The Neckar valley
The Neckar valley is the first scenic part of the *Burgenstrasse* (Castle Road). A route through several historic wine towns near ancient castles (many now restaurants and hotels), it leads from Mannheim via Heidelberg, Heilbronn and Rothenburg to Nürnberg. En route through some of Germany's most picturesque landscape, there are many places to sample the outstanding wines and cuisine of Baden, Franken and Württemberg.

Right: A Heidelberg panorama with a view of the castle. Boat trips through the scenic Neckar valley start from Heidelberg's Stadthalle daily, from Easter to Oct. Neckar-Steinach is 1½ hours away.

Below: The castle at Heidelberg contains Gothic, Renaissance and Baroque architectural features.

A suggested excursion

Leave Heidelberg from the Karlstor (gateway to eastern edge of Old Town) via the B37 and follow the Neckar to Neckarsulm, from where you can easily return to Heidelberg via the A6 or join the Baden Wine Road on the Bergstrasse near Wiesloch on the B3.

Most of the villages along the Neckar have interesting historic houses, churches and castles. Bad Wimpfen am Berg, one of the best-preserved walled towns of Germany, is highly recommended. The tourist office in the market square has maps for a one-hour walking tour.

While the Neckar is primarily associated with the Württemberg wine region, Heidelberg and its environs were ceded to the Grand Duchy of Baden in 1803. Hence, some of the vineyards are part of Baden, yet often border on Württemberg sites. You are likely to find wines from both regions in this area's shops and restaurants.

The chalky, shell-limestone soils yield spicy Müller-Thurgau, fruity Riesling and Silvaner and elegant Pinot wines from the Burgundy family. For something special, try a delicately spicy Muskateller or Traminer.

HEIDELBERG
Hirschgasse Hirschgasse 3. Tel: 06221/4540. Fax: 06221/454111. Mon-Sat from 1800. Hotel-restaurant (1472) opp. Karlstor.
Simplicissimus Ingrimstr. 16. Tel: 06221/183336. Fax: 06221/181980. Wed-Mon from 1800. Pretty courtyard.
Hotel Zum Ritter Hauptstr. 178. Tel: 06221/1350. Fax: 06221/135230. 1130-1430, 1800-2230. Renaissance house (1592).
Zum Roten Ochsen Hauptstr. 217. Historic student pub. Tel: 06221/20977. Fax: 06221/164383. Apr-Oct 1130-1400 and from 1700, Nov-Mar from 1700 (closed Sun, all year).
Zur Herrenmühle Hauptstr. 239. Tel: 06221/12909. Fax: 06221/22033. Mon-Sat from 1800. 17th-century house, idyllic courtyard.

ART AND HISTORY
Kurpfälzisches Museum Hauptstr. 97 (in Baroque Palais Moras). Daily 1000-1700 (except Mon). The 500,000-year-old jaw of Heidelberg man is on view. Garden restaurant.

NECKARZIMMERN
Burg Hornberg Tel: 06261/92460. Fax: 06261/924644. 1200-1400, 1800-2130. Closed Dec-Feb. 12th-century castle hotel with grand Neckar views.

The Kraichgau

ANGELBACHTAL
Schloss Michelfeld
Friedrichstr. 2. Tel: 07265/
7041. Fax: 07265/279.
Tue-Sun 1200-1400, 1800-
2200. Terrace. Hotel.
SULZFELD
Burg Ravensburg Tel:
07269/914191. Fax:
07269/914140. 1130-1400,
1730-2130 (except Mon).
Closed Dec-Feb.
WEINGARTEN
Walk'sches Haus
Marktplatz 7. Tel: 07244/
703700. Fax: 07244/
703740. 1200-1400, 1800-
2200 (except Tue; Sat
dinner only). Restaurant-
hotel in 16th-century house.

*Dining in an historic castle: Burg
Ravensburg near Sulzfeld.*

The large vineyard area near
Wiesloch marks the southern edge of
the Bergstrasse and the beginning of
the hilly region between the Oden and
Black Forests known as the Kraichgau.
It is a peaceful area, ideal for walking,
cycling, riding and fishing.

Route B3, on the western edge of
the wine-growing area, runs through
Bruchsal and Karlsruhe, each with a
splendid Baroque palace. The route
suggested below enables you to see
both. Don't miss the little wine
villages set among lush forests and
meadows in the valleys lining many
small streams (hence the frequency
of *Bach*, or stream, in many town
names).

Not only do grapes and other
fruits thrive in the warm Kraichgau
climate, but also tobacco and saffron,
which carpet the fields in pink, white
and purple flowers in the spring.

The heavy keuper soils yield
robust, full-bodied Riesling wines
with less acidity than their Rheingau
counterparts. Chalky loess is the
other main soil type, well-suited to the
Burgundy (Pinot) family – white wines
from Weissburgunder, Auxerrois and
Grauburgunder and red wines from
Spätburgunder and Schwarzriesling.
The principal variety, Müller-
Thurgau, is more delicate in
character from this part of Baden.

From Wiesloch, travel south on the
B39 to Eichtersheim, where Friedrich
Hecker, the Baden revolutionary
involved in attempts to form a
German republic (1848) was born in

the town's 16th-century moated castle. At nearby Schloss Michelfeld, you can sample top Kraichgau wines.

Turn west on the B292 to visit St Cecelia, 'Cathedral of the Kraichgau' in Östringen, then follow the signs to Odenheim. The late Baroque St Michael's Church, town hall and Siegfried's Fountain (the site where the Nibelung hero is said to have been killed) are worth a visit.

South of Odenheim, turn left to Tiefenbach, a good place to take the *Weinlehrpfad* (educational wine trail) through the vineyards, or to enjoy the quiet beauty of Kreuzbergsee, a nearby lake.

The route from Eichelberg and Elsenz to Eppingen is also most attractive. Many historic buildings and 14th-century frescoes in the Altstädter Kirche merit a stop in Eppingen, before you drive west to Burg Ravensburg, overlooking the steep Sulzfeld vineyards, for a wonderful view and a chance to sample the owner's wines. Then the idyllic wine village of Gochsheim is worth a small detour (via Flehingen).

Bretten and Bruchsal

Among the half-timbered houses lining Bretten's market square is the Melanchthon House, a memorial to the Reformation humanist and colleague of Luther. From here, it is a brief drive to Bruchsal on the B35.

Balthasar Neumann created Bruchsal's two Baroque masterpieces: St Peter's Church and the magnificent staircase in the palace built for a Schönborn prince bishop.

Karlsruhe

Legend says that Margrave Karl Wilhelm built his residence here after a dream in which he saw a fan-

shaped town 'grow' out of a fan lost by his wife. The town which developed along the roads radiating south of the palace (rebuilt by Margrave Karl Friedrich) became the capital of the Grand Duchy of Baden (1806-1918). The art and history museums in the palace grounds are first-rate.

Near Durlach (site of the original residence) there is a good view from the Turmberg, also the name of the 1200-year-old hillside vineyard.

Bretten's colourful market square. Friedrich II of the Pfalz is shown in knightly armour on the market fountain dating from 1555.

ETTLINGEN

A fascinating old town south of Karlsruhe (town hall, old paper mill, 18th-century palace). **Hotel Erbprinz**, Rheinstr. 1. Tel: 07243/3220. Fax: 07243/16471. 1200-1400, 1800-2200. Elegant. Classic and modern cuisine.

Baden-Baden and Ortenau

One of the many artistic features of Baden-Baden's elegant thermal baths.

The Ortenau district of Baden is situated in the western foothills of the Black Forest between Baden-Baden and Offenburg. The Baden Wine Road twists through the hillsides on country roads (rather than the B3), passing ancient castles and wine villages.

The vineyards stretch up to the forest-topped edges of the hillsides and nearly always face south. Weathered primitive rock (granite, gneiss) is the main soil type, yielding flavourful wines with fine, flowery bouquets and racy acidity.

Müller-Thurgaus often have a Riesling-like peach tone. Some of Baden's finest Rieslings are from vineyards near Baden-Baden, Bühl and Durbach. Traminer, with a delicate spiciness, and the Burgundy family are also at home here.

Baden-Baden

One of Germany's most luxurious resorts, Baden-Baden attracts the international set, reminiscent of the *Belle Epoque* a century ago, when Baden-Baden was a favourite spa and rendezvous of Europe's aristocracy.

The Romans discovered the healing powers of the thermal springs. You can visit the restored ruins of a Roman bath beneath the Römerplatz, site of the modern thermal baths.

The hub of social life is the Kurhaus, with its casino, pump room and restaurants in the grounds of the Kurpark (spa park). The park along the Lichtentaler Allee, converted into an English garden in 1850, and the Neues Schloss, with its bird's-eye view of town, are also well worth seeing.

Nearly 400 hectares (about 900 acres) of prime vineyards surround Baden-Baden in the suburbs of Varnhalt and Neuweier, Umweg and Steinbach. Together with the Baden wine towns of the Tauber valley, they are permitted to bottle their wines (Riesling) in the *Bocksbeutel*, otherwise reserved for Franconian wines. The privilege stems from tradition – a Neuweier family's ties with Franken.

Bühl to Waldulm

South of Baden-Baden, Riesling and Müller-Thurgau are the main white varieties, but Spätburgunder (red) becomes increasingly important. The highly prized Affentaler red wines are often bottled in a unique, triangular-shaped *Buddel* (rhymes with 'noodle').

From Bühl, drive to the Altwindeck fortress ruins for a good view, and follow the Baden Wine Road to Lauf (via Hub), Obersasbach and Sasbachwalden, a picturesque wine village. Continue through the steep hills to Kappelrodeck, famous for its Hex vom Dasenstein red wines with labels showing the *Hex* (witch). For a look at Schloss Rodeck, also the collective name of this area's vineyards, drive up the narrow road to St Albinus Church (with a pretty interior) on the hill in Waldulm.

BADEN-BADEN
-UMWEG
Bocksbeutel Umweger Str. 103. Tel: 07223/ 58031. Fax: 07223/60808. 1200-1430, 1800-2200 (except Mon). Vineyard setting. Guest rooms.
-NEUWEIER
Zum Alde Gott Weinstr. 10. Tel: 07223/55 13. Fax: 07223/60624. 1200-1500, 1830-2300 (except Thu, Fri lunch, Jan). Gourmet dining with vineyard views.
BÜHL
Grüne Bettlad Blumenstr. 4. Tel: 07223/ 24238. Fax: 07223/24247. 1200-1400, 1800-2130 (except Sun, Mon). 16th-century half-timbered house with guest rooms and garden. Very cosy.
Gude Stub Dreherstr. 9. Tel: 07223/8480. Fax: 07223/900180. 1200-1400, 1800-2200 (except Tue). Fine regional cuisine in a charming house. Garden.
-KAPPELWINDECK
Burg Windeck Kappelwindeckstr. 104. Tel: 07223/94920. Fax: 07223/40016. 1200-1400, 1830-2200 (except Mon). Excellent chef. Great views from terrace. Guest rooms.

Markgräflich Badisches Weingut Schloss Staufenberg, a wine estate in an ancient castle overlooking steep vineyards near Durbach. Enjoy the fabulous view with a bottle of wine and pretzels on the terrace. (Wine pub open Mar-Nov from 1000, except Mon in Mar and Nov. Wine shop open all year Mon-Fri 0930-1200, 1330-1730; Apr-Oct, also on Sat 1000-1600.)

Oberkirch to Offenburg

Renchtäler is the name of the large 310-hectare (766 acre) vineyard on the hills near Oberkirch, the gateway to the Renchtal (Rench valley). Grimmelshausen (c.1625-1676) wrote *Simplicissimus*, his satirical chronicle of the Thirty Years' War, here in 1669. The many art treasures in Lautenbach's Maria Krönung Church merit a visit.

Backtrack on the B28 to Gaisbach, to turn left on to the road to Durbach, where Riesling is known as Klingelberger and Traminer as Clevner. From Schloss Staufenberg (castle) there is a stunning view of Durbach, and a vast panorama, including Strasbourg cathedral's spire.

Historic buildings and modern sculptures blend well on Offenburg's market square, site of a wine festival (late September or early October) featuring wines from all of the Ortenau. The Rococo altars of gilded red and blue marble in the Heiliges Kreuz Church are superb.

BÜHLERTAL
Schlosshotel Bühlerhöhe Schwarzwaldhochstr. 1. Tel: 07226/550. Fax: 07226/55777. Gourmet restaurant **Imperial** Fri-Tue 1900-2200, Sun also 1200-1400. Superb wine list. Luxurious castle hotel in the forest. Closed mid-Jan to mid-Feb.
SASBACHWALDEN
Hotel Talmühle Talstr. 36. Tel: 07841/l001. Fax: 07841/5404. **Fallert** for gourmet dining, **Badische Stuben** for regional cuisine. 1200-1400, 1830-2130. Closed mid-Jan to mid-Feb.
DURBACH
Hotel Zum Ritter Tal 1. Tel: 0781/93230. Fax: 0781/9323100. 1200-1400, 1800-2200 (Sun lunch only).

Freiburg and Breisgau

GENGENBACH
Gengenbacher Winzergenossenschaft (WG)
This local co-operative has shops at Am Winzerkeller 2 and Hauptstr. 18, open Mon-Fri 0800-1200, 1330-1700 and Sat 0900-1200. Or sample them at the pub **Winzer-Stüble** Hauptstr. 18 (in the courtyard). 0930-2400 (except Tue).

LAHR-REICHENBACH
Adler Hauptstr. 18. Tel: 07821/7035. Fax: 07821/7033. 1200-1400, 1830-2200 (except Tue and Feb). Gourmet restaurant-hotel.

GLOTTERTAL
Hotel Hirschen
Rathausweg 2. Tel: 07684/810. Fax: 07684/1713. 1200-1400, 1800-2130 (except Mon). Traditional Baden cuisine. Friendly.

Hotel Schlossmühle
Talstr. 2. Tel: 07684/229. Fax: 07684/1485. 1130-1400, 1800-2130 (except Wed and Nov). Idyllic garden by the *Mühle* (mill). Black Forest specialities.

DENZLINGEN
Rebstock-Stube
Hauptstr. 74. Tel: 07666/2071. Fax: 07666/7942. 1200-1415, 1730-2130 (except Sun, Mon). Cosy ambience for gourmet dining. Guest rooms.

BADEN SPECIALITIES
Badisch Rotgold
Made only in Baden, this is said to have its origins in the Glottertal. It combines the elegance of the (red) Spätburgunder with the full body and rich bouquet of the (white) Grauburgunder.

Weissherbst
A rosé wine made from only one (red) grape variety. In Baden, it is usually Spätburgunder. Should be served chilled.

If you travel on the B3 south of Offenburg, you barely notice leaving the Ortenau and entering the Breisgau, for there is no break in the ribbon-like strip of vineyards and orchards on the foothills of the Black Forest. However, the hills are a little rounder and many of the Breisgau's vineyards are terraced with old stone walls.

Loess soils predominate, sometimes mixed with loam and/or limestone. Müller-Thurgau is the main grape variety, followed by members of the Burgundy family and the spicy Gewürztraminer.

Scenic route to the Breisgau
Travel the country road through the Kinzig valley from Offenburg to Ortenberg. The peaceful valley view from the castle above town belies a grim past – in the 16th and 17th centuries it was a centre of witch-hunts. Today it is a youth hostel.

The frescoes in the vineyard chapel Bühlwegkapelle (Käfersberg) are worth seeing, before driving to Gengenbach, a splendid medieval town with walls and gates, half-timbered houses and an impressive town hall on Rathausplatz.

At Biberach you can turn west on the B415 to Lahr (start of the Breisgau) or continue on the B33 to Haslach, to see ornate Black Forest costumes in the Schwarzwälder-

Trachten-Museum in the Kapuziner (Capuchin) monastery (closed Mon). Nearby, between Hausach and Gutach, is a *Freilichtmuseum* (open-air museum) with 16th to 18th-century farmhouses (Apr-Oct 0830-1800).

Lahr to Freiburg
The Baden Wine Road (B3) runs through the historic wine towns Mahlberg, Herbolzheim, Kenzingen and Hecklingen, with interesting features in their old town centres.

There is a panoramic view from the fortress ruins of Burg Lichteneck, the collective name of a large portion of the Breisgau's vineyards.

Enter Emmendingen through its 17th-century town gate, near the house where Goethe's sister, Cornelia Schlosser, lived. The main sights are between the Renaissance Margraves' palace and market square, with old patrician houses (see nos.4, 5, 8 and 10) and the Baroque town hall.

Before travelling to Freiburg, you can enjoy typically rural Black Forest villages and beautiful scenery by driving in a loop via Waldkirch, Kandel mountain and St Peter (where it is worth visiting the church, library and the Princes' Hall of a former Benedictine monastery). Then return to Denzlingen through the pretty Glottertal, a sheltered valley where red and white Burgunder vines thrive on slopes of weathered gneiss.

Freiburg

The Dukes of Zähringen founded the town in 1120. Except for several periods of French occupation, Freiburg was under Austrian rule from 1368 until its cession to the Grand Duchy of Baden in 1805.

The Münster (cathedral), built between 1200 and 1513, is the focal point of this old university town's many historical and cultural attractions. The *Official Freiburg Guide* (in English) has excellent information on local sights and customs. Contact: Freiburg Tourist Office, PO Box 1549, 79015 Freiburg. Tel: 0761/3881880. Fax: 0761/37003.

Important wine centre

There are c.740 hectares (about 1833 acres) of vines in Freiburg and its suburbs. The *Haus des badischen Weines*

A panorama of Freiburg, where the Breisgau, Tuniberg and Markgräflerland wine districts meet.

in the historic Alte Wache (1733) offers an extraordinary selection of wines, sparkling wines and spirits from this area.

For locals and visitors alike, the *Freiburger Weintage* (wine festival) in early July is an attraction, when the Münsterplatz becomes a showcase for wines from several Baden districts.

Alternatively, plan your visit in January or February for the *Fasnet* (carnival) festivities, rooted in Alemannic tradition. The costumes are legendary (visit the Carnival Museum, Turmstr. 14, Sat 1000-1400). On one popular mask, a bunch of grapes and grape leaves form a beard, symbolic of the desire to ward off evil from the vines.

FREIBURG
Colombi-Hotel
Rotteckring 16. Tel: 0761/21060. Fax: 0761/31410. Classic gourmet fare in the **Columbi-Restaurant** or regional specialities in the **Hans-Thoma Stube**. 1200-1500, 1900-2230. Terrace. One of Germany's top restaurants, with a comprehensive wine list.
Hotel Markgräfler Hof
Gerberau 22. Tel: 0761/32540. Fax: 0761/37947. 1200-1400, 1830-2200 (except Sun, Mon). Fine dining, superb wine list.
Oberkirchs Weinstuben
Münsterplatz 22. Tel: 0761/31011. Fax: 0761/31031. 1200-1400, 1830-2130 (except Sun and Jan). Historic wine restaurant and hotel. Outdoor seating on the Münsterplatz.

Kaiserstuhl and Tuniberg

BREISACH

Badischer Winzerkeller
(Central Cellars of Baden
Co-operatives) Zum
Kaiserstuhl 6. Produces wine
from one estate and 90 local
co-operatives. Vast selection
in the wine shop: Mon-Fri
0900-1200, 1300-1730. Also:
Apr-Oct 0900-1300 Sat.

Hotel am Münster
Münsterbergstr. 23. Tel:
07667/8380. Fax: 07667/
838100. 1200-1400, 1800-
2200. Closed Jan. Beautiful
view from terrace.

**VOGTSBURG
-BICKENSOHL**

Hotel Rebstock
Neunlindenstr. 23. Tel:
07662/93330. Fax: 07662/
933320. 1130-1400, 1800-
2130 (except Mon, Tue and
Jan). Terrace with view.

-BISCHOFFINGEN

Hotel Steinbuck
Steinbuckstr. 20. Tel: 07662/
771. Fax: 07662/6079. Thu-
Mon 1200-1400, Wed-Mon
1800-2200. Closed mid-Jan
to mid-Feb. Located in the
vineyards. Terrace.

-OBERBERGEN

Schwarzer Adler Badberg
Str. 23. Tel: 07662/93300.
Fax: 07662/719. Fri-Tue
1200-1400, 1900-2130.
Closed mid-Jan to mid-Feb.
Gourmet restaurant and
wine estate. Guest rooms.

GROWERS' CO-OPERATIVE

Winzergenossenschaft
(abbreviated WG) is a good
place to sample and buy
wine. Hours: Mon-Fri 0800-
1200, 1300-1700; Sat 0900-
1200. Also, Apr-Oct, Sat
0900-1800, Sun 1100-1800
during the *Offene Winzerkeller*,
or open house. Some co-ops
maintain a restaurant, where
you can enjoy the wines with
regional food (Ihringen,
Bickensohl, Bischoffingen,
and Oberrotweil).

The two land massifs of Kaiserstuhl
and Tuniberg are situated between
the Breisgau and the Rhine. The
Vosges Mountains ward off rain and
help to dissipate clouds, making this
one of Germany's warmest and
sunniest districts. The favourable
climate, together with heat-retaining
(volcanic tufa) and mineral-rich (loess)
soils, provide ideal growing conditions
for grapes.

With 5441 hectares (13,445 acres)
of vines, this is Baden's largest and
most concentrated wine-growing
area, with the highest number of full-
time growers. All of the villages
celebrate jointly at the huge wine
festival in Breisach in late August.

The powdery loess soils are prone
to erosion and so hillside viticulture is
only possible on terraced slopes.
Since 1950, the vast number of
narrow terraces has been consolidated
into broad, layered rows of terraces.
The new landscape is more efficient,
yet is almost surreal in appearance,
especially in the blue-violet shades of
dawn or dusk.

Hiking trails

Hikers can enjoy the exotic fauna and
flora, including 33 different types of
orchids in bloom (May and June), on
the Badberg near Oberbergen.

The signposted vineyard path in
Achkarren also explains much about

the region's geology. It begins opposite
the co-operative. Allow one hour for
this walk. At the Rhine crossing near
Sasbach is a fascinating trail through
the Limburg nature reserve that
highlights the area's natural resources
and history. Allow two hours.

The wines

The area is renowned for powerful,
full-bodied wines. The Burgundy
(Pinot) family is well represented:
fiery Spätburgunder red wines, with a
distinctive blackberry tone; neutral
but full-bodied Weissburgunder white
wines; and Grauburgunder, dry
whites with a more pronounced
acidity than Ruländer, the same
variety, but this synonym is used to
denote richer, honey-toned wines.

Spicy Gewürztraminer and
Muskateller are also grown here, as
well as milder, juicy Müller-Thurgau
and Silvaner.

The Tuniberg

This is an ancient chalky hill, famous
for wine and asparagus. From
Freiburg, drive west on the B31 to
Tiengen and Munzingen. The
vineyards are parallel to and east of
the road from Oberrimsingen to
Merdingen, whose attractions include
the pretty houses on the Langgasse
and the St Remigius Church, a jewel
of Baroque architecture.

The Kaiserstuhl

The Kaiserstuhl is an extinct volcano.
Viticulture here dates from the 8th
century, but vines were not planted
on the volcanic soils in the west until
a thousand years later.

From Wasenweiler, it is only
minutes to Ihringen, the largest wine-
growing community of Baden. The
spires of Breisach's cathedral come

BADEN

ERZEUGERABFÜLLUNG
BADISCHER WINZERKELLER EG · D-79206 BREISACH

KAISERSTUHL

Leiselheimer Gestühl

1995

RULÄNDER

SPÄTLESE

Qualitätswein mit Prädikat
A.P. Nr. 1/331-A-41-95

11%
0,75 ℓ

into view as you drive towards the Rhine. Among its art treasures are a Gothic altar, the Schongauer frescoes and an ornate reliquary.

The heart of the Kaiserstuhl is the Vogtsburg, which includes seven small but important wine villages. For an historical perspective on viticulture in the area, visit the wine museum in Achkarren (Easter-Oct, Tue-Fri 1400-1700 and Sat-Sun 1100-1700).

The richly carved Gothic altar in St Michaelis Church in Niederrotweil will interest art lovers. Burkheim and Endingen, with their ancient houses and old town gates, are best explored on foot. In Endingen's market square you will find a range of architectural styles. The old town hall (1527) has vaulted gables; the *Kornhaus*, or granary (1617), boasts high, stepped gables; and the new town hall is an elegant 18th-century manor house.

The country road from Riegel to Wasenweiler passes through the wine towns of Bahlingen and Bötzingen on the eastern edge of the Kaiserstuhl and completes the circuit.

If time permits, the historic train 'Rebenbummler' is a relaxing way to enjoy the landscape between Riegel and Breisach (round trips, May-Oct).

The unique terraced vineyards of the Kaiserstuhl, near Ihringen. Their collective name, Vulkanfelsen (volcanic rock), derives from the weathered volcanic soils that give the wines their fiery character.

Markgräflerland

The broad hills of the Markgräflerland stretch from Freiburg to Basel, with vineyards, orchards and fields nestling between the Black Forest and the Rhine. The river links the Upper Rhine area of Germany, Switzerland and France with their common heritage.

A thoroughfare for both merchants and soldiers since Roman times, the area suffered greatly during the medieval political and religious conflicts. A degree of stability came in the early 16th century, when the *Markgräfler* (Margraves or Marquises) came to power. From then on, it became known as the *Markgräfler Land* to distinguish it from the Hapsburg-ruled territory to the north (Freiburg and Breisgau).

Vineyards and grape varieties

A nearly uninterrupted band of vineyards parallels the B3 from Freiburg to Bad Bellingen. Further south, viticulture is patchy. Vines thrive in the chalky loess-loam soils (heavy clay in some sites) and the mild, humid climate.

The Markgräflerland is best known for two white varieties rarely found elsewhere in Germany: Gutedel, an ancient variety introduced to this area 200 years ago by Margrave Karl Friedrich, a progressive champion of quality wine-growing in Baden; and Nobling, a new crossing of Silvaner and Gutedel. Mild in bouquet and acidity, Gutedel wines are at their best when young and fresh. Nobling yields ripe, fruity wines with more body and acidity.

Nature, art and legend

Just minutes southwest of Freiburg (on the B3) you can explore six small wine villages bordering Batzenberg

hill (248 hectares/613 acres of vines) by walking the *Weinlehrpfad* beginning near Schallstadt, with lovely views.

In Oberkrozingen (Glöcklehof), near the pretty spa of Bad Krozingen, art lovers will appreciate the 9th-century wall paintings in St Ulrich's Chapel. Turning towards the Black Forest, you can see the imposing ruins of Staufen castle perched high on a vine-covered slope (Schlossberg). It overlooks the town of Staufen, with colourful houses, historic buildings, and a curious claim to fame: Faust is said to have succumbed to the devil in the Zum Löwen inn on the market square. You can enjoy a glass of wine here or, in early August, sample all kinds of Markgräflerland wines at the wine festival. The exquisite Baroque church of St Trudpert monastery is worth a detour to Münstertal, a former silver mining centre.

Staufen to Müllheim

Sulzburg merits a stop for the Ottonian (993) St Cyriak Church, stunning in its simplicity. In Laufen, you can visit an

The imposing ruins of Staufen castle crown the steep Schlossberg vineyard.

SCHWARZWÄLDER (BLACK FOREST) SPECIALITIES

Wässerle clear, distilled fruit spirits, eg *Kirschwasser* (cherry) or *Zwetschgenwasser* (plum).

Zibärtle a rare spirit made from mountain plums.

Kirschtorte chocolate cake layered with whipped cream and cherries flavoured with *Kirschwasser*.

Schäufele mit Kartoffelsalat lightly pickled and smoked pork shoulder with potato salad.

Wild game, eg *Rehrücken* (saddle of venison) served with pear halves filled with wild cranberry sauce.

Schinken smoked ham.

OTHER SPECIALITIES include clocks, wood carvings and pottery. (*Töpferei* is the name for a potter's studio.)

excellent co-operative and a world-famous nursery of perennial plants, especially iris (Staudengärtnerei Gräfin von Zeppelin). Neuenfels fortress ruins are visible as you drive towards Britzingen, where the co-operative has an outstanding wine shop.

Badenweiler's modern spa is set below the dramatic Hohenstaufen castle ruins. The Romans discovered the thermal springs in the first century and built extensive baths which can be visited in the spa park.

Baden's oldest wine market (1882) takes place every April in Müllheim, giving visitors a chance to sample several hundred different Markgräflerland wines. The museum in the old town hall in the market square has exhibits devoted to wine and to Adolph Blankenhorn, a great scientist who devoted his life to improving viticulture and helping small growers (Sun 1500-1800 and Apr-Oct also Tue and Thu 1500-1800).

Southern Markgräflerland

The Baden Wine Road continues south on the B3 to Auggen, whose co-op is a model of ecologically-oriented viticulture; Schliengen, with its picturesque town hall in the moated Entenstein castle; and Bad Bellingen, whose thermal springs were discovered during an unsuccessful search for oil.

Alternatively, you can travel via Kandern, then to Liel, to rejoin the B3 in Schliengen. Schloss Bürgeln, a Rococo castle situated back in the hills, offers a good view (tours of the period rooms Mar-Nov, except Tue, at 1100 and on the hour, 1400-1700). Kandern, nearby, is famous for wine, pottery and pretzels.

The southernmost vineyards of this district lie within the triangle of Efringen-Kirchen, Lörrach and Weil, opposite Basel. The moated castle in Inzlingen, east of Weil, is a wonderful setting for superb wine and food.

OBERMÜNSTERTAL
Hotel Spielweg Spielweg 61. Tel: 07636/7090. Fax: 07636/70966. Wed-Sun 1200-1400, 1830-2130. Mon-Tue light fare. Very picturesque house.
SULZBURG
Hirschen Hauptstr. 69. Tel: 07634/8208. Fax: 07634/6717. 1200-1400, 1830-2130 (except Mon, Tue). Top gourmet fare, great wines. Guest rooms.
MÜLLHEIM
Alte Post An der B3. Tel: 07631/5522. Fax: 07631/15524. 1200-1400, 1800-2130 (Sun, dinner only). Seasonal cuisine. Hotel.
EFRINGEN-KIRCHEN
Traube Alemannenstr. 19 (in suburb Blansingen). Tel: 07628/8290. Fax: 07628/8736. Thu-Mon 1200-1400, Wed-Mon 1830- 2200. Gourmet restaurant. Guest rooms.
INZLINGEN
Wasserschloss Riehenstr. 5. Tel: 07621/47057. Fax: 07621/2064. 1200-1430, 1900-2230 (except Tue, Wed and Feb). Gourmet dining in a 15th-century castle. Guest rooms.
WEIL AM RHEIN
Zum Adler Hauptstr. 139. Tel: 07621/98230. Fax: 07621/75676. 1200-1400, 1830-2200 (except Sun, Mon). Gourmet restaurant with guest rooms.

Badenweiler, with thermal springs discovered 2000 years ago.

The Bodensee

'The wine village of Hagnau welcomes its guests.' Visitors to Hagnau will find this cheerful greeting at the approaches to the town.

Bordered by Germany, Switzerland and Austria and not far from the Alps and the Black Forest, the Bodensee (Lake Constance) is surrounded by some of Europe's most beautiful scenery. It is a popular vacation spot, with many recreational opportunities and sights, not least of which is the lake itself. The lakeside promenades are lined with cafés where you can enjoy a panorama of graceful sailboats and windsurfers over a glass of *Seewein* (lake wine). A boat trip to Meersburg provides a good view of its medieval townscape and the steep vineyards below the Baroque palace. Steamers also cruise to Lindau, a delightful resort on the lake's eastern edge.

The islands of Mainau (famous gardens) and Reichenau (art treasures) and the historic town of Konstanz are worth visiting, as are the fascinating prehistoric lake dwellings on piles, near Unteruhldingen (tours daily from Easter to October).

The vine-covered shores of the Bodensee at Meersburg, with a view of the New Palace (far right) and its former riding stables (centre), now the Staatsweingut Meersburg. Spätburgunder Weissherbst (rosé) is a speciality of the estate.

The Bodensee's 480 hectares (1186 acres) of primarily Müller-Thurgau and Spätburgunder vines, concentrated on the northern shore from Meersburg to Hagnau, are the southernmost and highest in altitude of Germany.

The lake tempers the climate and reflects the sun's warmth. Most sites face south and are planted on hills of moraine gravel and chalky, sandy loam. At Hohentwiel, near Singen, however, a volcanic cone is the site of the highest vineyards of all (530m/1740ft). The castle ruins on the top of the hill are a good vantage point.

Bodensee wines are seldom available outside the area. Meersburg's popular wine festival in September features many towns' wines, and thus a good overview of *Seeweine* in general.

Art treasures en route to Meersburg

In Überlingen's Old Town are St Nicholas Church (magnificent altars) and town hall, famous for its Gothic Ratssaal (council chambers). The Gothic church (Baroque interior) and buildings of the former Cistercian monastery in Salem are worth a detour (open Apr-Oct). The cellars of Max Markgraf von Baden's wine estate are also in the grounds.

To see the small wine museum, ask at the wine shop (Mon-Fri 0900-1800, Sat 0900-1300). The estate's wines are served at nearby Gasthof Schwanen (1130-1400, 1800-2130, closed Jan-Feb). Return to the lake via Mendlishausen. The lavishly furnished church at Birnau is one of the finest Baroque buildings in Germany.

Meersburg

This medieval town is best explored on foot. Walk up the Steigstrasse to Marktplatz in the upper part of town to see the historic houses, such as

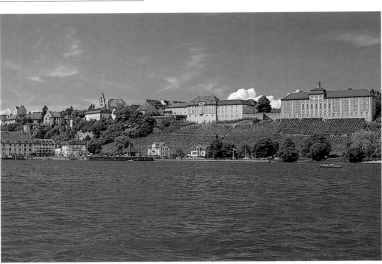

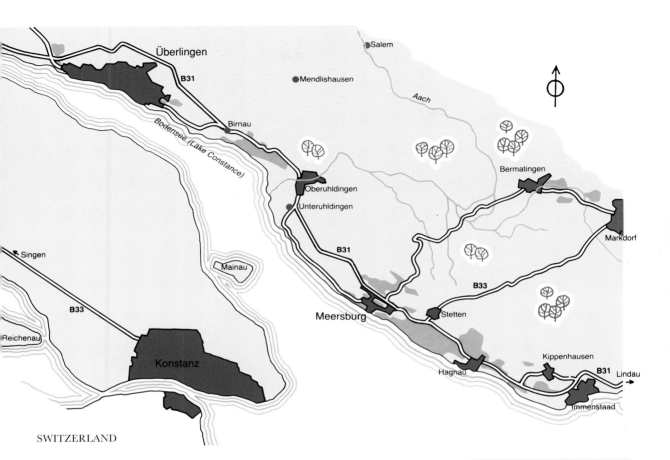

Weinstube Löwen and Hotel Bären (both are good places to sample wine). Also of interest are the dungeons and living quarters in the Altes (old) Schloss and the period rooms and stairway by Balthasar Neumann in the Neues (new) Schloss. The outdoor terrace of the café upstairs in the Altes Schloss offers a truly spectacular view of the Bodensee and the Alps.

The Staatsweingut, one of the oldest state-owned wine domains of Germany, is next door in the former riding stables of the palace (wine shop Mon-Fri 0730-1200, 1300-1800; May-Oct also Sat 0900-1300).

Hagnau to Lindau

Baden's first wine-growers' co-operative was founded in Hagnau in 1881. Hagnau, Kippenhausen and Immenstaad mark the end of Baden's vineyards along the lake. Further east, the landscape consists mostly of orchards and fields, although Württemberg claims a patch of vineyards near Kressbronn and Franken administers the three vineyards around Lindau. The lovely promenade of this island resort is a perfect place to enjoy a glass of Lindauer Seegarten while watching the boats sail in and out of the harbour.

MEERSBURG
Weinbau-Museum
(Museum of Viticulture) Vorburggasse 11. Easter to mid-Oct, 1400-1700 Tue, Fri, Sun. Historic casks, old press, coopers' workshop.
Haus der Guten Weine
Schützenstrasse 1. Mon-Fri 0800-1200, 1330-1800, Sat 0830-1200. Shop with vast selection of Baden and Bodensee wines.
Weinlehrpfad
In Meersburg: from near 'Wetterkreuz' at eastern edge of town, there is a vineyard path to Hagnau (5km / 3 miles), with superb views of the lake and the Alps. In Hagnau: vineyard path near Wilhelmshöhe.

Saale-Unstrut

The Herzoglicher Weinberg on the slopes below Freyburg's Neuenburg castle – today, a model vineyard to demonstrate the steep stairways, dry stone terraces and grape varieties typical of the region.

Vines have lined the slopes of the Saale and Unstrut river valleys for ten centuries. Today, Saale-Unstrut is Germany's northernmost wine-growing region, straddling the 51° of latitude between Leipzig and Weimar. It is a gentle landscape of hills ringed by forests, poplar groves and broad plateaus. Vineyards and orchards are scattered on the slopes, while corn and wheat fields dominate the flatter expanses. Much of the region lies within the Saale-Unstrut-Triasland nature park, a haven for rare fauna and flora (especially orchids, at Laucha-Krawinkel and Kleinjena-Toten Täler).

Freyburg, Naumburg and Bad Kösen are the main wine centres, but really to discover the region, travel on the *Weinstrasse* (wine road). It follows the Unstrut from Nebra to Grossjena, then continues westward along the banks of the Saale and the Ilm to Bad Sulza. Sections of the route are identical with the *Strasse der Romanik* (the Romanesque Road), with signposts to historical castles, monasteries and churches. The *Radwanderweg* (bicycle trail) along the rivers' banks, the *Wanderweg* (hiking trail) through the vineyards, as well as trips by boat and train are pleasant alternatives, particularly since many roads are being repaired and detours abound. Don't let this deter you, though – there are lots of friendly people to help show you the way.

No one really knows when viticulture was introduced into this eastern outpost of the Frankish kingdom, but vineyards were first documented in Emperor Otto III's deed of gift to the monastery in Memleben in AD 998.

The forests were *gerodet*, or cleared, (town names that end with *-roda* reflect this fact) and monasteries and churches were built throughout the region as it was colonized 'by the sword and by the plough'. Vineyards were necessary to ensure the supply of Communion wine. It was at the hand of the Cistercian monks, in particular, that viticulture thrived here. In 1137 they established a monastery near Bad Kösen and by 1153 had planted vines on the Köppelberg hill – an outstanding site to this day.

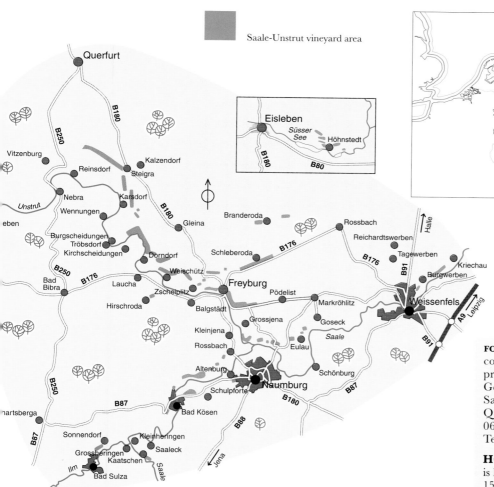

Saale-Unstrut vineyard area

By the mid-16th century, there were c.10,000 hectares (24,710 acres) of vineyards in greater Thuringia, including the vineyards of Saale-Unstrut. The centuries that followed were less auspicious for wine.

Wars, competition from imported wines and other beverages, as well as migration to better-paying jobs in the cities all contributed to the decline of viticulture that culminated with the arrival of the phylloxera (vine louse) here in 1887.

Much of the German research to combat the phylloxera was done in viticultural institutions in Naumburg. The regional co-operative (founded in 1934) and the State Wine Domain have helped keep the region's viticultural tradition alive.

Today, there are 447 hectares/ 1105 acres of vines, half of which are Müller-Thurgau, Silvaner and Weissburgunder. Small amounts of the white varieties Riesling, Kerner, Bacchus and Traminer, and the red grapes Portugieser, Dornfelder and Spätburgunder are also cultivated. Limestone and sandstone are the main soil types.

FOR FURTHER INFORMATION
contact the regional wine promotion board:
Gebietsweinwerbung Saale-Unstrut Querfurter Str. 10, 06632 Freyburg.
Tel/Fax: 034464/26110.

HÖHNSTEDT

is known for vines (c.60 ha/ 150 acres) and orchards. Drive north from Freyburg on B180 via Querfurt to Eisleben, where you can visit the houses where Martin Luther (1483-1546) was born and died: Seminarstr.16 and Andreaskirchplatz 7 (except Mon). Then drive east on B80 and turn left 3.5km/ 2 miles past Süsser See (lake).
Weingut Born
Wanslebener Str. 3. Tel: 034601/22930. Open daily 0800-2000.
Weingut Hoffmann
Wanslebener Str. 11. Tel: 034601/22932. Mon-Fri from 1600 and open all day Sat and Sun.

VITZENBURG
Schweizerhaus Am Weinberg 4. Tel: 034461/22562. Fax: 034461/24255. 1100-1400 (except Tue and Thu), 1700-2200 (except Thu). Terrace. Hotel.
Zum Unstrutblick Parkstr. 3. Tel: 034461/23891. 1030-2200 (except Thu). Terrace views. Hotel.

ZSCHEIPLITZ
Gasthaus Pretzsch Am Anger 6. Thu-Tue from 1130, Sat-Sun from 1030.

FREYBURG
Weingut Pawis Ehrauberge 12 (south of town, via Mühlstr.). From 1400 (except Tue). Cosy pub, vine-clad terrace.
Berghotel z. Edelacker Schloss 25 (adjacent to Neuenburg castle). Tel: 034464/350. Fax: 034464/35333. From 1130. Superb views. Terrace dining.
Hotel Unstruttal Markt 11. Tel: 034464/7070. Fax: 034464/70740. Daily from 1100. Historic house with a pretty courtyard.
Zum Künstlerkeller Breite Str. 14. Tel: 034464/70750. Fax: 034464/70799. Daily from 1100. Historic house and cellars. Hotel.

NAUMBURG
Hotel Stadt Aachen Markt 11. Tel: 03445/2470. Fax: 03445/247130. From 0700 daily. Historic house.
Zur Alten Schmiede Lindenring 36. Tel: 03445/24360. Fax: 03445/243666. 1700-2200 (except Sun). Charming hotel-restaurant.
Zum Alten Staats-gefängnis (the old prison) Mühlgasse 18. Tel: 03445/200940. Tue-Sun 1130-1400 and from 1800. Very cosy, historic restaurant.
Weingut Herbert Vökler Allmersstr. 3. Wine pub. May-Oct 1800-2200.

One of Germany's most successful brands of Sekt is Rotkäppchen (red capsule), trademarked in 1894.

The Unstrut valley
Memleben was the site of an imperial monastery and a *Pfalz* (palace) that was a favourite residence of King Heinrich and his Ottonian successors. A visit to the ruins, idyllically set in a garden, and the crypt, is a good place to start a journey on the *Weinstrasse*.

It zigzags across the Unstrut from Nebra, where the valley narrows and tall sandstone cliffs rise up from the water's edge, to Karsdorf, important for cement. The same chalky soils yield excellent wines. From Wennungen to Kirchscheidungen the *Weinstrasse* is nestled between the river and woods. The Hahnenberge vineyards line the slopes on the opposite bank, but are not always visible from the wine road.

Between Laucha and Dorndorf – with an interesting bell museum and a centre for hang-gliding – the road crosses the river again, skirting the vineyards as it winds to Freyburg.

Historical sites with views
Regal lions adorn the bridge you will cross at Nebra en route to Vitzenburg, where a detour uphill (via the B250,

Schloss Neuenburg (1090), the eastern bastion of the Landgraves of Thuringia. The castle is well worth a visit (1000-1700 except Mon).

then the first left turn) to the castle affords a fine view of the valley.

At Tröbsdorf, cross the Unstrut to Burgscheidungen. The Baroque palace and its Italian gardens, now in the hands of an absentee landlord, still exude an air of splendour and the view from the terrace is beautiful.

Zscheiplitz offers an impressive panorama of the Schweigenberge hills' terraced vineyards, extending as far as Freyburg and the Neuenburg castle. The 12th-century monastery church and Weissenburg castle ruins are worth seeing and on the path to the *Kalkbrennofen* (historic lime kiln) there are lovely views of the meadows and forests in the valley below.

From Zscheiplitz to Freyburg
Follow the road next to the river to the Eckstädter Turm, a tower that belongs to Freyburg's 13th-century fortifications. This town is the region's viticultural centre and the site of its largest wine festival (2nd weekend in

Sep). The Winzervereinigung (co-operative, open daily 0900-1800) and the Rotkäppchen sparkling winery's historic *Domkeller* with a 120,000-litre carved cask merit a visit (tours Mon-Sat 1000-1400, Sun 1000-1200). The beautiful altar and baptismal font in the St Marien Church (Sun 1330-1530), the Neuenburg castle and the Jahnmuseum, devoted to the 'father of gymnastics', are also of interest.

Blütengrund and Naumburg

Depart Freyburg via the Mühlstrasse and bear right at the fork in the road towards Grossjena, Blütengrund and the *Fähre* (ferry) at the confluence of the Unstrut and Saale rivers. Here you can see the monumental reliefs carved into the stone hillside (1722), historic villas and the studio where the artist Max Klinger worked – all set amidst the Sonneck site. You can also travel this pretty route on the boat 'Fröhliche Dörte' (two-hour round trip, Wed-Sun).

From here it is but minutes to Naumburg, famous for its cathedral with exquisite art treasures, such as the life-sized statues of its patrons. The town square and St Wenzel's Church are also striking in appearance.

A detour north-east of Naumburg will enable you to see the vineyards and historical buildings at Goseck, Weissenfels and Burgwerben that are not on the *Weinstrasse* – to which we now return via the Kleinjena bridge.

The Saale valley

From Kleinjena to Rossbach and the Saale crossing at Altenburg, the site Steinmeister is on the right, followed by a nearly uninterrupted succession of top sites (Saalhäuser and Schöne Aussicht) all the way to Bad Kösen. The wine road, however, crosses the

The Steinernes Bilderbuch (stone album) depicts wine-related Biblical motifs carved in stone at Grossjena.

Saale to enable you to visit Kloster Pforta, a Cistercian monastery from 1137 until it was converted in 1543 into a renowned state school, now called Schulpforte. Its Romanesque and Gothic buildings merit a visit.

You will pass by the Köppelberg site en route to Bad Kösen, a spa with thermal saline springs. Don't miss the remarkable collection of Käthe Kruse dolls in the history museum in the 12th-century Romanisches Haus (closed Mon). To visit the State Wine Domain, turn right after crossing the bridge in Bad Kösen and drive next to the Saale (ie backtrack) to Saalhäuser.

From Bad Kösen the *Weinstrasse* follows the Saale to Saaleck, where you can visit the romantic Rudelsburg (1171) and Saaleck (1050) castle ruins.

You can enjoy the trip to the castles by boat (allow two hours). The wine road continues along the Ilm river from Grossheringen, passing by the Sonnenberg site on the opposite heights, to its end at Bad Sulza.

FESTIVALS WITH WINE
Grossjena: mid-Jun.
Naumburg: late Aug.
Bad Kösen: Jun and Sep.

BAD KÖSEN
Landesweingut Kloster Pforta (State Wine Domain) Saalhäuser: wine pub from 1000. Wine festivals early May, late Sep. Schulpforte: sales shop 1000-1800.
Weingut Lützkendorf Saalberge 31 (near State Wine Domain). Wine pub daily from 1000. Terrace.
'Himmelreich' Bergstr. 46 (watch for right turn at Lengefeld, west of town). From 1100 May-Sep daily, Oct-Apr except Mon, Tue. Views of the castles.
Schöne Aussicht Ilskeweg 1 (across the bridge). Tel:034463/27367. Fax: 034463/27365. From 1100. Nice terrace. Hotel.
SONNENDORF **Sonnenburg** (watch for right turn after Unter-Neusulza but *before* the railway underpass). Tue-Fri from 1400, Sat and Sun from 1100. Great views.

Sachsen

S achsen, Germany's smallest and easternmost wine-growing region, is nestled in the Elbe river basin some 200km (125 miles) south-east of Berlin and 150km (95 miles) north-west of Prague. The *Sächsische Weinstrasse* (Saxon Wine Road), the *Elbe-Radweg* (bicycle path) and the *Weisse Flotte*, the world's oldest (1836) fleet of paddle-wheel steamboats, travel the length of the wine country as they follow the course of the river from Pirna, south of Dresden, to Diesbar-Seusslitz, north of Meissen.

Along this route, a mere 55km (34 miles), there is an extraordinary number of art and architectural treasures to admire, from historical fortresses to sumptuous palaces surrounded by elaborate parks or gardens. These were financed by revenues from Saxon's wine and the silver mined in the Erzgebirge (Ore Mountains), and from 1710, the 'white gold' produced in Meissen's renowned porcelain manufactory.

At present, the many roadworks and detours can make travel by car quite an adventure. However, your efforts to seek out Sachsen's vintners and restaurateurs will be rewarded with good wine, food and hospitality second to none. The warmth of their welcome is genuine.

FOR FURTHER INFORMATION contact the regional wine promotion board: Weinbauverband Sachsen Niederauerstr. 26/28, 01662 Meissen. Tel: 03521/763530. Fax: 03521/763540.

Pöppelmann designed both the Weinbergkirche (below) and the Baroque Schloss in Pillnitz.

Vines have been cultivated in the mild climate of the Elbtal (Elbe valley) since the 12th century. Here, as elsewhere in Europe, viticulture initially thrived under the Church and the aristocracy. Later, wealthy citizens bought vineyards and built as summer houses the little 'huts' that still dot the landscape.

Viticulture and wine-related jobs were vital to the region's economy. At the turn of the 19th century, Sachsen had more than 1600 hectares (c.4000 acres) of vines. However, competition from other beverages, severe weather, wars and two 'imports' from the USA (vine mildew and phylloxera, a vine louse) took their toll: by 1945 only 67 hectares (166 acres) remained.

Hobby vintners
Today, hobby vintners tend most of Sachsen's 350 hectares (865 acres) of vines and deliver their grapes to the regional co-operative in Meissen. The State Wine Domain in Radebeul is the region's other large producer.

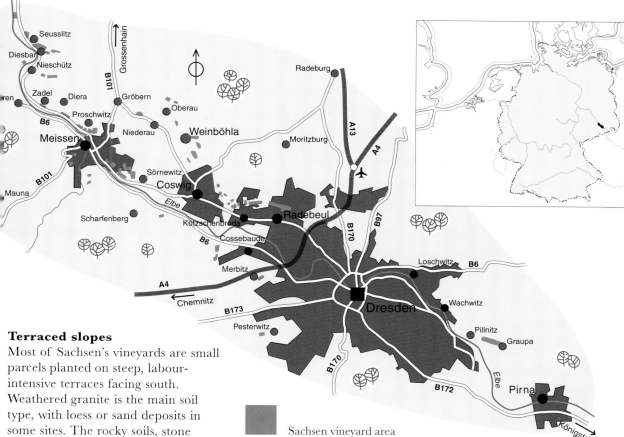

Sachsen vineyard area

Terraced slopes

Most of Sachsen's vineyards are small parcels planted on steep, labour-intensive terraces facing south. Weathered granite is the main soil type, with loess or sand deposits in some sites. The rocky soils, stone terraces and sun-reflecting surface of the Elbe all provide warmth, yet an early spring can be deadly: there can be frost as late as mid-May.

White grapes, eg Müller-Thurgau, Riesling, Weissburgunder, Ruländer and Kerner, predominate. Specialities include the spicy Traminer and the Riesling-Muscat crossing Goldriesling.

Spätburgunder and Portugieser are the main red varieties. *Schieler* is an old speciality dating from the days when red and white grapes were planted side by side in the vineyards, then pressed and fermented together to make a rosé-coloured wine (cf. *Schillerwein*, page 115).

Yields are quite low. Marketed as varietals, the wines are almost always dry in style with an agreeable acidity.

Sachsen – *einfach stark*

Sachsen's slogan, 'simply strong', is a reminder of the powerful Saxon dynasty (Germany's first kings and emperors were Saxons) and of one of its most illustrious rulers, August the Strong (1670-1733). Sachsen's superb art collections and Baroque buildings and gardens are his legacy. The sculptor Permoser, the architects Pöppelmann and Bähr, the organ builder Silbermann and Böttger, the inventor of porcelain, are all names you will encounter during your visit.

Other names you'll see here derive from Sachsen's 6th-century Slavic past, such as town names ending in 'a' (Pirna), 'en' (Meissen), 'itz' or 'witz' (Pillnitz, Seusslitz, Proschwitz).

ESPECIALLY RECOMMENDED
The 25 restaurants/hotels awarded this *Gütesiegel* (seal of quality) offer Saxon wine and food in a friendly atmosphere. They are also knowledgeable about the local wines and sights, and happy to be of assistance.

Hoflössnitz, where much of Sachsen's viticultural history was made. The Goldener Wagen site sweeps up the adjacent hillside to the Spitzhaus, accessible via the stairway designed by Pöppelmann in 1747.

DRESDEN

Wettiner Keller An der Frauenkirche 5 (Hilton Hotel). Tel: 0351/86420. Fax: 0351/8642725. Tue-Sat from 1800. Cosy cellar.

Hotel Pattis Merbitzer Str. 153 (from Altstadt via the B6 to the suburb of Merbitz). Tel: 0351/42550. Fax: 0351/4255255. Regional fare in **Erholung** 1100-1500 and 1800-2400. **Gourmet Restaurant** 1800-2400 (except Sun). Idyllic setting.

Hotel Schloss Eckberg Bautzner Str. 134. Tel: 0351/8042571. Fax: 0351/8045379. Daily 1100-2300. Closed Jan. Neo-Gothic castle in a riverside park. Great views. Pretty garden.

PIRNA

Hotel Deutsches Haus Niedere Burgstr. 1. Tel: 03501/443440. Fax: 03501/ 528104. Mon-Fri from 1600, Sat-Sun from 1500. Historic house with lovely garden courtyard.

Hotel Pirna'scher Hof Am Markt 4. Tel/Fax: 03501/44380. Restaurant daily from 0630, cellar pub Mon-Sat from 2000.

Dresden and the Elbhang

From an old Slavic fishing village Dresden evolved into a splendid city of art and culture, giving rise to the nickname 'Florence on the Elbe'. Wine revenues helped line the royal coffers and by 1500, vineyards were an integral part of the landscape between Dresden and Pillnitz, an area known as the Elbhang.

Today, hobby vintners have taken the initiative to restore some of Dresden's viticultural tradition. They have replanted the riverside terraces of two palatial mansions near Loschwitz as well as two parcels of the Königlicher Weinberg (royal vineyard) in Wachwitz and Pillnitz.

In Loschwitz, you can reach the heights for a good view via two venerable cable cars. Or, in Wachwitz, walk through the royal vineyard on the Panorma Weg and up the steep steps called the Himmelsleiter, the 'ladder to heaven'. Garden fans can visit the Rhododendrongarten nearby.

Pillnitz

From the Blaues Wunder, the blue suspension bridge at Loschwitz, it is a brief drive to Pillnitz via the *Sächsische Weinstrasse* (Pillnitzer Landstrasse). The street is the site of the *Elbhangfest*, a huge folk festival in late July. A more scenic option is to take an historic steamer from Dresden, arriving near the majestic stairway of Baroque Schloss Pillnitz (about two hours).

Pöppelmann designed the twin palaces with decorative chinoiserie for August the Strong in 1721. A 200-year-old camellia is but one of many rarities in the magnificent gardens (tours of the grounds daily, May-Oct).

Cross the road and walk past the historical press house (1827) to see another Pöppelmann gem (1725), the Weinbergkirche at the foot of the Königlicher Weinberg. Gilded grapes decorate its sandstone altar and there are concerts on Sundays (May-Oct).

Both the church and the vineyard were restored by local initiatives. A walk along the Leitenweg path at the top edge of the vineyard affords a good view. It begins behind the cosy restaurant Weinbergschänke (daily, from noon) via An der Schäferei.

Gateway to 'Saxon Switzerland'

The *Weinstrasse* loops through Graupa, where Wagner composed *Lohengrin* while convalescing in a farmhouse (now a museum, Tue-Sun 0900-1600), before resuming its riverside course to Pirna. Here, at the southern end of the *Weinstrasse*, vines are also being replanted. As you explore the market square and its side streets, look up to see the decorative gables, portals and oriels. The late Gothic St Marien Church is also worth seeing. Just minutes to the south the splendid scenery of 'Saxon Switzerland' begins.

The Lössnitz hills of Radebeul

Near the Dresden-Neustadt *Bahnhof* (train station) drive under the railway tracks to reach the *Weinstrasse* (Leipziger Strasse) and proceed to Radebeul. Turn right at Hoflössnitz Strasse and watch for the signs to Hoflössnitz, an historic wine estate. Research carried out here in the early 1900s was instrumental in reviving Saxon viticulture after the havoc wreaked by the vine louse.

In the wine museum you can actually see a vine louse (and wine-related items) as well as remarkable paintings on the walls and ceilings (exotic birds) in the rooms upstairs.

There are concerts, exhibitions, wine tastings and festivals at Hoflössnitz throughout the year.

Schloss Wackerbarth and its beautiful park (above) is the home of the Sächsisches Staats-Weingut (State Wine Domain) and the setting for many festivals and concerts. It was built in 1730 by Johann Knöffel.

Before visiting western Radebeul, don't miss the historic wine estates and villas on the Weinbergstrasse and the panorama from the Spitzhaus.

Steep vineyards rise up behind the historic houses on the Obere Berg-strasse. From the Volkssternwarte (planetarium) walk to the Jakobstein hut for a superb view of the Schloss Wackerbarth palace at the foot of the terraced vineyards, now the State Wine Domain (open daily 1000-1800).

Also recommended is the scenic path through the vineyards on Zechsteinweg (near Barkengasse).

RADEBEUL SIGHTS
Hoflössnitz Knohllweg 37. **Wine Museum** Tue-Fri 1400-1700, Sat and Sun 1000-1700 and the cosy wine pub **Schoppenstube** from 1400 (except Mon).
Karl-May-Museum Karl-May-Str. 5. Mar-Oct 0900-1800, Nov-Feb 1000-1600. Closed Mon. North American Indian artifacts and author's memorabilia.
Puppentheatersammlung Barkengasse 6 (in historic Hohenhaus). Tue-Fri 0900-1600. Also last Sun of the month 1000-1700 (with performances). Famous collection of marionettes.
'Lössnitzdackel' Historic narrow-gauge train between Radebeul Ost, Moritzburg and Radeburg.

WEINBÖHLA

Peterkeller Kirchplatz 19. Pub in the cellar (1794) of former wine estate that also houses the wine and history museum. Thu 1700-2200, Fri-Sat 1700-2400, Sun 1400-2000.

SÖRNEWITZ

Förster's Stammlokal Zaschendorfer Str. 15. Tel: 03523/73060. Fax: 03523/73071. Mon-Thu 1130-1400, 1700-2200. Fri only lunch. Sat-Sun from 1130. Farmstead from 1845, with courtyard and guest rooms.

Elbtalkellerei Meissen Wein-Café Dresdnerstr. 314. Tel/Fax: 0351/4411694. From 1500 (except Mon). Light fare served with estate's own wines. Guest rooms.

MEISSEN

Bauernhäus'l Oberspaarer Str. 20 (right bank of the Elbe). Tel: 03521/733317. Fax: 03521/738715. Tue-Sat 1200-1430. Daily (except Sun) from 1800. Very cosy, historical decor. Garden.

Domkeller Domplatz 9. Tel/Fax: 03521/457676. Daily from 1100. Closed Jan. Superb terrace views.

Meissner Burgstuben Freiheit 3. Tel/Fax: 03521/453685. Tue-Sun 1100-1800. Restaurant-café with estate's own wines. Terrace. Guest rooms.

Vincenz Richter An der Frauenkirche 12. Tel: 03521/453285. Fax: 03521/453763. Tue-Sat 1600-2300, Sun 1200-1800. Historic house (1573) with lovely courtyard.

Weingalerie (in the castle grounds) Apr-Dec, Wed-Sun 1100-1800. Wine shop of Schloss Proschwitz wine estate. Excellent selection from all of Sachsen.

Weinböhla and Schloss Moritzburg

From Radebeul the *Weinstrasse* (Meissner Strasse) follows the Elbe to Meissen, but there is a secondary route from Coswig that takes in the old wine towns of Weinböhla, Niederau and Gröbern. Their vineyards, all in the Gellertberg site, were renamed in honour of the 18th-century writer Gellert, a frequent visitor. By 1840, this was the largest continuous vineyard area of Sachsen. After the vine pest, however, the alluvial sandy soils were replanted with asparagus and orchards.

In Weinböhla there is a wine and history trail that starts at the town hall. After the walk, relax over a glass of local wine at the Peterkeller.

One other 'detour' is recommended – a visit to the palace at Moritzburg. It is 7km (4 miles) east of Weinböhla. Or, from the Radebeul Ost train station, you can enjoy a 30-minute ride on the 'Lössnitzdackel' train.

It is to August the Strong and his architect Pöppelmann that the palace owes its Baroque appearance and majestic lake setting. The splendid furnishings and impressive collection of hunting trophies are well worth a visit (May-Oct 1000-1700, Nov-Apr closed Mon).

Given their passion for hunting, it is not surprising that the Saxon rulers set up a stud farm here. You can see the horses with riders in period costumes at the festive *Hengstparaden* (stallion parades) in September.

The Spaar Hills

The slopes of the *Spaargebirge* between Sörnewitz and Meissen boast not only the excellent vineyard sites of Kapitelberg and Rosengründchen, but also very scenic hiking trails. Old vineyard walls and the remains of historic wine estates share the landscape with the woods and vines. Ascend the heights to the Boselgarten, a botanical garden, and the vantage points Boselspitze, Juchhöh and Karlshöhe. These afford great views of Old Meissen and, on a clear day, as far south as 'Saxon Switzerland'.

Meissen – on the right bank

In Meissen the *Weinstrasse* (Dresdner Strasse from Coswig) runs under the railway tracks left of the train station, then turns right into the B101 (Grossenhainer Strasse).

To visit the *Winzergenossenschaft*, the regional co-operative and Sachsen's largest producer, follow the B101 to the left turning into the Bennoweg.

The co-op was founded in 1938, but its philosophical origins date from 1799 and 1811, when the first private viticultural society and a school for wine-growers were founded here – the first of their kind in Europe.

Today, the co-op's 2500 members cultivate one third of the region's vineyards and offer a comprehensive selection of wines. To sample them, visit the shop (Mon-Fri 0930-1745, Sat 0930-1300) or the wine restaurant 'Probierstube' (open daily from 1700) in the grounds at Bennoweg 9. Here, Sachsen specialities are served on Meissen porcelain with the green vine-leaf pattern.

The co-op's other shop, the Küfertheke, is on the market square (no.10) in the Old Town (open daily 1000-1800).

Historical Meissen

Cross the Elbe on the B101 and park on the river bank to visit Old Meissen, founded in 929, when the Saxon Duke Heinrich, Germany's first king, built a fortress on the Burgberg (castle hill) as a defence against the Slavs.

The Albrechtsburg castle is its successor. From the second-storey windows of the north wing you can see a vineyard in the Meisa valley, where viticulture in Sachsen was first documented in 1161. The castle was never used as a residence, but from 1710 to 1864 it housed Europe's first porcelain manufactory. The interior vaulting, paintings and draped-arch windows are remarkable (open daily from 1000, except Jan).

The other magnificent Gothic structure on the Burgberg is the cathedral, whose origins date from 968, when Heinrich's son Otto, the first German emperor, made Meissen a diocese (open daily from 0900).

Gems of 'white gold'

Descend the Burgberg via the steps to the Burgstrasse to the market square. It is ringed by an ensemble of beautiful Renaissance houses, the town hall and the Frauenkirche, with a 37-bell porcelain Glockenspiel.

From here it is a brief walk along the Triebisch river to the porcelain manufactory at Talstrasse 9. Here you can admire three centuries of art treasures in the Schauhalle (museum) and see the artists at work in the Schauwerkstatt (display workshop). There is also a shop in the grounds (all are open daily 0900-1700).

Nearby, in a small memorial church, the Nikolaikirche, the unique porcelain furnishings (2.5m [8ft] high figures) are worth seeing (May-Sep, Tue-Thu and Sun 1400-1600).

From Meissen to Seusslitz

Opposite Old Meissen the *Weinstrasse* (Hafenstrasse/Elbtalstrasse) skirts the Bocksberg, a granite outcrop with the Schloss Proschwitz site on the heights, and the terraced Katzensprung site below. The Katzenstufen (200 steps) rise to scenic views from the heights.

Where the Elbe bends at Nieschütz the dramatic cliffs of Diesbar-Seusslitz come into view. There is a pleasant walk through the Heinrichsburg site, starting either at Diesbar or at the Schlosspark in Seusslitz. You can enjoy the local hospitality at concerts and festivals in the grounds of the palace or at the family wine estates on the *Weinstrasse* (Meissner Strasse). Or cross the Elbe (ferry) for a glass of wine at the Elbklause for a splendid view of this idyllic landscape.

DIESBAR-SEUSSLITZ
Merkers Weinstuben Meissner Str. 10. Tel: 035267/50780. Fax: 035267/50317. Tue-Thu 1700-2200, Fri-Sun 1100-2200. Wine estate, gourmet fare. Terrace. Guest rooms.
Rosengarten Meissner Str. 4. Tue-Sun from 1100. Wine estate's restaurant. Terrace and garden.
Lehmann's Seusslitzer Weinstuben Weinstr. 26. Tel: 035267/50236. Mon-Fri from 1700 (except Thu), Sat-Sun from 1200. Wine estate. Cosy pub, lovely garden. Guest rooms.
Seusslitzer Hof Weinstr. 15. Wed-Mon from 1100. Wine estate's restaurant.

The Baroque palace and church at Seusslitz designed by George Bähr.

Summary of Appellation of Origin

THE THIRTEEN *QUALITÄTSWEIN* REGIONS	GERMAN QUALITY WINES (*Qualitätswein b.A.*)	*increasingly individual character*	EXAMPLE:
Ahr	**13 wine-growing regions** (*bestimmtes Anbaugebiet* [**b.A**])divided into:		**Mosel-Saar-Ruwer**
Baden			
Franken	**c.40 districts** (*Bereich*) divided into approximately:		**Bereich Bernkastel**
Hessische Bergstrasse			
Mittelrhein			
Mosel-Saar-Ruwer	**160 collective vineyard sites** (*Grosslagen*) divided into approximately:		**Bernkasteler* Badstube**
Nahe			
Pfalz	**2650 individual vineyard sites** (*Einzellagen*)		**Bernkasteler* Graben**
Rheingau			
Rheinhessen			
Saale-Unstrut			
Sachsen			
Württemberg			

* The name of individual and collective vineyard sites is usually preceded by the name of a village + 'er'.

BEREICH (District)

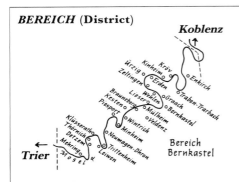

Bereich

A *Bereich* includes the collective and individual vineyards of many wine-growing villages. It usually takes its name from the best-known village (eg **Bereich Bernkastel**).

GROSSLAGE / EINZELLAGE (Collective / Individual Vineyard Site)

***** boundary of collective vineyard site (*Grosslage*) **Badstube**

Bratenhöfchen
Doctor
Lay
Matheis-Bildchen
Graben
Alte Badstube am Doctorberg*

} individual vineyard sites (*Einzellagen*) within **Badstube**

Grosslage / Einzellage

A *Grosslage* is a collection of *Einzellagen* (individual vineyard sites) which have similar soils and microclimates and therefore yield wines of a similar character. Some sites consistently yield riper, richer wine than others, due to a favourable microclimate, location, exposure and soil structure (eg **Bernkasteler Doctor**).

The boundaries between appellations of origin are determined by climatic and geological factors which differ from region to region and within an individual region. These differences are reflected in the character of the wine. For example, a Riesling *Kabinett* from the steep slaty soils of a northerly region, such as the Mosel-Saar-Ruwer, is likely to be lighter and more delicate than a Riesling *Kabinett* from gentler slopes of loam and sand of a more southerly region, such as the Pfalz. The latter is likely to be fuller in bouquet, body and flavour.

In general, the more narrowly defined the appellation of origin, the more distinctive the character and taste of the wine. However, small vineyards yield limited quantities of wine and most of Germany's 2650 vineyard names are known only locally. For marketing purposes it often makes sense for a producer to label wine with a broader appellation which is better known and can ensure a greater continuity of supply.

The interplay of natural factors and the grower's attitude to quality determine a wine's character.

Summary of Quality Categories

There are two broad quality categories for wine produced in the European Union: table wine and quality wine. A wine's classification is based on several factors, including appellation of origin and the amount of natural sugar in the grapes at harvest. The second determines the wine's potential alcoholic content.

Germany's wine country consists of nearly 105,000 hectares (260,000 acres) of vineyards. This area is divided into five broad table wine regions which serve as appellations of origin for German table wine. This same area is also divided into 13 more narrowly defined regions which serve as the appellations of origin for German quality wine.

An important difference between Germany and France, for example, is that every German vineyard can produce either table or quality wine. There are no vineyards reserved for one or other category as in France. A German wine's classification depends primarily on the ripeness of the grapes (natural sugar) at harvest. Riper grapes yield more concentrated wines.

If the grapes ripen sufficiently to produce a quality wine, then other factors come into play. The grapes must all come from one of the 13 specified regions, for example, and the wine must pass official analytical and sensoric tests. Approval is signified on the label by the quality control test number (A.P. Nr.). About 95 per cent of an annual German harvest falls into the quality wine category.

If the grapes only ripen enough to produce a table wine, then the grapes may come from one of the five broad table wine regions. Table wines are exempted from the official quality control tests. Most German table wine is consumed locally.

Quality categories

The terms used to indicate increasing levels of ripeness at harvest are:

Table wine
Made from normally ripe grapes.
Deutscher Tafelwein is equivalent to French *Vin de Table*.
Deutscher Landwein is equivalent to French *Vin de Pays*.

Quality wine
Made from ripe, very ripe, or overripe grapes, selectively harvested:
Qualitätswein b.A. (QbA) quality wine from one of the 13 specified regions, made from ripe grapes; everyday wines to enjoy with or without meals (equivalent to French A.C. wines).
Qualitätswein mit Prädikat (QmP) quality wine with special attributes from one district (*Bereich*) within one of the 13 regions. Made from riper, very ripe and overripe grapes; superior wines to drink with or without meals and on special occasions (equivalent to French A.C.+*cru*).
Kabinett fully ripe grapes; the lightest of the *Prädikat* wines; good with most foods.
Spätlese riper, late-harvested grapes; richer in body and taste; *trocken* or *halbtrocken* styles go well with many dishes; the classic style (with slight sweetness) harmonizes well with richer foods.
Auslese very ripe grapes selected bunch by bunch; rich, noble wines with more intense bouquet and flavour.
Beerenauslese very ripe, individually selected berries; luscious rarity with ripe, natural sweetness.
Eiswein very ripe grapes harvested and pressed while still frozen; wines with intense sweetness and acidity.
Trockenbeerenauslese overripe individually selected berries, often dried up (*trocken*) by a fungus which imparts a honeyed tone to the wine; extremely rich, nectar-like rarity.

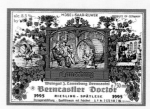

Region Mosel-Saar-Ruwer
Village Berncastel
Vineyard site Doctor
Grape variety Riesling
Ripeness *Spätlese*
Style not mentioned
Note: traditional spellings of Bernkastel and Doktor use a 'c' rather than a 'k'.

143

Grape Varieties

There were grapevines on earth long before people – as long as 130 million years ago – and the descendants of ancient wild vines still entwine trees in a few places on the upper Rhine. The Romans introduced the systematic planting of vines (viticulture) in Germany shortly before the birth of Christ.

By the Middle Ages, vineyards stretched as far north as Denmark, and red grape varieties predominated. Today, about 50 grape varieties (of the nearly 8000 in existence) are cultivated in Germany (80 per cent white, 20 per cent red), roughly between Bonn and the Bodensee.

Viticulture is highly regulated. Vineyards are permitted only on sites where grapes are likely to ripen sufficiently to yield quality wines. Furthermore, only approved varieties are allowed and the list varies from region to region. Except for a few experimental plots (registered with the authorities) the cultivation of Cabernet Sauvignon, for example, is illegal.

Scientific research has contributed greatly to the high quality of German wine. Through clonal selection and breeding, scientists try to develop grapes which are more resistant to frost, disease and pests; ripen earlier; and achieve a higher sugar content and/or greater yields without compromising quality.

It takes 15-20 years of carefully monitored growth to decide whether a new crossing can be added to the list of approved varieties.

There has been a gradual increase in the number of Riesling vines and red grape varieties. No changes occur overnight, however, for newly-planted vines first bear fruit suitable for wine after three years. Most vineyards are replanted every 25-30 years.

CLASSIC WHITE VARIETIES

Elbling possibly pre-dates the Romans in Germany. It is an early-ripening, prolific variety grown primarily on the upper Mosel near Luxembourg. Elbling yields light, neutral wines with a high acidity. It is well-suited for making *Sekt*.

Grauburgunder yields wines with a mild acidity and a distinctive bouquet. It denotes a more food-compatible, sleeker and drier style wine than its synonym **Ruländer**, which is used for richer, fuller-bodied and more fragrant wines. (Synonyms: Pinot Gris or Pinot Grigio, Tokay d'Alsace, Malvoisie.)

Gutedel is an ancient variety grown in the Markgräflerland of Baden and in Sachsen. Low in acidity, Gutedel yields light, pleasant quaffing wines. (Synonyms: Chasselas, Fendant.)

Müller-Thurgau, or **Rivaner**, is a crossing of Riesling and Gutedel developed by Dr Müller (from the Swiss canton of Thurgau) in 1882 at Geisenheim. A prolific variety which ripens early (September) it is very widely planted in Germany. The wines are milder in acidity than Riesling and have a flowery bouquet and light muscat flavour. They are best consumed while young and fresh.

Riesling produces Germany's finest wines. Late to ripen (October-November) it yields a small quantity of high-quality wine with a pronounced acidity that gives wines piquancy, structure and ageing potential. The bouquet is fruity but not obtrusive. When young, the wines can be austere; with maturity, the bouquet and flavour develop fine nuances and complexity. Riesling harmonizes well with food.

Silvaner, once the predominant grape of Germany, is traditional in Franken, Rheinhessen and Saale-Unstrut. The wines are full-bodied, neutral and mild.

Vinified dry, Silvaner is excellent with meals. The wines often mature early.

Traminer is prized for its spicy bouquet, often compared to roses, and flavour. A shy bearer, it is grown as a speciality, in Baden, the Pfalz, Saale-Unstrut and Sachsen. (Synonyms: Clevner [in Baden], Gewürztraminer.)

Weissburgunder, grown primarily in Baden, the Pfalz, Saale-Unstrut and Sachsen, produces neutral wines with more acidity than Grauburgunder. It is well-suited to making dry wines. (Synonym: Pinot Blanc.)

NEW WHITE VARIETIES

Bacchus, a crossing of (Silvaner x Riesling) x Müller-Thurgau, is the Latin name of Dionysos, the Greek God of Wine. The wines are fragrant, with a light muscat flavour.

Faberrebe is a crossing of Weissburgunder and Müller-Thurgau. The wines are classical in character, ie not too exotic, with a lively acidity and a light muscat tone.

Huxelrebe, a crossing of Gutedel and Courtillier musqué, yields elegant wines with good acidity and a delicate muscat tone. It usually yields very ripe wines, often peachy in bouquet and flavour.

Kerner, a crossing of the red variety Trollinger with Riesling, is named after the poet and physician Justinus Kerner. The wines are similar to Riesling, with a fresh, racy acidity, but a more pronounced bouquet.

Morio-Muskat, a crossing of Silvaner and Weissburgunder, is named after its breeder, Peter Morio. This very prolific, perfumed variety is often used to add spice to blends.

Ortega, a crossing of Müller-Thurgau and Siegerrebe, is an early-ripening variety which nearly always yields *Auslese*-type (very ripe) wines with a peachy bouquet and a long aftertaste.

Scheurebe, a crossing of Silvaner and Riesling, is named after Georg Scheu (pronounced 'Shoy'), a grape breeder whose research in the 1920s produced many of Germany's new crossings. Rich in acidity, the wines have a distinctive bouquet and flavour reminiscent of blackcurrants. Riper or mature Scheu has a delicate spiciness. It is delicious with blue cheese.

CLASSIC RED VARIETIES

Lemberger is a speciality of Württemberg. The wines are fresh, racy and full-bodied. (Synonyms: Limberger, Blaufränkisch.)

Müllerrebe, a mutation of Spätburgunder, ripens earlier but generally does not achieve the same quality. Württemberg has the most plantings. (Synonyms: Schwarzriesling, Pinot Meunier.)

Portugieser, an old and prolific variety, yields light, mild quaffing wines. It probably originated in the Danube valley, not in Portugal.

Spätburgunder is the great Burgundy grape that produces the finest red wines in Germany. The wines are velvety and full-bodied with a bouquet reminiscent of blackberries. Its fruity, rather than tannic, acidity is typical of most German red wines. (Synonym: Pinot Noir.)

Trollinger is a speciality of Württemberg. Late to ripen, it yields high quantities of light, fragrant wine with a pronounced acidity.

NEW RED VARIETY

Dornfelder is a new crossing (1955) that yields deep red, full-bodied wines with a rich black cherry fragrance and a fairly tannic acidity.

Pronunciation Guide and Glossary

THE THIRTEEN WINE REGIONS

Ahr
(*Are*)
Baden
(*Bah*-d'n)
Franken
(*Frahn*-k'n)
Hessische Bergstrasse
(*Hess*-iss-sheh *Bearg*-shtrah-sseh)
Mittelrhein
(*Mit*-tel-rhine)
Mosel-Saar-Ruwer
(*Mo*-z'l *Czar Roo*-vair)
Nahe
(*Nah*-heh)
Pfalz
(*Pfaults*)
Rheingau
(*Rhine*-gow)
Rheinhessen
(Rhine-*hess*-en)
Saale-Unstrut
(*Zah*-leh *Oon*-stroot)
Sachsen
(*Zahk*-ss'n)
Württemberg
(*Vyurt*-tem-bearg)

QUALITY CATEGORIES

(in ascending order of the
ripeness of the grapes at harvest)
Tafelwein
(*Tah*-fel-vine)
Landwein
(*Lahnt*-vine)
Qualitätswein bestimmter
Anbaugebiete, or QbA
(Kvah-lee-*tayts*-vine be-*shtimmt*-
air *ahn*-bough-geh-beet-eh)
Qualitätswein mit
Prädikat, or QmP
(Kvah-lee-*tayts*-vine mit *Pray*-
dee-kaht)
*Kabinett
(Kah-bee-*net*)
*Spätlese
(*Shpate*-lay-zeh)
*Auslese
(*Ouse*-lay-zeh)
*Beerenauslese
(*Bear*'n-ouse-lay-zeh)
*Eiswein
(*Ice*-vine)
*Trockenbeerenauslese
(*Traw*-k'n *bear*'n ouse-lay-zeh)

GERMAN PRONUNCIATION

During your visit to Germany's wine country, particularly to some of the more remote villages, the guidelines below may help communication.

* Look at the parts rather than the whole of long, compound words, eg
  Trocken / beeren / auslese
dried (up)/berries/selective harvest.

* There is no silent 'e' in German; it is pronounced roughly as 'eh' or 'uh'. *Probe* (tasting) does not rhyme with 'robe'; it has two syllables – '*pro*-beh'.

* In the pronunciation guidelines that follow, 'oo' rhymes with 'moon'.

German	Approximate English equivalent
b (at end of syllable)	= p
ch (at end of syllable)	= Lo*ch* Ness
d (at end of syllable)	= t
j	= y
s (before a vowel)	= z
sch	= sh
sp	= shp
st	= sht
v	= f
w	= v
z	= stree*ts*
ä (ae)	= l*a*te
äu (aeu)	= b*oy*
au	= h*ou*se, h*ow*
ei	= *eye* (long 'i')
eu	= b*oy*
ie	= *ee* (long 'e')
ö (oe)	= *er*
ü (ue)	= m*ew*, y*ou*

Note: See pages 142-145 for definitions of appellations of origin, quality categories and grape varieties.

GLOSSARY OF GERMAN WINE TERMS

Abfüller (*Op*-fuel-air) bottler.
Amtliche Prüfungsnummer (*Ahmt*-lich-eh *Prew*-foongs-*noom*-mair) quality control test number, signifying that a wine has passed official analytical and sensoric tests. Not a prize, but rather it indicates that at least minimum standards have been met. Abbreviated 'A.P.Nr.'
Anbaugebiet (*Ahn*-bough-geh-beet) one of 13 specified wine-growing regions in Germany. (See page 142.)
Bad (*Bahd / t*) a spa, eg Baden-Baden, Bad Kreuznach, Wiesbaden.
Bereich (Beh-*rike*) one of c.40 districts. (See page 142.)
Berg (*Bearg*) hill or mountain.
Bocksbeutel (*Bawks*-boyt'l) flagon-shaped bottle used for quality wines of Franken and a few parts of northern Baden.
Burg (*Boorg*) fortress.
Deutsche Landwirtschaft Gesellschaft or **DLG** (*Doytch*-eh *Lahnt*-veert-shahft Geh-*zell*-shahft) German Agricultural Society that awards prizes and seals for outstanding wines and organizes an annual national wine competition. The prize-winning wines and producers are named in a catalogue available from the German Wine Institute.
Deutsche Weinstrasse (*Doytch*-eh *Vine*-shtrah-sseh) German Wine Road. It runs the length of the Pfalz region, from Bockenheim to the French border.
Edelfäule (*Aid'l*-foy-leh) noble rot or *Botrytis cinerea*, a fungus that pierces the skins of ripe grapes, thereby causing the water content to evaporate and the grapes to shrivel. The concentrated acids and sugars that remain yield luscious dessert wines, eg *Beeren*- and *Trockenbeerenauslese*. *Edelfäule* imparts a honeyed tone to the wine.

Einzellage (*Ine*-ts'l-lah-geh) one of the approximately 2650 individual vineyard sites. (See page 142.)

Erzeugerabfüllung (Air-*tsoy*-gair-*op*-fuel-loong) producer-bottled, ie the grapes were grown and the wine was produced and bottled by one individual or a collective of individuals.

Federweisser (*Fay*-dair-vice-air) milky coloured, nearly fermented grape juice available for only a few weeks during the harvest in autumn. Since most of the natural sugar has been converted to alcohol and CO_2, it has a pleasant tang. It is often served with *Zwiebelkuchen* (onion quiche).

Grosslage (*Gross*-lah-geh) one of the approximately 160 collective vineyard sites. (See page 142.)

Gutsabfüllung (*Goots*-ob-fuel-loong) estate-bottled, a term referring to an individual grower or estate. Same as *mis en bouteille au Château*.

Halbtrocken (*Hahlp*-traw-k'n) medium dry style. (See page 143.)

Keller (*Kell*-lair) cellar.

Kelter (*Kell*-tair) wine press.

Lese (*Lay*-zeh) harvest. Harvest dates vary according to grape variety and weather conditions. Müller-Thurgau, an early-ripening variety, is usually harvested in mid or late September; the later-ripening Riesling about three weeks later. The grower can risk leaving the grapes on the vine longer to achieve higher levels of ripeness. *Spätlese* is a 'late' harvest, ie the fully ripened grapes are picked days or even weeks later than those picked during the normal harvest. *Auslese* is a 'selective' harvest, which can take place at any time (ie normal or late harvest), depending on the grapes' ripeness.

Oechsle (*Erx*-leh) scale developed in the 19th century by Ferdinand Oechsle to measure how much sugar has developed in a grape (an indication of ripeness) by comparing the specific gravity of grape juice to that of water. The weight of the grape juice, or must, is expressed in degrees Oechsle. Every quality category is based on Oechsle levels that are specified according to grape variety and wine region.

Prädikat (*Pray*-dee-kaht) special attribute that indicates the ripeness of grapes at harvest. There are six Prädikats, from *Kabinett* to *Trockenbeerenauslese*. These descriptive terms reflect facts of nature, whereas the terms indicating degree of dryness (*trocken, halbtrocken*) reflect the winemaker's style. (See page 143.)

Schloss (*Schlaws*) castle or palace.

Sekt (*Zeckt*) sparkling wine. (*Sekt b.A.* is made entirely from German grapes.)

Strausswirtschaft (*Shtrouss*-veert-shahft) wine pub in a grower's home, where for four months of the year he can sell his own wines (no others) and light food or snacks. Look for a *Strauss* (wreath) hung over the door, or, in Württemberg, a *Besen* (broom).

Trocken (*Traw*-k'n) dry style. (See page 143.)

Weinbaulehrpfad (*Vine*-bough-lair-pfaht) educational path through the vineyards, signposted with information about growing conditions, grape varieties, work in the vineyards, etc.

Weingut (*Vine*-goot) wine estate.

Weinkellerei (*Vine*-kell-lair-eye) winery that buys grape must (to make wine) or wine from a grower, and then bottles and markets the wine.

Winzer (*Vin*-tsair) grape farmer.

Winzerfest (*Vin*-tsair-fest) wine festival. The German Wine Institute publishes a calendar of them annually.

Winzergenossenschaft (*Vin*-tsair-geh-*naws*-sen-shahft) co-operative of grape farmers who deliver their grapes to a winery that will make, bottle and market the wine.

WHITE GRAPE VARIETIES

Bacchus (*Bah*-koos)

Elbling (*Elb*-ling)

Faber (*Fah*-bear)

Grauburgunder (*Grow*[how]-boor-goon-dair)

Gutedel (*Goot*-aid'l)

Huxel (*Hoox*'l)

Kerner (*Kair*-nair)

Morio-Muskat (*Mo*-ree-oh Moose-*kaht*)

Müller-Thurgau (*Mew*-lair *Toor*-gow)

Ortega (Or-*tay*-geh)

Riesling (*Reez*-ling)

Ruländer (*Roo*-len-dair)

Scheurebe (*Shoy*-ray-beh)

Silvaner (Zill-*vah*-nair)

Traminer (Trah-*mee*-nair)

Weissburgunder (*Vice*-boor-goon-dair)

RED GRAPE VARIETIES

Dornfelder (*Dorn*-fell-dair)

Lemberger (*Lem*-bear-gair)

Portugieser (Por-tyou-*gee*[hard 'g']-zair)

Spätburgunder (*Shpate*-boor-goon-dair)

Trollinger (*Trawl*-ling-air)

WINE TYPES

Weisswein (*Vice*-vine): white wine

Rotwein (*Wrote*-vine): red wine

Weissherbst (*Vice*-hairpst): rosé wine

Sekt (*Zeckt*): sparkling wine

Further Information

WHERE TO WRITE OR CALL

Canada
German Wine Information Service, 160 Bloor Street East. Suite 500, Toronto, Ontario M4W 1B9.
Tel: (416) 964-8014.
Fax: (416) 964-6611.

Germany
German Wine Institute, Gutenbergplatz 3-5, 55116 Mainz.
Tel: (49) 6131/28290.
Fax: (49) 6131/282950.

UK
German Wine Information Service, Lane House, 24 Parson's Green Lane, London SW6 4HS.
Tel: 0171-331 8800.
Fax: 0171-331 1970.

USA
German Wine Information Bureau, 245 Fifth Avenue, Suite 2204, New York, NY 10016. Tel: (212) 896-3336.
Fax: (212) 896-3342.

PUBLIC HOLIDAYS

1 Jan, Good Friday, Easter Monday, 1 May (Labour Day), Ascension Day, Whit Monday, 3 Oct (Unity Day), 25-26 December. (Check locally about other, regional holidays.)

OPENING HOURS

Shops are permitted to be open Mon-Fri 0600-2000 and Sat 0600-1600. In small towns, many close for lunch (1300-1500). Shops at train stations are open Sun and after hours. Most museums close Mondays.

THE GERMAN WINE INSTITUTE

The **Deutsches Weininstitut** in Mainz is the generic promotion board for German wine. The Institute and its information services around the world distribute educational brochures, books, maps, posters, calendars of events, video-cassettes and slide shows – all of which can help you plan your visit to German wine country.

Check with the organizations listed to the left to clarify any fees for postage and/or the cost of the materials.

What's available

• *Deutsche Winzerfeste/German Wine Festivals* A calendar of more than 500 festivals, listed region by region. (Note for U.S. readers: the day precedes the month, eg 10.09 is 10 Sep, not 9 Oct.)
• *Vintners to Visit* Guides with maps and charts to help you find visitor-friendly wine estates and vintner-operated restaurants, pubs and accommodation. (When ordering, be sure to mention which region[s] you'll be visiting.)
• *DLG Preisträger-Verzeichnis* Annual catalogue of award-winning wines, wine estates and co-ops in Germany's national wine competition, plus addresses and phone numbers.
• *German Wines – A Correspondence Course* Home study course (with a certificate for successful completion of the exam).
• *The Wines of Germany* Full-colour atlas of the wine regions, including road and vineyard maps.

THE ASSOCIATION OF *PRÄDIKAT* WINE ESTATES – VDP

This group of quality-oriented estates sponsors auctions, tastings and events. For a list of the members' names and addresses and an events calendar, contact: VDP, Schloss Wallhausen, 55595 Wallhausen. Tel: (49) 6706/944411. Fax: (49) 6706/944424.

SAMPLE LETTER T0 A GROWER

[Sender's name, address, telephone and fax numbers and the date.]

Sehr geehrte Damen und Herren,

ich habe in *A Traveller's Wine Guide to Germany* über Ihr Weingut gelesen und würde es gerne kennenlernen. Wäre Ihnen mein Besuch am [date] um [time] angenehm?

Ich reise allein/Ich reise nicht allein. Wir würden gerne mit insgesamt [total number in party] Personen kommen. *(Delete where not applicable.)*

Bitte benachrichtigen Sie mich kurz per Brief, Fax oder Telefon, wenn mein Terminvorschlag ungünstig für Sie liegt. Herzlichen Dank für Ihre Bemühungen im voraus.

Mit freundlichen Grüssen
[signature]

Dear Madam/Sir,

I have read about your wine estate in *A Traveller's Wine Guide to Germany* and would like to visit it. Would a visit on [date] at [time] be convenient?

I will be travelling alone/I will not be travelling alone. We are a party of [number] persons in all. *(Delete where not applicable.)*

If the suggested date and/or time are not convenient, would you please be so kind as to notify me by letter, fax or telephone? Thank you very much for your help.

Yours sincerely,
[signature]

Index

Page references in *italic* type
indicate illustrations.

Abtswind, 102
Achkarren, 126, 127
Affentaler wines, 122
Ahr, 16-19
Ahrweiler, 16, 17, 18
Albersweiler, 88
Albrechtsburg castle, 141
Alf, 35
Alken, 33
Alsenz, river, 47
Alsheim, 73
Alsterweiler, 87
Altenahr, 16, 17, 18, 19, *19*
Altenbamberg, 47
Altenburg, 135
Altleiningen, 80
Alzey, 75, *75*
Amorbach, 98
Angelbachtal, 120
Annweiler, 88
Arenfels, Schloss, *23*, 24
Armsheim, 77
Aschaffenburg, 98
Asperg, 110
Assmannshausen, 66, *66*
Auen, 50
Auerbach, 91, 92
Auggen, 129
Auslese, 55, 143
Autobahn, 15
Auxerrois grape, 31, 120
Ayl, 42, 43

Bacchus grape, 46, 94, 133, 145
Bacharach, 26, *26-7*, 28, 29, 67
Bachem, 18
Bad Bellingen, 128, 129
Bad Bergzabern, 89
Bad Bertrich, 35
Bad Breisig, 24
Bad Cannstatt, 108
Bad Dürkheim, 81, 82, *82*, 84
Bad Ems, 29
Bad Honnef, 24
Bad Hönningen, *23*, 24
Bad Kösen, 132, 135
Bad Kreuznach, 44, 46, *46-7*, 49, 53
Bad Krozingen, 128
Bad Mergentheim, 99
Bad Münster am Stein, 48, *48*, 53
Bad Neuenahr, 16, 17, 18
Bad Schwalbach, 67
Bad Sobernheim, 49, 50
Bad Sulza, 132, 135

Bad Wimpfen am Berg, 119
Baden, 90, 92, 98, 116-29
Baden-Baden, 116, 122, *122*
Badenweiler, 129, *129*
Badisch Rotgold, 124
Badische Bergstrasse, 92
Bahlingen, 127
Basel, 128
Bechtheim, 75
Beckstein, 99
Beerenauslese, 143
Beilstein (Mosel), 34, *34*
Beilstein (Württemberg), 110
Bendorf, 23
Bensheim, 90, *90*, 92, 93
Bereich, 142
Bergstrasse, 90-3
Bermersheim, 75
Bernkastel-Kues, 30, 34, 37, *37*, 37-8
Besenwirtschaft, 106; *see also* *Strausswirtschaft*
Besigheim, 106, 110
Beutelsbach, 114
Bickensohl, 126
Biebelried, 100, 101
Biebrich, 57
Bietigheim-Bissingen, *112-13*, 113
Billigheim, 88
Bingen, 20, 28, 53, 68, 76
Bingerbrück, 44, 52
Birkweiler, 86
Birnau, 130
Bischoffingen, 126
Blütengrund, 135
Bockenau, 50
Bockenheim, 78, 80
Bocksbeutel, 94, 98, 100, 122
Bodenheim, 72
Bodensee, 14, 116, 130-1
Bonn, 16, 20
Boppard, 26, 27, 28
Bottwar valley, 110
Bötzingen, 127
Brackenheim, 112
brandy, 24
Braubach, 29
Brauneberg, 38
Braunweiler, 51
Breisach, 126-7
Breisgau, 124-5
Bremm, 35
Bretten, 121, *121*
Bretzenheim, 53
Briedel, 36
Britzingen, 129
Brohl, 19
Bronnbach, 99

Bruchsal, 120, 121
Bruttig, 34
Bühl, 122
Bühlertal, 123
Bullenheim, 103
Bundesstrasse, 15
Bunte Kuh, 18
Buoch, 114-15
Burg Are, 19
Burg Arras, 35
Burg Ebernburg, 48
Burg Eltz, *32*, 33
Burg Gutenfels, 29, *29*
Burg Hohenbeilstein, 110
Burg Lahneck, 29
Burg Landshut, 38
Burg Layen, 53
Burg Lichtenberg, 110
Burg Metternich, 34, *34*
Burg Ravensburg, 120, *120*, 121
Burg Rheinfels, 28
Burg Thurant, 33
Burg Trifels, 88
Bürgeln, Schloss, 129
Burgen, 32
Burgenstrasse, 14, 118
Burgscheidungen, 134
Burgsponheim, 50
Bürgstadt, 98, 99
Burgundy grape family, 31, 46, 106, 119, 120, 122, 124, 126
Burgwerben, 135
Burkheim, 127
Burrweiler, 86, 87

Cabernet Sauvignon grape, 144
Castell, 102, *102*
Charlemagne, 68, 76
Charta, 67
Cleebronn, 112
Clevner grape, 106, 123; *see also* Gewürztraminer; Traminer
co-operatives; *Winzergenossenschaften*, 11, 16
Cochem, 33, *33*, 34, 35
Cologne, 19, 25, 33, 73

Darmstadt, 90
Daubach, 50
Deidesheim, 82, 83, 84
Denzlingen, 124
Dernau, 17, 18, 19
Dettelbach, 104, 105
Detzem, 39
Deutsche Weinstrasse, 78, 80, 82, 86, 87, 88, 89
Deutsches Eck, 22, *22*
Dieblich, 33
Diesbar, 136, 141

Dirmstein, 80
Dittelsheim-Hessloch, 74
Dorndorf, 134
Dornfelder grape, 17, 79, 133, 145
Dörrenbach, 89
Dörscheid, 29
Dorsheim, 53
Dotzheim, 57
Drachenblut, 24
Drachenfels, 24, 25, *25*
Dreis, 38
Dresden, 138
Duchroth, 49
Durbach, 122, 123
Durlach, 121

Ebernburg, 48, 50
Edenkoben, 86, 87
Edesheim, 86
Ediger-Eller, 34-5
Efringen-Kirchen, 129
Ehrenbreitstein fortress, 22
Ehrenfelser grape, 65
Eibelstadt, 100
Eichelberg, 121
Eichtersheim, 120-1
Einzellagen, 142
Eisleben, 133
Eiswein, 13, *36*, 143
Eitelsbach, 42
Elbe, river, 14, 136
Elbhang, 138
Elbling grape, 31, 43, 144
Ellerbachtal, 50
Elmstein, 83
Elsenz, 121
Eltville, 60, *60*
Emmendingen, 124
Endingen, 127
Enkirch, 36, 38
Eppingen, 121
Erbach (Bergstrasse), 93
Erbach (Rheingau), 60-1
Erden, 37
Erlenbach, 98
Erpel, 24
Eschbach, 88
Escherndorf, 105
Esslingen, 108-9
Ettlingen, 121

Faberrebe grape, 145
Fankel, 34
Fellbach, 114
Felsengärten, 106, *110*
festivals, wine, 13, 147, 148;
Ahr, 16, 17; Baden, 123, 125, 126, 128, 130;

Index

festivals, wine, (cont.)
  Bergstrasse, 90, 92; Franken, 97, 104; Mittelrhein, 21, 23; Mosel-Saar-Ruwer, 33, 34, 37, 42, 43; Nahe, 44, 47, 48, 52, 53; Pfalz, 80, 81, 82, 83, 88; Rheingau, 54, 56, 60, 61, 62; Rheinhessen, 70, 72, 73, 77; Saale-Unstrut, 134, 135; Sachsen, 138, 139, 141; Württemberg, 108, 111
Filzen, 42
Flein, 111
Flonheim, 77
Flörsheim, 56
Flörsheim-Dalsheim, 74, 75
Forst, 82, 83, 84
Franken, 56, 94-105, 131
Frankweiler, 86
Frauenstein, 57
Freiburg, 116, 124, 125, *125*, 128
Freinsheim, 80-1, *81*
Freudental, 112
Freyburg, 132, *132*, 134, 135
Frickenhausen, 100
Frühburgunder grape, 18

Gau-Bickelheim, 77
Gau-Bischofsheim, 72
Geilweilerhof, 88
Geisenheim, 60, 63, 65
Gengenbach, 124
Genheim, 52
Gerlachsheim, 99
German Wine Academy, 59
Gerolzhofen, 104
Gewürztraminer grape, 79, 124, 126; *see also* Clevner, Traminer
Gimmeldingen, 86
glasses, wine, 17, 30, 44, 55, *55*, 78, 90, 106, *114*
Gleisweiler, 87
Gleiszellen, 89, *89*
Glen, river, 47
Glottertal, 124
Gochsheim, 121
Goethe, J.W. von, 61
Goldriesling grape, 137
Gondorf, 32, 33
Goseck, 135
Graach, 37
Gräfenbach valley, 52
grape varieties, 11, 144-5
Grauburgunder grape, 144; Baden, 120, 126; Bergstrassse, 90; Mosel-Saar-Ruwer, 31; Nahe, 45; Pfalz,

79; Rheinhessen, 68; *see also* Ruländer
Graupa, 138
Gröbern, 140
Gross-Umstadt, 90, 92
Grossbottwar, 110
Grossheringen, 135
Grossheubach, 98
Grossjena, 132, 135, *135*
Grosskarlbach, 80
Grosslage, 142
Grunbach, 114-5
Grünstadt, 80
Güglingen, 113
Guldenbach valley, 52
Guldental, 52
Guntersblum, 73
Gutedel grape, 116-17, 128, 144
Gutenberg, Johannes, 60, 70
Gutenburg fortress, 52

Haardt, 86
Haberschlacht, 112
Hackenheim, 76
Hagnau, 130, *130*, 131
Hahnheim, 75
Halber, 90
Hallburg, Schloss, 105
Hallgarten, 61
Hambach, 85
Hambach, Schloss, 86, *86*
Hangen-Wahlheim, 73
harvest, selective/late, 11, 62
Harxheim, 72
Haslach, 124
Hattenheim, 55, 60, 61
Hecklingen, 124
Hefebrand, 12
Heidelberg, 87, 116, *118*, 118-19, *118-19*
Heilbronn, 106, 111
Heimersheim, 17, 18
Heppenheim, 90, 92, 93, *93*
Heppingen, 17, 18
Herbolzheim, 124
Herrnsheim, 75
Herxheim-Hayna, 88
Hessigheim, 106, 110
Hessische Bergstrasse, 90, 92
Hildegard, St, of Bingen, 47, 63
Hochheim, 55, 56, *57*
Hock, 56
Hoflössnitz, *138*, 139
Hohenlohe, 111
Hohenneuffen fortress, 109
Hohentwiel, 130
Höhnstedt, 133
Horrheim, 112
Hüffelsheim, 51

Hüttenheim, 103
Huxelrebe grape, 145

Idar-Oberstein, 44
Ihringen, 126
Ilbesheim, 88
Ilm, river, 132, 135
Immenstaad, 131
Ingelheim, 68, 76-7
Inzlingen, 129
Iphofen, 102, 103, *103*
Ippesheim, 102, 103
Irsch, 42

Jagst valley, 111
Johannisberg, 62, 63
Johannisberg, Schloss, 55, 62, 63, *63*, 76
Jugenheim, 77

Kabinett, 55, 143
Kaiserstuhl, 126-7, *127*
Kallstadt, 80, 81
Kamp-Bornhofen, 29
Kandern, 129
Kanzem, 42
Kappelrodeck, 122
Kappelwindeck, 122
Karden, 32, 33
Karlsruhe, 120, 121
Kasel, 42
Kastel-Staadt, 43
Kaub, 29
Kenn, 39
Kenzingen, 124
Kernen-Stetten, 114
Kerner grape, 106, 145; Franken, 94; Mittelrhein, 21; Nahe, 45, 46; Pfalz, 78; Saale-Unstrut, 133; Sachsen, 137; Württemberg, 106
Kesten, 38
Kiedrich, 58, 60
Kippenhausen, 131
Kirchscheidungen, 134
Kirn, 44, 53
Kitzingen, 100, 101
Kleinbottwar, 110
Kleinjena, 132
Kleinkarlbach, 80, 81
Klingelberger grape, 123
Klingenberg, 98
Klingenmünster, 89
Kloster Disibodenberg, 47
Kloster Eberbach, 55, *58*, 58-9, *59*
Kloster Lorsch, 58
Kloster Maulbronn, 113
Kloster Pforta, 135

Klüsserath, 39
Knittlingen, 113
Kobern, 33
Koblenz, 20, 22, *22*, 23, 26, 30, 34
Kocher valley, 111
Königsbach, 86
Königswinter, 23, 24, 25
Konstanz, 130
Korb, 115
Korlingen, 42
Kostheim, 56
Kraichgau, 120-1
Krausberg hill, 19
Kressbronn, 131
Kreuzwertheim, 98
Kröv, 36-7
Kues, *see* Bernkastel

Lahn, river, 20
Lahnstein, 20, 29
Lahr, 124
Landau, 86, 88
Landskrone, 16, *16*, 17
Langenlonsheim, 53
Laubenheim, 53
Laucha, 132
Lauda, 99
Laudenbach (Tauber valley), 99
Lauf, 122
Lauffen, 128-9
Lautenbach, 123
Leinsweiler, 87, 88
Leistadt, 81
Leiwen, 39
Lemberger grape, 106, 111, 112, 145
Leutesdorf, 24
Liebfrauenstrasse, 72
Liebfraumilch, 68, 74, 75, 144
Lieser, 38
Lindau, 130, 131
Linz, 24, *24*
Longuich, 39
Lorch, 64, 66-7, *67*
Lorchhausen, 55, 66
Loreley cliffs, 28, 29
Loreley-Burgenstrasse, 29
Lörrach, 129
Lorsch, 44, 48, 58, 93
Lörzweiler, 72
Loschwitz, 138
Löwenstein, 110
Ludwigsburg, 108, 110, 113
Ludwigshöhe, Schloss, 87, *87*

Machern, 37
Madenburg fortress, 88-9

Mahlberg, 124
Maikammer, 87
Main, river, 14, 56, 97, 105
Mainau, 130
Mainbernheim, 102
Mainschleife, 104-5
Mainz, 39, 68, 70-71, *71*, 72
Mandel, 51
Marbach, 108, 110
Maria Laach, 19
Marienberg fortress, 94, 96, *96*, 97
Marienburg, 35
Marienthal, 17, 18-19
Maring-Noviand, 38
Markelsheim, 99
Markgräflerland, 128-9
Markgröningen, 112, *113*
Marksburg fortress, 29
Markt Einersheim, 103
Marktbreit, 100
Marktheidenfeld, 99
Martinstein, 50
Martinsthal, 58, 60
Marx, Karl, 41, 46
Mayschoss, 16, 17, 19
Meddersheim, 50
Meersburg, *130*, 130-1
Mehring, 39
Meisenheim, 47
Meissen, 136, 137, 140, 141
Memleben, 132, 134
Merdingen, 126
Mertesdorf, 42
Merxheim, 50
Mettenheim, 72, 73
Metzingen, 106, 109, 110
Michelstadt, 93
Miltenberg, 94, 98
Minheim, 38
Mittelheim, 61
Mittelrhein, 20-9
Möglingen, 112
Mönchsondheim, 102, 103
Monsheim, 75
Monzingen, 50
Morio-Muskat grape, 78, 88, 145
Moritzburg, 139, 140
Mosel, river, 14, 30, 34
Mosel-Saar-Ruwer, 30-43
Mülheim, 38
Müller-Thurgau grape, 63, 144, 147; Ahr, 17; Baden, 119, 120, 122, 124, 126, 130; Bergstrasse, 90; Franken, 94, 95, 98, 100, 102, 104; Mittelrhein, 21, 23; Mosel-Saar-Ruwer, 31; Nahe, 45,

46, 51, 52, 53; Pfalz, 78; Rheinhessen, 68; Saale-Unstrut, 133; Sachsen, 137; Württemberg, 106; *see also* Rivaner
Müllerrebe, *see* Schwarzriesling
Müllheim, 129
Mundelsheim, 106, 110
Münster-Sarmsheim, 52, 53
Münstermaifeld, 33
Münstertal, 128
Muscat grape, 137
museums, wine: Ahr, 18; Baden, 127, 129, 130, 131; Franken, 97; Mittelrhein, 22; Mosel-Saar-Ruwer, 30, 33, 36, 37, 38, 40; Pfalz, 78, 83, 85, 86; Rheingau, 59, 64; Rheinhessen, 70, 73, 74; Sachsen, 139, 140; Württemberg, 108, 109, 112
Muskateller grape, 79, 117, 119, 126
Mussbach, 85, 86

Nackenheim, 68, 72
Nahe, 44-53
Naumburg, 132, 133, 134, 135
Naurath, 39
Nebra, 132, 134
Neckar, river, 14, 106, 108, 118-19
Neckarzimmern, 119
Neipperg, 112
Nennig, 43
Neu-Bamberg, *76*, 77
Neuenburg, Schloss, 134, *134*, 135
Neuffen, 109
Neuleiningen, 80, *80*
Neumagen-Dhron, 38, 39
Neustadt, 83, *83*, 84, 85, 86
Neuweier, 122
Niederau, 140
Niederburg fortress, 33
Niederhausen, 44, 49
Niederlahnstein, 29
Niederrotweil, 127
Niederstetten, 99
Niederwald monument, *64*, 65, 66
Nierstein, 68, *72*, 72-3
Nobling grape, 128
Nordheim (Franken), 105
Nordheim (Württemberg), 113
Norheim, 48
Nürburgring, 19
Nürtingen, 109

Oberbergen, 126
Oberburg castle, 33
Oberhausen, 49
Oberkirch, 123
Oberkrozingen, 128
Obermünstertal, 129
Oberrotweil, 126
Obersasbach, 122
Oberstenfeld, 110, 113
Obersulm-Willsbach, 110, *111*
Oberwesel, 26, 28, 29
Ochsenbach, 113
Ochsenfurt, 100, *101*
Ockfen, 42
Odenheim, 121
Odernheim, 47
Oestrich, 61, *61*
Offenburg, 122, 123, 124
Öhringen-Zweiflingen, 113
Olewig, 42
Oppenheim, 73, *73*
Ortega grape, 145
Ortenau, 122-3
Ortenberg, 124
Osann-Monzel, 38
Osthofen, 75
Östringen, 121

Partenheim, 77
Perl, 30, 43
Perle grape, 94
Pfalz, 78-89
Pfalz fortress, *28-9*, 29
Pfingstwiese, 47
Pforzheim, 113
phylloxera, 133, 136
Piesport, 30, 38, *38*
Pillnitz, *136*, 137, 138
Pirna, 136, 137, 138
Pleidelsheim, 110
Plochingen, 109, 110
Pokal, 17, 44
Pommersfelden, 103
Portugieser grape, 145; Ahr, 17; Franken, 94, 98; Mittelrhein, 23; Pfalz, 79; Rheinhessen, 68, 77; Saale-Unstrut, 133; Sachsen, 137
Prichsenstadt, 104, *104-5*
Proschwitz, 137
Pünderich, 36

QbA, 143
QmP, 143

Radebeul, 136, 139, 140
Radeburg, 139
Randersacker, 100
Ranschbach, 87

Rauenthal, 55, 58
Rech, 17,19
Reichenau, 130
Reicholzheim, 99
Reichsburg fortress, *33*, 34
Remagen, 16
Remis'chen, 44
Rems valley, 114-115
Remshalden, 114
Repperndorf, 101
Rhein Terrasse, 68, *72*, 72-3
Rheinbrohl, 24
Rheingau, 54-67
Rheingoldstrasse, 29
Rheinhessen, 68-77; 'Rheinhessen's Switzerland', 76, *76*, 77
Rhens, 26-7
Rhine, river, 8, 14, 15, 20, 27, 29; 'Rhine in Flames', 22, 29, 67
Rhodt, 86, 87, *88*
Rhöndorf, 24
Rieslaner grape, 94
Riesling grape, 56, 144, 147; Ahr, 17; Baden, 119, 120, 122, 123; Bergstrasse, 90; Franken, 94, 96, 100, 102; Mittelrhein, 21, 23, 24, 28, 29; Mosel-Saar-Ruwer, 31, 32, 34, 37, 39, 41, 42; Nahe, 45, 46, 47, 48, 49, 51, 52, 53; Pfalz, 78, 81, 82; Rheingau, 54, 55, 56, 58, 61, 62, 63, 65, 66, 67; Rheinhessen, 68, 76; Saale-Unstrut, 133; Sachsen, 137; Württemberg, 106, 110, 111, 114
Rietburg fortress, 87
Rivaner grape, 21, 144; *see also* Müller-Thurgau
roads, 15
Rockenhausen, 47
Rödelsee, 102
Romantische Strasse, 14, 99
Römer, 17, 44, 55, *55*
Rossbach, 135
Rotenfels, 48, *48-9*
Rotliegendes, 68, 72
Röttingen, 99
Roxheim, 51
Rück, 98
Rüdesheim (Nahe), 51
Rüdesheim (Rheingau), 15, 28, 54, 55, 63, 64-5, *65*, 67
Ruländer grape, 126, 137, 144; *see also* Grauburgunder
Ruwer, river, 30, 42

Index

Saale, river, 14, 132
Saale-Unstrut, 132-5
Saaleck, 135
Saar, river, 30, 42-3
Saarburg, 42, 43, *43*
Sachsen, 136-41
St Alban, 72
St Aldegund, 35
St Goar, 28, 29
St Goarshausen, 15, 29
St Johann, 77
St Katharinen, 51
St Martin, 86, 87
St Peter, 124
Salem, 130
Samtrot grape, 106
Sasbachwalden, 122, 123
Saulheim, 76
'Saxon Switzerland', 138, 140
Scheurebe grape, 46, 51, 78, 94, 145
Schieler, 137
Schierstein, 57
Schiller, J.C.F. von, 110
Schillerwein, *114*, 115
Schliengen, 129
Schlossböckelheim, 48, 49
Schnait, 114
Schönburg fortress, 28
Schoppen, 78
Schriesheim, 92, 93
Schwaigern, 112, 113
Schwanberg, 102-3
Schwarze Katz, 34, 50
Schwarzriesling grape (Müllerrebe), 106, 111, 112, 113, 120, 145
Schweich, 39
Schweigen, 78, 80, 88, 89
Schweppenhausen, 52
Seinsheim, 103
Sekt, 12, 21, 60, 64, 144
Serrig, 42
Seusslitz, 136, 137, 141, *141*
Siebeldingen, 88
Siebenborn, 38
Silvaner grape, 144, 145; Baden, 119, 126, 128; Bergstrasse, 90; Franken, 94, 95, 96, 98, 100, 102, 104; Nahe, 45, 46, 47, 51, 52, 53; Pfalz, 78, 81, 87; Rheingau, 63; Rheinhessen, 68; Saale-Unstrut, 133; Württemberg, 106
Sommerach, 104, 105
Sommerhausen, 100
Sonnendorf, 135
Soonwald, 150

Sörnewitz, 140
Spaar hills, 140
sparkling wine, *see Sekt*
Spätburgunder grape, 144, 145; Ahr, 17; Baden, 120, 122, 124, 126, 130; Franken, 94, 98; Mittelrhein, 23; Nahe, 45; Pfalz, 79; Rheingau, 54, 56, 58, 66, 67; Rheinhessen, 68, 77; Saale-Unstrut, 133; Sachsen, 137; Württemberg, 106, 112
Spätlese, 55, 143
Speyer, 71, 78, 84, *84*, 85, 87
Spezial, 17
spirits, 12
Sponheim, 51
Sprendlingen, 77
Stahleck fortress, *26-7*, 28
Starkenburg fortress, 92, *92*
Staudernheim, 51
Staufen, 128, *128*
Staufenberg, Schloss, 123, *123*
Steeg, 28
Steigerwald, 102-3
Steinbach (Baden), 122
Steinbach (Bergstrasse), 93
Steinheim, 110
Stetten, *see* Kernen
Stockheim, 112
Stocksberg, Schloss, 112
Stolzenfels, Schloss, 26
Strasbourg, 123
Strasse der Romantik, 132
Strausswirtschaft, 68, 86; *see also Besenwirtschaft*
Stromberg, 49
Stromburg fortress, 49, 52
Strümpfelbach, 114, *115*
Stuppach, 99
Stuttgart, 106, 108, 109, *109*
Sulzburg, 128, 129
Sulzfeld (Baden), 120, 121
Sulzfeld (Franken), 100
Süsser See (lake), 133

Talheim, 111
Tauber valley, 98-9, 101, 106, 111, 116, 122
Tauberbischofsheim, 99
Tauberrettersheim, 99
Tauberzell, 99
Tiefenbach, 121
Traben-Trarbach, 34, 35, 36
Traisen, 48
Traminer grape, 87, 105, 119, 122, 123, 133, 137, 145; *see also* Clevner; Gewürztraminer
Traubengelee, 12

Traubenkernöl, 12
Traubensaft, 12
travel, 14-15
Trechtingshausen, 28, 29
Trester, 12
Treveris, 30
Trier, 30, 31, 33, 34, 37, 39, *40*, 40-1, *41*, 42
Trittenheim, 34, 39, *39*
Trockenbeerenauslese, 143
Trollbach valley, 52-3, *52-3*
Trollinger grape, 106, 110, 112, 113, 114, 144, 145
Tuniberg, 126

Überlingen, 130
Uffenheim, 103
Uhlbach, 108
Umweg, 122
Ungstein, 78, 81
Unkel, 24
Unstrut, river, 14, 132, 134
Untertürkheim, 108
Unteruhldingen, 130
Ürzig, 37

Vaihingen, 112, 113
Varnhalt, 122
Veitshöchheim, 97
Venningen, 12
Victoria, Queen, 56
Viertele, 106, *114*
Vitzenburg, 134
Vogelsburg, 104, 105
Vogtsburg, 126, 127
Volkach, 104, 105, *105*
Vollrads, Schloss, 55, 61, 62, *62*, 63
Vulkanfelsen, *127*

Wachenheim, 78, 82, 83, 84
Wachwitz, 138
Wackerbarth, Schloss, 139, *139*
Waiblingen, 115
Waldböckelheim, 51
Waldkirch, 124
Waldlaubersheim, 53
Waldrach, 42
Waldulm, 122
Wallhausen, 52
Walluf, 57, 58
Walporzheim, 17, 18, 19
Wehlen, *36*, 37
Weibertreu, 111
Weikersheim, 99, 106, 111
Weil, 129
Weinböhla, 140
Weinbrand, 12
Weindorf, 22

Weinessig, 12
Weingarten, 120
Weingelee, 12
Weinhefe, 12
Weinheim, 92
Weinsberg, 110, 111
Weinsheim, 51
Weisenheim am Berg, 81
Weissburgunder grape, 145; Baden, 120, 126; Mosel-Saar-Ruwer, 31; Nahe, 45; Pfalz, 79; Rheinhessen, 68; Saale-Unstrut, 133; Sachsen, 137
Weissenfels, 135
Weissherbst, 124, 144
Wendelsheim, 77
Wennungen, 134
Wertheim, 98, 99
Westhofen, 75
Wicker, 55, 56
Wierschem, 33
Wiesbaden, 54, 56-7
Wiesenbronn, 102
Wiesloch, 90, 92, 93
Willsbach, *see* Obersulm
Wiltingen, 42
Windesheim, 52
wine: appellation of origin, 142; labelling, 8, 10; output, 8; quality categories, 11, 143; regions, 11; style, 11, 143; tasting, 8, 13; vintages, 145
Winkel, 60, 61, 62
Winnenden, 115
Winningen, 32-3
Wintrich, 38
Winzenheim, 53
Winzerbrände, 12
Winzergenossenschaften, *see* co-operatives
Wisper valley, 67
Wolf, 36
Wöllstein, 77
Wonnegau, 75
Wonsheim, 77
Worms, 68, 71, 72, 74, *74*, 75, 87
Württemberg, 98, 106-15, 131
Würzburg, 94, 95, *96*, 96-7, *97*

Zell, 30, 32, 34, 35
Zeltingen, 37
'Zeppelin' wine, 38
Zornheim, 72
Zscheiplitz, 134
Zweiflingen, *see* Öhringen
Zwingenberg, 90, 91, 92